C0-AXE-731

PROMOTION AND CONTROL OF
INDUSTRY IN POSTWAR FRANCE

PROMOTION AND CONTROL OF INDUSTRY IN POSTWAR FRANCE

John Sheahan

HARVARD UNIVERSITY PRESS

CAMBRIDGE MASSACHUSETTS | 1963

Distributed in Great Britain by Oxford University Press, London

Publication of this work has been aided
by a grant from the Ford Foundation

Library of Congress Catalog Card Number 63-7592

Printed in the United States of America

TO DENISE

PREFACE

If there is a place on earth more satisfying to the human spirit than Beaulieu-sur-Dordogne, it is probably somewhere else in France. If there is a society on earth more frustrating to those who wish it well than the French, it must be, to anyone not French, his own.

Both the American and the French societies operate with collective myths that provide some measure of internal consistency in their choices but at the same time impose what appear to the outside observer to be ridiculous limitations. Within the sphere of economic preferences, the two myths contrast sharply on the relative roles of individual and collective action. The French seem in many respects to be obsessed with the necessity of preventing the chaos that would occur if the uncivilized forces of independent competition, or the unstabilizing effects of private choice in determining the pattern of production, were allowed to assert themselves without immense precaution. These preferences have their costs. But the intent here is not to disparage failure to follow the American path. It is rather to suggest that the limitations imposed by the American myth itself may become clearer, more completely subject either to rational defense or in some cases to change, if the empirical consequences of alternative approaches are made more evident.

The French economic experiments discussed here are most disorderly, possibly even dangerous. Some of them probably were unhelpful, and some perhaps helpful there but less relevant in the American situation. Still, the combination of new forms of government intervention with maintenance of private enterprise has been consistent with the best performance that the French economy has achieved in at least the last century. There might well be something here.

The American economy has undertaken noble experiments in the past, and retains enormous vitality. But the great enterprise which settles down in the channels established by past success is rarely the one that the future rewards. French economic history suggests that a tendency to slow down leads easily to the generation of rising handicaps to economic and social flexibility: inability to sustain growth fosters reliance on protective institutions inhibiting its revival. But the decade of the 1950's added a more promising indication. Intelligently directed effort, blessed by favorable external conditions but creating many of its own advantages, proved able to turn the historical trend around in a more positive direction.

The present study aims at an exploration in detail of choices in the area of governmental and private control of industry. It emphasizes contrasts between the organization of particular industries in France and in the United States, and attempts to trace out some of their major consequences for performance. It is focused on the manufacturing sector, and on the decade from 1950 to 1960.

This investigation was made possible by a National Research Professorship grant from the Brookings Institution for the academic year 1959–60. It was practically feasible only because of the high degree of cooperation received from scores of French officials of both government and industry. In the interests of free criticism of the efforts with which they are associated, it is perhaps best to acknowledge their vitally necessary assistance collectively rather than by name.

Chapters 7, 9, and 12 are revised in varying degree from articles published respectively in the *Journal of Industrial Economics, Bulletin SEDEIS*, and *American Economic Review*. Permission of these journals to draw on the same material is gratefully acknowledged.

Among the many French and American economists who were helpful either in sharing their own thoughts, in opening the way to fruitful sources of information, or in advising on various drafts of this material, particular thanks are due to Jean Fourastié, Jacques Houssiaux, François Perroux, Jo Saxe, and all the members of the economics department of Williams College. Professor C. P. Kindleberger had the patience to make detailed and extremely helpful suggestions on the entire manuscript, making possible a number of corrections and forcing the use of considerable ingenuity to preserve some positions with which he disagrees.

On a level so far removed from the text itself that they may well disassociate themselves entirely, two economists bear a great deal of responsibility for the attempt to reach toward an application of the study of industrial organization to problems of national growth. They are Professors Edward Mason and Emile Despres. Professor Mason did consider and offer excellent advice on a draft of this book. But well before this he provided a more essential basis, by presenting the subject of economics in concrete applications as a way toward better social organization through respect for fact as well as independent thought.

Emile Despres has never been afflicted with this text, and will if he does see it take it apart most effectively. That process of taking apart by going beyond the level at which others would be satisfied to stop, using accepted conclusions as a point of departure for original questions leading the mind in new directions, has been a constant pleasure to observe and a major stimulus to this inquiry.

Williamstown, Massachusetts
June 1962

CONTENTS

I THE POSTWAR ECONOMY

II INDUSTRY STUDIES

III POLICIES

IV EMPIRICAL RESULTS AND ECONOMIC THEORY

LIST OF TABLES

PART I | The Postwar Economy

All franc values are expressed in new francs, denoted NF, regardless of whether or not the reference is to a period following their adoption. To convert to the standard francs in use prior to 1960, multiply by 100. To convert to dollars, some care is necessary. The franc was devalued repeatedly in the early postwar years, then held officially stable from 1949 to August 1957. In that period, the official exchange rate was 3.50 NF, or 350 francs, per dollar.

In August 1957 the value of the franc was decreased in a complicated manner extending over several months, in an effort to disguise the operation and to control its effects selectively. This was followed by an open and effective devaluation in December 1958. The official value of the NF since that time, pending further change now conceivable in either direction, has been 4.9 per dollar.

References in square brackets in the text correspond to item numbers in the Bibliography.

1 | The Main Questions

French industry has been written off as being so hopelessly slow-moving for such good reasons by so many acute observers that its vigor since World War II is as puzzling as it is pleasing to behold. The evidence of thwarted competition, of distortions caused by erratic government intervention and a costly degree of protection, has long provided a rich mine of bad examples to drive home traditional lessons of economic policy. Interferences with domestic and international markets did indeed seem to yield a rigid economic system with unusually low vitality. But, in their invariably contrary way, the French have clouded this neat picture during the last decade by a rate of progress considerably outpacing that of the American economy. This has had the happy incidental result of converting apparently clear-cut answers into a more interesting set of open questions.

The central question here is the relevance of market organization to aggregate expansion. If private and governmental interferences with free markets have been as prevalent as pictured in most of the available studies of the French economy, the expansionary record of recent years suggests either: (1) that market organization is not very significant, (2) that it has changed greatly for the better without adequate recognition of the fact, or (3) that at least some of the forms of intervention practiced in France have had positive results offsetting genuinely harmful obstacles to progress. These possibilities may be jointly minimized by a simple conclusion that the aggregative performance remains thoroughly unsatisfactory. The first empirical question considered is therefore the record of performance since the war. The evidence is mixed. The economy is in the process of rapid transition. But dead economies are not in transit. This one is very much, if quite unevenly, alive.

The contrasting character of the postwar changes within the manufacturing sector offers a particularly promising opportunity to explore the functional connections between market organization and economic growth. The vast differences in the responses of individual firms and industries to the new opportunities opened up since the war suggest that aggregative factors are insufficient to explain the process of long-run economic stagnation and revival. The position here is not that market organization determines aggregate expansion, but that it is a vital part of any reasonably adequate explanation. Recalcitrant choices in noncompetitive markets can thwart an otherwise promising basic situation, just as positive microeconomic choices with respect to investment, innovation, export effort, and pricing act to create favorable aggregate conditions. This is a supply-oriented study, founded on the belief that supply decisions, while far from uniquely determinant, are crucially important.

Supply decisions of individual firms are constrained jointly by relatively fixed structural determinants, such as the technological factors which set lower limits to the scale of efficient production and govern the possible economies of size, and by discretionary institutional arrangements. Such institutional arrangements may be matters of private agreement, such as the use of joint selling agencies, or of group discussions to divide markets and establish common policy on investment. They may also be matters of government intervention intended to inhibit or to promote private cooperation, to discourage or to stimulate new entry, to block or to facilitate competition from imports, or to shape investment plans by direct action in individual markets. The term market organization is used here to refer to the whole set of external facts which the individual firm must consider in making its decisions, including both the relatively fixed structural factors and the legal or conventional restraints imposed by government or by private arrangements.

Questions involving possible changes in market organization continuously pose issues of limited choice. Preferences consistent with particular social goals may be imposed easily in some industries, at the same time as they prove prohibitively costly in others. Policy formulated without concern for structural limitations is either futile or unduly expensive. But such limits rarely determine all the important aspects of organization in a given market. The element of choice remains open even with respect to such a key structural factor as the number of firms. It is inconceivable that the real limits on efficient operations with known techniques in the production of primary aluminum, for example, would permit as many firms in this field as in the textile industry. It is probable that average costs would be much higher with eighty producers than with eight. But the technology is perfectly consistent with complete monopoly, as in the United States before the war, or with two firms, as in France, or with the six producers that a combination of government policy and private initiative have now created in the United States. No aspect of the production structure in either country dictates that there need be a joint selling agency for the producers and government supervision of pricing, as in France, or that such arrangements be avoided, as in the United States. The central concern here is the area of open choice in such matters, and particularly that of choices which have been different in France and in the United States.

The only way to deal with the questions chosen for consideration is to explore individual markets, one by one; to establish and attempt to explain the main facts of their organization and behavior. This is an impossible program, if the objective is to be a definitive study covering all important sectors. The core of this book constitutes a compromise between such an objective and the practical possibilities open to the author. It consists of a set of condensed inquiries into five manufacturing industries, supplemented by a set of statistical contrasts placing them in relation to the rest of French manufacturing and to their American counterpart industries, followed by consideration of major policies affecting all manufacturing. The industry studies are highly selective, in the double sense of the choice of fields considered and the particular aspects stressed in each. The choices among industries were guided first by an effort to include both highly successful and less dynamic fields, secondly by the inclusion of industries particularly associated with special techniques of government intervention, and thirdly by an effort to include cases representing widely different degrees of concentration and competition. Within each discussion, attention is concentrated on material bearing on the areas of interest specified above.

The intent here is not so much to add information on the operation of French industries as it is to explore them for evidence illuminating the effects of organization on expansion. Perhaps the most troublesome aspect of the approach used is a conscious effort to draw inferences from French experience applicable to the American economy. Performances of each of the five industries in France and America are compared whenever feasible, not simply to provide a standard of reference but to bring out possible reasons for differences in behavior. Sometimes these comparisons suggest that forms of private cooperation or direct intervention practiced in France are seriously detrimental to performance, and point toward alternatives that the American economy has done well to avoid. Sometimes they suggest the opposite. In all cases these comparisons are treacherous: the external environments and internal response mechanisms of these economies are different in too many respects to permit easy transfer of evidence from one to the other. On the other hand, manufacturing is in both countries predominantly in the hands of private business guided by a roughly similar complex of motivations. The weights attached to security as against rising profits, or collaboration with other firms and the government as opposed to resolute independence of action, certainly differ between the two societies. The basic search remains the same. Structure and choices in the French automobile industry resemble those in the American automobile industry more closely than they do those of the French cotton textile producers. The attempt to transfer evidence across countries lends itself to debate and correction but it is not inherently impossible.

The real differences between the French and the American economies may be diminishing. On the French side, the revival of vigor since the war has carried some industries toward the production scale and aggressive techniques long considered to be typical of American industry. Living standards have risen faster than those in the United States since 1950, and expenditure patterns have moved in directions taken earlier here. On the American side, some industries that were particularly dynamic seem to have drifted toward acceptance of a more modest rate of progress, guided by a greater interest in statesmanlike cooperation as opposed to impolite competition. The degree to which "managerial" direction of the economy has increased in importance relative to impersonal market forces is a valid subject for debate. The reality of a significant element of administrative guidance, both private and government, is hardly subject to doubt. This is precisely the type of organization with which the French economy has been coping for much of the twentieth century. Long-established firms resolved mutal differences, learned to adjust to a slow pace of growth, and in the process adopted decision patterns which insured slow growth. Many of the postwar experiments in government intervention were explicitly designed to attack the defects arising from a situation which may now be developing in the United States. It will be dismal indeed if the American economy repeats all the mistakes that were made in France, and unfortunate if we cannot profit from more recent experience on the positive side.

Although government controls and techniques of promotion have always been more important in the French economy than in the American, the manufacturing sector was allowed a great deal of freedom up to the period immediately preceding the second world war. Business was not even bothered by any government efforts to enforce competition. Price controls for manufactured goods were introduced in the short period of social reform toward the end of the 1930's, but they were being abandoned when the war came. The real period of innovation in controls of manufacturing began at the end of the war. Price controls were then established on a permanent basis. Alternatively applied rigorously or allowed to become inoperative, they are now back in the latter stage. A brief wave of nationalizations in 1944–45 was largely confined to power, transport and finance, but it did introduce a highly interesting case of government competition in the automobile industry. Economic planning, backed by extensive public funds for investment and selective credit controls, was introduced in 1946 and is still in effect. Administrative variation of export assistance, import permits, taxes and credit terms applicable to individual industries, and a host of informal levers for shaping business choices have made French manufacturing much more nearly a joint business-government operation than is true in any other industrialized Western economy. These experiments have all the haphazard and inconsistent aspects of efforts to deal with varied problems from differing viewpoints and uncoordinated control agencies. It would be distinctly surprising either if they all worked smoothly or if these well-intentioned measures did not include some positive achievements. Much of the effort here is concerned with disentangling their effects; not to second-guess French officials but rather to inform Americans.

Though statistical material on French industry has improved greatly since the war, it remains less complete, less mutually consistent, and less well organized than that available for the

United States economy. The gaps relevant to this study have been partially compensated by the high degree of cooperation received from both industry and government officials who often made unpublished data available for general guidance. Still, it was occasionally necessary to choose among several official estimates of a given set of facts and to rely on incomplete clues to an uncomfortable degree. The worst handicap has been the absence of any thorough census of manufactures. The problems have been least for physical production and exports, worst for financial accounts. Company reports vary from clear disclosure exceeding the norm for American corporations in a few cases to carefully guarded secrecy concerning such dangerous information as sales and profits.

The main empirical criteria used here as a basis of judging performance are the expansion of production, ability to export, and restraint on prices. All of these factors can be measured, at least to an acceptable degree of approximation. Moreover, the measures can to some extent be compared internationally. The effort is to provide the discipline of aggregate results, international comparisons, and inter-industry contrasts to make explicit the basis of judgment. The conclusion must, in the end, invite debate rather than impose answers.

It is particularly necessary in this changing situation to be explicit with reference to time. The French economy has been changing away from a particular set of institutions which were not well suited for rapid growth, toward another set of institutions which may or may not turn out in the end to be much better. The process of change is itself the crucial area of discussion. It is possible that institutions which would inhibit progress when and if they became fully stabilized may stimulate healthy change as they are introduced and worked out through repeated trial and error. The key to the ability to keep moving may be the ability to keep changing the methods of promoting motion.

The period emphasized here is the decade of the 1950's.

This was a very special decade: sufficiently special to transform French industry from one of the weakest in the west to one of the more dynamic. The research involved was carried out chiefly in 1959 and 1960. These two years were in no sense "normal." They do have the useful characteristic of applying to conditions of external balance. The devaluation of December 1958 was accompanied by sufficient price stability to permit maintenance of an equilibrium exchange rate for the first time since the war. But the correction of previous currency overvaluation itself constituted an unusual stimulus to exports, generating an improvement which should not be confused with a trend. At the same time, deliberate attempts to shift current income from households to firms acted to restrain consumption temporarily and produced an unusually pronounced change in output composition. All years are periods of transition, but 1959 and 1960 were more so than most.

An attempt to forewarn of all the difficulties here would yield an appalling list. Better to emphasize the positive intent: to disturb familiar ideas, to force a selection among sound and dubious elements, by the process of confronting them with the results of a varied set of experiments going beyond the boundaries of the familiar.

2 | Aggregative Trends

The widespread belief that the French economy is singularly incapable of sustained expansion seems to be, or should be, disintegrating under the impact of the postwar evidence. The performance of the decade 1950–60 does not fit easily with any hypothesis that fundamental social factors in this country, or institutional rigidities emerging in the process of advanced industrial development, preclude vigorous growth. It is undeniable that real braking factors have been and still are present. The performance has remained inferior to identifiable possibilities. It has simply been a significant improvement, comparing fairly well with current achievements elsewhere and extraordinarily well with the long-term trend in France itself.

The rate of advance in the 1950's is most easily described in terms of changes in total output. For this purpose, the country's national accounts are at least as reliable as those of other nations. They provide an informative and reassuring score. But they do not measure the degree of structural change going on behind today's output totals, determining the reaction system and growth possibilities of the coming years. Some of the factors handicapping economic growth have proven more tenacious than one might deduce from the aggregate results, while others clearly have entered phases of rapid improvement. The future is open to conceivable disaster in multiple forms, but the foundations of the French economy are more favorable for continued forward movement at the beginning of the 1960's than they were in 1950.

1. Comparative Growth Rates

Between 1950 and 1960 the gross national product increased 53 percent in the aggregate, or 41 percent on a per capita basis [178]. The rate of gain in production per capita was approximately three times the average achieved in the preceding century, and one-third greater than the expansion in the best single decade during that century [174, pp. 13, 60]. These quantitative estimates are subject to a wide margin of error. Their general validity is supported by John Sawyer's conclusion from detailed historical study that it is necessary to go back to the 1850's to find another decade in which economic behavior showed comparable vitality [45].

It is possible to argue that the postwar achievement represents no amazing change for the better, either by stressing the positive side of the preceding record in France, or by emphasizing that other industrialized nations have exhibited even greater strength in recent years. In fact, the long-term record of French economic growth is considerably less bleak than depicted by most discussions of the country's entrepreneurial and social problems. National product per capita increased about 14 percent per decade from the mid-nineteenth to the mid-twentieth centuries. This growth rate was not significantly different from those of Germany and the United Kingdom, though well below those of Canada and the United States [174, p. 13]. This evidence should be qualified by the point that the French gains in output per capita were achieved with a nearly stable population, while other Western countries successfully combined equal or greater increases in production per capita with rising populations.

If two countries achieve equal rates of increase in production per capita, one with rapidly expanding and the other with a stable population, it is for some purposes inadequate to conclude that their accomplishments are equivalent. The country with the rising population may find it easier to raise output per capita because of the mobility of new entrants to the labor force, and the reassurance that population growth gives to business firms considering long-term investment. But it is also handicapped by claims on resources for housing, education and capital equipment for the rising population, and it must ordinarily resolve technological problems more effectively if it is to secure simultaneously rapid increases in employment of labor and production per man. If it does succeed, it is in effect making more human life possible without doing any less to raise material standards for each person.

It is fairly clear that population trends themselves may be affected by the attitudes and opportunities generated in the process of economic growth. If the restriction of population in France were partially a response to lack of economic opportunity, and to a corresponding loss of social flexibility as the economy failed to evolve, then reliance on comparisons in terms of output per capita would convert a consequence of relative failure into a symbol of success.

However one may judge the French performance up to 1929, the two following decades were unambiguously dismal. Simon Kuznets' data show that net national product per capita made no significant gain between the periods 1924–33 and 1949–53 [174, p. 60]. From 1929 to 1955 the rate of growth of output per capita was less than one-third that of the United States [37, p. 215]. Industrial production in France fell 17 percent between 1929 and 1938, while rising 16 percent for all OEEC members combined [179].* Much of the belief that the French

* In this instance and throughout the present study the corresponding change for combined members of the Organization for European Economic Cooperation is taken as a particularly useful basis of comparison against which to match changes in France. For the period covered here, the data include the seventeen West European countries that were originally members of the Organization. They do not include Spain, Canada, or the United States. The OEEC was replaced in 1961 by the Organization for Economic Cooperation and Development, with different membership.

economy was organized to resist progress relates to observed behavior in this period. It is not in fact surprising that the economic collapse of the 1930's strengthened all social forces counseling protection of existing positions. The adaptive capacity of the economic system was absorbed by problems of survival rather than stimulated by possibilities of expansion.

The immediate postwar years were marked by rapid enough recovery but also by extreme inflation and wasteful resource allocation [30]. It was still possible in the early 1950's to consider the postwar trend as completely consistent with a picture of long-run incapacity. This was in fact the most frequent conclusion of students of the French economy. Harold Lubell was able to document signs of genuine change as early as 1951 [104], but this was distinctly a minority view. By 1957, the optimistic and the pessimistic could comfortably coexist: the April issue of *World Politics* carried two successive articles, by Wallace Peterson and by David Landes, the first emphasizing that the French economy was making important new progress and the second that it was not [108] [41]. By the end of the decade, it remained easy to identify probable sources of future difficulty, but hardly reasonable to question the fact that the movement from reconstruction into a new world of aggregate growth had been successfully accomplished.

When the basis of comparison is changed from France's own history to that of the record of other industrialized nations in the 1950's, it becomes clear that the factors at work in this decade were far too general to be assigned entirely to domestic causes. The increase in GNP per capita between 1950 and 1960 in France was slightly less than that for all OEEC members combined. England and the United States were not in the class of the continental economies with respect to growth in this period, but among the latter France did not especially stand out. It was almost exactly in place in an interesting international pattern: for the major industrial countries of the west, growth rates in the 1950's were inversely correlated with income per capita in 1950. Of the five countries for which Milton Gilbert and Irving Kravis estimated comparative income levels in 1950, France was third, below the United Kingdom and the United States. For the same five countries, its growth rate from 1950 to 1960 was third highest, below those of Germany and Italy. Table 1 summarizes the two types of information.

TABLE 1. Comparisons of GNP Per Capita: Absolute Levels in 1950 and Growth from 1950 to 1960

	(1) GNP per capita in 1950, based on U.S. price weights (dollars)	(2) Increase in GNP per capita from 1950 to 1960 (percentages)
United States	1830	16
United Kingdom	1133	24
France	968	41
Germany	782	85
Italy	545	67
All OEEC member countries	—	43

Sources: Milton Gilbert and Associates, *Comparative National Products and Price Levels*, Paris, OEEC, 1959, table 2, p. 23, for column 1. OEEC, *General Statistics*, July, 1961, p. III, for column 2.

The markedly higher growth rates of the continental European countries shown in Table 1 reflect an element of belated postwar reconstruction, as distinct from sustained expansion beyond earlier capacity. The English-speaking countries are entitled to some consolation on this account. But the picture does not change radically if the period of comparison is shifted to later years. For 1955–60, when all five of these countries were well beyond prewar income peaks, the ranking of expansion rates remains much the same. The chief differences are that the Italian growth rate becomes the highest of the five, and the French growth rate appears higher relative to both Germany and the United States. France and Italy maintained almost exactly the same growth rates in the last half of the decade as they did in the first half, while Germany and the United Kingdom slowed up slightly and the United States slowed up drastically.

Restricting comparisons of progress to industrial production also has the effect of making the French expansion appear more impressive. From 1950 to 1960 industrial production increased 89 percent, compared to 80 for all OEEC members combined. The fact that the index of industrial production rose more rapidly than the OEEC average while the growth of GNP was below that average may be partly a statistical mirage, given the permissibility of doubt on the precision of both sets of estimates. It may nevertheless reflect genuinely slower progress in the agricultural-trade-service sectors of the French economy, as compared to other OEEC members.

The global indicators for the French economy show that performance was good relative to those of other industrialized nations, not necessarily that the underlying complex of behavior and policy was in any sense optimal. If one looks at details of the economy, evidence of successful resistance to increasing efficiency, or trouble caused by misguided effort to improve it, is about as easy to find as evidence of helpful action. François Perroux has made the point most forcefully with respect to the nineteenth century in France: the global indicators show continuing growth, and compare reasonably well with other economies, but historical study of behavior reveals a poorly integrated society actively and often effectively *resisting* progress [44, p. 73].

The facts do not dictate a single conclusion. It may be that the basic statistics indicating growth are incorrect, or it may be that activities which did maintain inefficient organization, or block specific desirable changes, were of trivial long-run significance. A third possible interpretation seems, in the light of the 1950's, to be better than either of these. The rate of growth indicated was simply far below the potentials of the society, in France as in all other western countries. This is probably also true of the 1950 decade itself. Growth was so much better than that of the past that it shows earlier performance to have been far below potential, but it was still so handicapped that it is reasonable to locate the optimum far above the achievement.

2. Output Composition and Relative Prices

The percentage increase in private consumption between 1950 and 1960 was identical to that of the gross national product. Investment rose a little more rapidly, and government consumption slightly less. The only striking departures from the pattern of parallel movement were provided by the markedly greater increases in both export and import volume. The national accounts for 1960, and volume changes for the period 1950–60, are summarized in Table 2.

Table 2. French National Accounts, 1960, and Changes from 1950 to 1960

	1960 Aggregate Values Billion NF	1960 Sector Use as Percentages of GNP	Percentage Increase in Volume 1950–60
Private consumption	185.2	65	53
Government consumption	41.6	15	44
Investment	55.1	19	57
Exports	45.5	16	76
Imports	(−42.4)	(−15)	75
GNP	285.0	100	53

Source: Ministère des Finances et des Affaires Economiques, Service des Etudes Economiques et Financières, *Rapport Sur Les Comptes de la Nation, de l'Année 1960*, Paris, 1961, pp. 152–53.

Note: 1960 aggregates and percentage distribution are expressed in current prices. The percentage increase in volume is based on calculations in 1956 prices.

The picture of change shown in the last column of Table 2 is subject to possible distortion by particular cyclical characteristics of the end years cited, but their similarity as years of moderately above-average growth makes this problem minimal.

More serious interpretive difficulties, applying particularly to government consumption and to investment, arise from the characteristics of the French price structure.

Official calculations of government consumption indicate that its claim on output has been relatively reduced since 1950. The estimates are based on re-evaluation of actual expenditures to express them in constant 1956 prices. But both the level and the rate of growth of government consumption are thereby understated relative to other French accounts. The level is understated because, in 1956 as in all other years of the period considered, a major component of government consumption was the use of arbitrarily paid manpower in military service. This labor is priced far below its value in productive employment, so a given level of government consumption is equivalent to the sacrifice of a greater value of private consumption or investment. Further, the process of capital accumulation in the 1950's has significantly raised the scarcity and value of labor relative to other factors of production. Government consumption is pre-eminently labor intensive. Evaluating its increase on the basis of constant prices contradicts the reality of the increasing opportunity cost of labor utilized. The problem applies to all the accounts, but the systematic bias is particularly important for government consumption.

With respect to investment, the French price structure raises a different difficulty. Table 2 indicates that the ratio of gross investment to GNP was equal to 19 percent in 1960. Data for preceding years show an oscillation of investment around a trend slightly steeper than that of GNP, with a peak ratio of 21 percent in 1957 and 1958. These ratios compare well with those in the United States and other western countries. They correctly indicate a major sacrifice of alternative uses of the national product in order to increase and modernize productive capacity. But the gain achieved by the loss of alternative consumption has been undermined by the fact that prices of capital goods in France are higher relative to other domestic prices than is true in the United States or the other major West European countries.

The ratio of prices of investment goods to those of consumer goods in France was approximately 25 percent higher than in the United States in both 1950 and 1955.* This relationship is discussed as to fact, and explored as to cause, in Chapter 6 below. It began to alter after 1955, but remained throughout the decade one of the most important restraints on the French growth rate. This relationship means that a given ratio of investment expenditure to national income results in an unusually low real gain in productive equipment. Because of the country's comparative disadvantage in the production of capital equipment, it also means that attempts to secure rising investment have had a particularly direct effect on the balance of payments.

As measured in constant 1954 prices, the rate of gross fixed capital formation in France increased 63 percent between 1950 and 1960, and that in machinery and equipment fully 75 percent [178]. Compared to the 53 percent rise in GNP, these figures indicate a powerful effort toward the modernization of industry, which must have contributed significantly to the rate of growth. But a comparison with other OEEC countries again puts the French effort in more modest perspective. The rate of fixed capital formation for combined OEEC countries, measured similarly, increased 91 percent between 1950 and 1960. The volume of investment in machinery and equipment rose 94 percent. This makes the increase in France look less dramatic, and also makes the fact that American investment in machinery and equipment was only one percent higher in 1960 than in 1950 look somewhat ominous.

* Calculated from [115], p. 40, using European quantity weights. Based on their respective expenditures in national currency, the ratio of investment to GNP in France was 103 percent of that in the United States in 1955 [178]. When corrected for prices, the French ratio was only 82 percent of the American using U.S. weights, or 95 percent using European weights [115, pp. 36, 53].

If the preceding figures on growth of investment and GNP are turned on their heads, they suggest that the marginal efficiency of capital may have been higher in France than in the other OEEC countries in this period. The ratios of increases in GNP to increases in gross fixed capital formation were .84 in France and .62 for all OEEC members combined. This comparison is on shaky grounds in any case because it neglects capital consumption, but it may still be a genuine consequence of the relatively greater emphasis in France on investment in machinery and equipment. It also leaves room for the possibility that changes in the efficiency of the productive structure, as distinct from capital formation, contributed relatively heavily to the growth of output in France.

As indicated in Table 2, exports and imports have risen at nearly equal rates, greatly exceeding the rate of increase of GNP. The difference between the growth of trade volume and that of domestic production is an important and beneficial structural change. The French economy has become less insulated. It has taken greater advantage of the possibilities of gains from specialization and scale through the production of goods for foreign as well as domestic markets, while allowing a greater share of internal demand to be met by foreign supplies in areas of particularly high domestic costs.

The improvement in export volume shown in Table 2 has been one of the brightest aspects of the economy. Part of the gain does reflect a simple transition from the early postwar period of acute supply difficulties to an era of greatly expanded capacity. But in the course of the early 1950's sheer capacity became much less important than the country's ability to provide export goods competitive in price and quality. Under these conditions, export volume did rise slowly from 1952 through 1955. In the 1956–57 domestic inflation, exports actually fell, despite strong external demand conditions. Following the correction of inflation in 1958, an extremely well-conceived program combining devaluation with fiscal adjustments and reduction of trade barriers was prepared by a special advisory committee under the chairmanship of Jacques Rueff [88]. This program was implemented at the end of 1958 and had an immediate, highly beneficial, impact on both the domestic economy and the balance of payments. It was followed by an increase of 20 percent in commodity export volume in 1959, and a further increase of 17 percent in 1960 [178].

Trade with foreign countries outside the franc zone has risen much more rapidly than trade with countries in the zone. In value terms, exports to foreign countries have gained markedly relative to imports. With exports valued f.o.b. and imports valued c.i.f., the ratio of exports to imports climbed from 67 percent in 1949 to 93 by 1955, plunged back to 71 percent in 1956 and 1957, and then slightly exceeded 100 percent for 1959 and 1960 [18, p. 239] [82].

For the purposes of this study it is more meaningful to discuss changes in trade with countries outside the franc zone than to refer to total trade. Exports to countries within the franc zone cannot be considered to represent any competitive achievement, since they have been sold under conditions excluding free recourse to alternative sources by the importing countries. Further, much of the trade within the franc zone has been conducted at highly artificial prices. Finally, such trade does not directly affect success in dealing with balance of payments restrictions on the growth of the French economy, since such limitations refer only to foreign currencies. This is not to say that trade within the franc zone has been irrelevant to French economic expansion. On the positive side, it has supplied necessary raw materials. On the negative side, it has represented a persistent distortion of resource allocation in both the metropole and the colonies, and a net export of resources that might otherwise have facilitated domestic expansion.

Considering only trade with countries outside the franc zone, finished industrial products have played a larger role in imports and a smaller role in exports for France than for most other industrialized nations. Further, a key aspect of trade in finished goods which has long tormented French economists is that imports of industrial equipment have nearly always been greater than exports of such equipment. Table 3 summarizes the trade balances for the main product categories during the period of the Second Plan, 1952–57.

TABLE 3. Trade Balances by Product Category, 1952–57 (Billion NF)

Net export categories		Net import categories	
Industrial products for consumers	+ 4.5	Raw materials	−10.5
Semi-processed goods	+ 6.0	Energy	−10.3
Food	+ .3	Industrial equipment	− 1.3
	10.8		22.1

Source: Commissariat Général du Plan, *Rapport Annuel*, 1958, I, 19.

Note: The net deficit indicated for this period was divided almost equally between the dollar zone and EPU countries.

After 1957, the deficit progressively decreased and the structure of trade moved toward greater emphasis on manufactured goods. Finished industrial products were equal to 30 percent of all exports to foreign countries in 1950, 33 percent in 1957, and 40 percent in 1960. They also rose from 20 percent of imports in both 1950 and 1957 to 25 percent in 1960 [12, pp. 207–10] [82]. The increase in exports was led by the automobile industry in 1958 and 1959, but then the correction of the currency value and the reduction of trade barriers within the Common Market led to a more general increase of both exports and imports. In 1960, for the first time since the war, exports of industrial equipment to countries outside the franc zone actually exceeded imports.

3. Sector Origin of National Product

Both the long record of limited participation in world export trade of manufactured products and the relative weakness of the equipment industries have been properly regarded as signs of an unusually slow adaptation of the French economy to modern production possibilities. One of the best studies of this subject, prepared by the United Nations Economic Commission for Europe in 1954, spelled out in detail the evidence of the economy's strong resistance to structural change [49]. There can be little question that in general the French have not exhibited any great degree of long-run economic flexibility, either in shifting away from agriculture or in seizing new opportunities within the industrial structure.

The percentage of the labor force employed in the industrial sector showed little growth during the first half of the twentieth century, and the percentage active in agriculture rose relative to other West European countries in this period [49, charts 10 and 11, p. 173]. But there was a shift toward industry up to the time of the depression: the percentage of the active labor force employed in the industrial sector rose from 29 to 34 percent between 1906 and 1931. It was cut back to 30 percent by 1936. By 1954 it was up to 36 percent [18, pp. 38–39].

By 1959, the share of the French national income produced in the industrial sector, including mining, energy, and construction as well as manufacturing, was approximately equal to that in the other OEEC countries. France derived 45 percent of its national income from industry in that year, including 34 percent from manufacturing. These ratios were slightly above those for the United States, though below those for England and Germany. But the share of agriculture in France was 12 percent, as against 4 in the United States and England, and 7 in West Germany [179, p. 3].

The greater relative importance of agriculture in France might partially be explained by the fact that the supply of arable land per capita is higher than in the other two European countries. But this is not a sufficient explanation. The land-labor ratio is still higher in the United States, where the share of national income originating in agriculture is only one-third that in France. The additional explanatory factor, and the more important one for the future, is the level of income. As incomes rise, the distribution of demand shifts away from agriculture and its relative contribution to national income falls. The unusually slow shift of the French distribution of employment and income away from agriculture in the first half of the twentieth century was a result of the slow long-term rise in income, rather than a necessary consequence of the proportion of basic resources.

The 1950's have shown considerable improvement in the balance between agriculture and the rest of the economy. Between 1949 and 1958, income produced in agriculture rose only 4 percent while net national income in constant prices increased 52 percent. Emigration of labor from agriculture permitted income per capita within the sector to increase 24 percent, as against a rise of 46 percent outside the sector [16e, p. 1072]. Discontent within agriculture is understandable in the circumstances, but the process at work is fundamentally an accelerated transition toward a production structure consistent with a higher-income economy.

The movement of labor out of agriculture during the 1950's helped ease the strain of a population structure peculiarly adverse to expansion. The population increased steadily as a consequence of the higher birth rates beginning in 1945, but the active labor force remained practically constant. By the end of the decade, the first postwar children were just on the verge of entering the labor market. Between 1960 and 1966 the number of annual entrants in the labor force should rise more than 50 percent, greatly enhancing the flexibility and further growth potential of the economy [175, December 24–25, 1961] [176].

The organization of the industrial sector shows anachronistic traits inherited from preceding stagnation, accompanied by clear signs of positive transformation in the 1950's. The concentration on this sector in the present study is intended to permit a more specific explanation of the causes and impediments involved in this industrial transformation, not to imply that independent factors operating in agriculture and services are irrelevant to the growth process. But the primary engine of change at this stage of the French economy is the industrial sector. The rate of progress in industry largely determines the possible rate of transition away from agriculture and strongly affects the possibilities of raising the efficiency of the commercial sector through increases in the volume handled by each outlet. The importance of change in the industrial sector is probably underestimated by its present relative contribution to national income, and even more strongly so by its present share of total employment.

4. Monetary Problems and the Capacity to Resolve Them

The process of structural adaptation has been obscured by sometimes violent but perhaps less important monetary crises. Domestic inflation and external deficits were worse in France in the early postwar years than in other industrialized countries, and did get seriously out of control again in 1956–57. But it would be incorrect to regard these twin problems as chronic aspects of the economy, in a degree any worse than in most other countries.

Prices were brought under fairly good control from 1952 through 1955, and again after their brief explosion in 1956–57. Since 1957 they have behaved as a continuing minor irritant, in much the same sense as in nearly all western countries. The balance of payments was consistently adverse up to 1955 because domestic prices were out of contact with external price levels. Devaluation in 1949 proved unhelpful because the inflation of 1950–51 promptly wiped out its effects. The conviction that a new devaluation would merely stimulate renewed inflation, plus a widespread preference for administrative techniques of checking imports and stimulating exports, led to acceptance of continued currency overvaluation. This seriously handicapped restoration of external balance. In 1957, an inadequate devaluation applied selectively among industries was used to permit reduction of export subsidies, but it did not restore any equilibrium between domestic and world prices. Finally, at the end of 1958, devaluation in conditions of very moderate excess capacity, accompanied by some administrative control of prices, worked beautifully. It was followed in 1959 and 1960 by simultaneously rising exports, aggregate demand, and foreign exchange reserves.

That the economy followed a major devaluation by expansion without inflation in 1959 and 1960, when it had proven unable to do so on earlier attempts, might be explained by stressing either that the government was more able and ready to use monetary and fiscal restraints on inflation, or that the supply elasticity of the productive system has greatly increased. Since the operation was accompanied by expansion of demand and production, it would seem reasonable to place primary emphasis on the ability to accomplish this rather than on the availability of restraints. The change on the supply side has been real and has been more than a mere correction of wartime disorganization. It has included a major alteration of attitudes toward, and capacity for, sustained expansion of production without inflation.

The proposition that French attitudes toward expansion changed markedly under the impact of the second world war has been most effectively developed by C. P. Kindleberger [39].*

* The positive change in attitudes emphasized by Kindleberger may be viewed as a natural reaction to the economic and military defeats of the 1930's and early 1940's: old methods and interests favoring the status quo were too badly discredited to stand effectively against those who sought change. But Gordon Wright suggests that the strength of the move forward was hardly inevitable. "Any nation's morale can easily disintegrate, its outlook can become badly distorted, if at moments of crisis it fails to discover within itself a civic-minded elite possessed of deep convictions and courageous enough to fight for them . . . if France

It is certainly consistent with postwar economic behavior, and strikingly underlined by the reversal of a demographic trend of more than a century. The net reproduction rate, which followed a declining trend all through the nineteenth century, and reached .87 in the years 1935–37, was never below 1.24 in any year from 1946 through 1959 [17d, p. 251]. Change in this direction has certainly not been confined to France, but here again the indication is that a previous extreme in a negative direction has been replaced by positive preferences more closely comparable to other advancing western countries.

A change in attitudes apparently did occur and was a helpful factor in most areas of economic performance, but an attitude is not enough. It is better that French business and government officials want to improve the capital equipment industries than that they be satisfied with inferior results, but beyond this it is necessary that the methods used be appropriate to the problem. In this particular area, the methods chosen were for a long time very ill-advised. What needs examination is the economic environment and the reasons for success or failure of particular attempts to improve it. Better results are possible when people actively seek them, and most of the postwar economic results have been good, but some of the methods tried have proven much better than others.

France has been able to breathe without either inflation or external deficits since 1958. This new situation has been established without any significant reduction in the rate of domestic expansion. Future mistakes may wreck the present achievement, but the changes of the 1950's did secure a genuine improvement in the possibility of expansion without monetary crises.

As compared either to its own past or to contemporary progress in other western countries, the French economy pros-

---

since 1945 has shown some healthy trends and signs of renewal, they are to be traced neither to the men of Vichy nor to the straddlers, but to the men, the action, the ideals of the wartime resistance" [50, p. 526].

pered most hearteningly in the 1950's. The major indices of performance were decidedly positive. The changes in underlying structure have been in directions favorable for the continuance of such progress. The results were by no means uniformly brilliant. Policy mistakes can be discerned at least as easily as in any other country. Among the major industries, progress varied from outstanding to decidedly weak. It is just such differences which provide a basis for investigation of the causes of partial failure and particular success.

3 | The Omnipresent State

The government has long been vastly more entangled in the operation of the economy in France than has been true in either England or America. The combination of stimulus and protection surrounding the initial stages of manufacturing in the seventeenth and eighteenth centuries proved highly resistant both to domestic revolution and to the onslaught of laissez-faire thought. "Save for a momentary aberration from about 1860 to about 1880, France has always been, as it was in 1700, true in the main to the tradition of Colbert" [33, p. 272].

The postwar interventions discussed here represent a turn to new forms and more intense state action rather than any drastic change in the traditional sphere of governmental authority. Those forms of intervention which have had a direct bearing on organization and behavior of industry since the war include: (1) economic planning, (2) the postwar nationalizations and extensions of state enterprise, (3) price control, (4) selective promotion and protection, and (5) policies concerning competition and concentration.

1. Planning

The French approach to planning has been aimed from the start at finding a new path between centralized control and individual market decisions. It has no more than a slight, formal resemblance to the system of centralized control practiced in Russia. It is based on group consultation and persuasion. Within the government, the Planning Commission acts as an advisory agency somewhat on the lines of the Council of Economic Advisers in the United States. It has no authority over the operating agencies. It does have the strength of an independent voice concerned with coordination of policy. In dealing with the private business sector, the Commission does not issue directives. It establishes a set of guiding hypotheses on the possible evolution of the economy during the period to be considered, and invites individuals from leading firms, trade associations, labor unions, and other government agencies to discuss their plans against this background. The purpose of the discussions is less to commit participants to fixed programs than to influence their thinking by emphasizing opportunities and problems arising from the interdependent results of their decisions.

Although the Commission cannot force private firms to take any specific actions, it can use persuasion from a position as an influential agency of a government possessing vast powers of selective promotion and control. Most importantly, it can do a great deal to affect availability of financing through its role in the allocation of public funds to assist private investment. It can act on private preferences, and thus to some extent shape choices without giving orders.

The first plan initially concentrated on "basic industries," meaning chiefly the nationalized industries plus steel. The second plan, starting in 1954, went on to include in its scope practically all sectors of the economy. It is possible to interpret this change as a substantial improvement. "From relatively modest beginnings in the immediate postwar period French short-term plans have evolved into a comprehensive scheme of resource allocation for Metropolitan France" [110, p. 268]. It is also possible to view the process as a change from active redirection of the economy to formalized description.

There is no consensus on the effects of the planning system. Published evaluations range from wholehearted approval [100]

[102] [108], to strong criticism [30], by way of interestingly nuanced dissection [110]. Informal discussion with government and industry officials adds further contradictions. Some of the sharpest criticism comes from within the government and some of the strongest support from private industry. The approach here is to study its application in the industry most closely associated with the planning process, steel, to note some of the incidental effects of the plans as relevant in the cases of the other industries and then to explore the general question in Chapter 10.

2. Nationalizations and State Enterprise

When the French Government returned to power in 1944, its approach to economic problems was dominated by a mood of resentment against the past and determination to make a new future. To a considerable degree, the element of bitterness against past abuses overshadowed the simultaneous effort to plan coherent steps toward an improved organization of the economy. The result included a wave of nationalizations, mostly carried out by executive decree, that could not by any stretch of the imagination be termed a "program" for reform.

The postwar nationalizations centered on gas, electricity, coal, and a small group of the most important banks and insurance companies [30, pp. 174–80] [92] [93] [98]. Radio and telephone communications, as well as air and rail transport, were state operated before the war; trucking was not then and has not since been brought under state ownership. Government firms were set up freely to carry out oil exploration and development; these have since extended to a government role in distribution. None of the steel firms were taken over. The only instance of nationalization within manufacturing which enters directly in the following industry discussions was that of the Renault automobile company. This was a pure case of retaliation against the particular producer. It provides an example differing fundamentally from the industry-wide nationalizations: state ownership here did not institute monopoly but instead led to competition.

In the first years after the war the possibility of further nationalizations served as a powerful stimulant to cooperation with the government, especially in the case of the steel industry. But its role as a specter rapidly lost importance in the late 1940's as it became clear that further moves in this direction were most unlikely. An implicit truce seems to have been established since 1946. No more firms have been threatened with nationalization, and no movement has developed to promote denationalization. But the existing state firms have continued to expand both in their own industries and, through new investment, in associated areas, and the issue of possible government investment to create additional firms in fields believed to be lagging has been very much alive [28] [91, pp. 168–69, 177] [175, June 17 and 18, 1960].

The control of business financing possibilities through nationalization of major credit institutions and establishment of new government agencies was crucially important in the early postwar years, but became much less so as business profits and private credit sources grew through the 1950's. From 1947 through 1949, roughly two-thirds of all investment financing was provided either directly from public funds or by state-owned credit agencies [18, p. 98] [30, p. 34]. In 1949, public funds used for investment in metropolitan France were three times as great as those secured through internal financing by business enterprise. By 1959, the relationship had been reversed: internal financing was 1.7 times as great as that provided by public funds. The relative use of public funds declined steeply during the first half of the 1950's, but then levelled off. It remained within a range of 23 to 26 percent of total metropolitan investment from 1956 through 1959 [4, p. 12].

In the first instance, nationalization of credit agencies and of nonfinancial firms was considered to be associated with the goal of planned modernization of the whole economy [95, pp. 21–30]. It was expected that the state firms would provide enormous direct leverage for implementation of an over-all program. This concept included the seeds of a potent conflict of interest. The managements of the firms went vigorously to work to improve efficiency and expand the scale of their operations, trying to cut costs and raise revenues much as individual private enterprises might be expected to do in the same market conditions. Government agencies external to the firms found that the managements of the state-owned firms were by no means eager for outside advice on what they should do. On the level of practical control, the state firms are more open to supervision than private companies are, but at the same time the channels are open for the firm itself to shape the governmental choices that control its own environment. On the level of basic principle, questions of the means and objectives of control of the state firms lead directly to the same fundamental issue as planning itself, the relationship of over-all coordination to decentralized managerial decision.

3. Price Control

In the same initial postwar burst of loosely associated moves to increase government direction of the economy, wartime price controls were placed on an explicitly continuing basis. This was not a radically new departure. Price regulation had been established in 1936 as a means of supervising revisions resulting from the new social legislation of the Popular Front. Wartime controls followed almost immediately, and the French took the opposite path of the United States by deciding to hang on to them in peacetime. The administrations which have come and gone since then have included many people determined to reduce or eliminate controls, but their collective effort has done little more than create variations in the intensity with which regulations are exercised. To quote the director of the control agency, "Despite the end of grave shortages, despite a general spirit hardly favorable to the maintenance of price regulation . . . recent history shows that such regulation has a real vitality. . . . Without wishing it, perhaps without realizing it, we finally constructed, piece by piece, a solid and permanent instrument of governmental action" [111, pp. 30–31].

The system of control might be summarized by stating that the "Direction Générale des Prix," acting under the authority of the Minister of Finance, can issue orders at any time to any industry or individual firm establishing ceiling prices for their products at or below prevailing levels. In practice a complex but flexible system allows most industries a high degree of freedom most of the time.

Regulations divide industries into three main groups: (1) those subject to direct price fixing by authority, (2) those allowed complete freedom, and (3) the Orwellian-flavored category of "controlled liberty." Firms in this third class must submit explanations of any proposed increases, or of initial prices for new products, and must delay application of the new prices for a fifteen-day examination period. The control agency can reject or attempt to alter the proposals, or do nothing and allow them to go into effect at the end of the waiting period. The three broad regulatory categories include numerous subdivisions to facilitate administration, but the basic point is perhaps that the control agency has the authority to alter the classification of any industry by decree.

During most of the postwar period, stricter forms of regulation have been applied to aluminum, steel, sulfuric acid, fertilizers, wood pulp, and some paper and pharmaceutical products. Industries subject to "controlled liberty" have included agricultural equipment, automobiles, combustion motors, household equipment, oils and paints, tires and other rubber products. Complete freedom has usually been allowed for cement, porcelain, textiles, toys, watchmaking and wood products, and in general for any dispersed group of small producers too difficult to supervise [111, pp. 39–51]. In principle, prices of steel products have been free of regulation since the establishment of the Coal-Steel Community. In practice they have remained a matter of government-industry negotiation.

The control agency maintains a representative on the commission dealing with monopolistic practices, and endeavors to keep track of suspect cases as particularly likely candidates for strict regulation. But it would be going too far to suggest that monopolistic industries are controlled and competitive ones are not. Administrative convenience, concern with input cost changes which would become widely diffused, and consideration of the relative weight of particular products in the major price indices, cut across any division of industries by degree of competition.

Whatever the form of control applying to any group of producers, they are subject to the possibility of a general "blockage" of all prices at existing levels. Attempts to freeze all prices have been made repeatedly, but exceptions allowed for legitimate reasons to one group after another have usually rendered such attempts meaningless within a few months. The one important exception was the general freeze imposed in the 1952 recession. The usual practice has been to go on dealing with specific cases and to leave the "blockage" in effect until its defeat is consecrated by an order for another freeze at the new price level then in existence.

In the early postwar years, the regulatory agency carried out independent studies of costs as a basis for its pricing decisions, endeavoring to set prices at levels permitting profits for firms with costs near the industry average, but not necessarily for the highest-cost producers. Authority to carry out such studies remains, but they are not now common. In the usual case, the agency is asked to judge the permissible increase that would compensate for given increases in costs. The judgment in such issues is based on cost breakdowns provided by the industries, showing the net effect of price increases for specific inputs. It is standard practice, emphasized repeatedly to unions and to firms, to refuse authority to pass on wage increases in the individual industry going significantly beyond those in manufacturing generally.

Pricing decisions inevitably go beyond measurement of costs to consider the desirability of changing allowed profit margins. Under some governments, decisions frequently forced the companies concerned to accept lower margins. More recently, policy has favored increasing margins in order to encourage investment. In all important cases involving this issue, the Planning Commission, the Ministry of Industry, the Ministry of Finance, and interested government purchasing agencies, are consulted and play active roles in the decision process. Officials concerned with these internal debates are emphatic in insisting that the results constitute a balance of conflicting judgments and negotiating skills rather than any abstract optima determined by clearly defined criteria.

Decisions reached by the control agency are transmitted to an advisory board of twenty-seven men, including representatives of agriculture, business, labor and consuming groups. This "Comité National des Prix" accepts most of the decisions automatically. For a few particularly sensitive items, or for any special case the Committee wishes to debate, it may undertake a general investigation and establish new policy directives. The Committee's advice is not binding but is usually followed. The price directorate thus retains wide scope for action, within broad limits set occasionally by the review board and—implicitly but fundamentally—by the cabinet.

The intensity with which controls have been exercised has varied greatly with changes in economic conditions. Controls were generally relaxed during the first postwar recession in 1949, tightened up following the inflationary jump in 1951, then maintained quite actively through recession, recovery, and the renewed inflation of 1956–57. Since 1957, with inflationary pressures greatly quieted, they have been reduced to a point allowing almost complete pricing freedom. The regulatory agency remains in place, the discretionary powers remain, but most industries need do little more than file notices of intended price changes. The possibility of genuine control remains in the ambiguity beloved of French administration.

4. Selective Promotion and Protection

The interventions in particular markets practiced by the Planning Commission and price control agency do not by any means exhaust the techniques of direction practiced by the government. The Finance Ministry, the Ministry of Industry, public lending institutions working partly with the Planning Commission, and specialized agencies concerned with exports, have been actively applying selective promotional methods. The main lines of direction have concerned efforts to foster investment and influence location, develop exports, and replace imports by domestic production. Monetary and fiscal powers include many devices intended to facilitate this directive process. They have been complemented by frequent recourse to all the traditional methods of export promotion and import restriction.

In the immediate postwar period, the French Government rejected the possibility of applying aggregative monetary and fiscal restraints to curb inflation, partly under the influence of an understandable desire to avoid at all costs any return to the stagnation of the 1930's. This choice quickly led to a complementary emphasis on direct restriction of recourse to capital markets, as well as controls over construction and allocation of raw materials, as the inflationary process got completely out of hand [89]. Interest rates were officially kept low to encourage investment, but only those firms able to secure support of government agencies were able to get credit at all. This provided a powerful opening for the influence of investment by the

Planning Commission, and the basis for a disproportionate allocation of investment resources between the public and private sectors. At the same time, the overwhelming inflationary pressures made it practically impossible to allow any genuine freedom to import. The inflation plus shortages of key inputs within France kept the balance of payments in a critical state despite import restrictions, and no one whatsoever doubted the necessity of a prolonged drive to make the economy more self-sufficient.

By 1949, with the help of foreign aid and a rapid recovery of production in those basic industries able to carry out investment, it was possible to drop much of the apparatus of direct supervision of industry. Credit rationing, with selective access to funds through investment in line with government objectives, remained common. Such aid has been associated particularly with modernization of basic industries, movement of plants from Paris into areas of little industrial development, reorganization of scattered facilities of subnormal efficiency, and reconversion of plants from older to new industries.

Most of this financial aid has been only loosely coordinated. It has not been handled as an integral part of economic planning, but more as a series of allotments of help among those applicants sufficiently well organized to make their needs clear to one of the many agencies operating the various aspects of these programs. The degree of government coordination and initiative in these activities may well increase: a new "Society for Conversion and Industrial Development" was created in 1960 to centralize the process [4, p. 15].

The combination of generally tight credit with special help for particular applicants acts to favor firms able to maintain good contacts with government. Coupled with a general administrative preference for larger firms, it provides one of the more important routes by which government intervention has been used to favor size and concentration. But at the same time fiscal legislation has worked in the opposite direction.

Both the design of business taxes and the methods of collection have placed most of the burden on the larger companies. Here too the postwar changes have been working in a direction more favorable to them. One of the best reforms was the shift from reliance on turnover taxes to taxation based on value added. This acted to correct the previous bias of French business toward the maximum degree of internal self-sufficiency, accentuated by the effort to escape the pyramiding effect of turnover taxes leveled each time inputs passed through the market. The change in taxation encouraged a shift toward larger-volume specialized production, and aided the more capital-intensive firms by making business taxes more nearly proportional to labor costs. It also embodied a new method of discretionary intervention, since the fiscal legislation included authority for selective variation of the rate (between limits of 20.5 and 27.5 per cent), applied to each industry.

The intent of the provision for administrative variability of the tax on value added was to improve stability by making it possible for the Minister of Finance to reduce or raise the rates for individual products in response to conditions of recession or excess demand in each case. Apart from its use for this purpose, the variable tax quickly became a method of altering industry choice on such matters as exports and investment. It has provided a basic incentive to export at all times, by the practice of waiving the tax on value added on all export sales. In addition, a reduction of the rate of tax applied to domestic industry sales may be traded for an agreement by the industry to carry out specific investment or export programs favored by the Ministry of Industry or the Planning Commission. Unlike the selective credit aids, the tax does not differentiate among firms within a given industry.

The selective element in the system of business taxes goes well beyond the administrative variability allowed by the tax on value added. It includes several varieties of depreciation allowances: a basic system resembling that of the United States, allowing choice between straight line or moderately accelerated depreciation; a more generous system applicable to industries exporting a large proportion of their production; a variety of particular techniques for special industries, along the lines of the privileges accorded extractive industries in the United States but here extended to the manufacturing sector, most notably to the steel industry; and, for a time, extra depreciation for expenditure on equipment manufactured in France. The complexity of the depreciation rules itself acted to bias opportunities in favor of larger firms, as Martin Norr has pointed out. "The proliferation of special rules in fact made the system, although workable by the larger enterprises, difficult for the smaller, who were often confined as a practical matter to normal straight-line depreciation" [87, p. 396]. A major revision of depreciation rules in 1959 did greatly simplify them, without eliminating special aids to export industries.

Efforts to help exporters have been frequently revised. In 1960 they were centralized through a reorganization of the *Centre National du Commerce Exterieur*. Firms exporting at least 20 percent of their production, or undertaking to do so in the future, are given "La Carte d'Exportateur," which is used to open the way to privileges of the type indicated above [74].

The counterpart of the varied measures used to encourage exports was, until 1959, a persistent effort to maintain strong import barriers against manufactured goods. Repeated rounds of devaluation and inflation left average French prices too high to permit external balance without a disproportionate reliance on direct measures to push exports and restrain imports. The fiscal system proved too feeble, and the supply elasticity of French industry too low, to secure an improved foreign balance without provoking inflation. Import barriers were reduced temporarily when the balance of payments improved, but great care was taken to maintain a high level of protection for particularly weak fields such as industrial equipment and textiles.

The essential basis of a movement toward open trading conditions was finally achieved by the successful devaluation that came at the end of 1958. Progress toward removal of quantitative restrictions on trade within the Common Market, and reduction of tariffs against imports from all sources, has since been rapid. As before, the first steps toward the removal of restrictions maintained some protection for the weakest industries, but all were informed that quotas would be removed before the end of 1961. In European trade at least, France has come closer to removing protection than seemed even remotely conceivable five years ago.

In foreign trade, the basis of selective intervention seems to be disappearing. In domestic matters, the use of price controls has been greatly relaxed, but selective promotional techniques remain very much in action. They keep alive a much stronger possibility for government guidance of industry than the United States has ever known in peacetime.

5. Competition and Concentration

It is about as easy to find inconsistencies in public policy in France as in the United States. The same entangled choices and conflicting purposes, with recurrent partial changes in methods as older techniques become sufficiently unbearable, haunt both sides in their efforts to deal with the social control of business. This does not mean that the emphasis is often the same in the two countries. The French have been on a roughly parallel track, but well over to the side of active intervention. Both societies swung toward peaks in their acceptance of laissez faire during the nineteenth century, but the French for a shorter time and with less enthusiasm. Both moved in the direction of greater intervention in the first half of the twentieth century, but the French with less reluctance. Both bought policies of supervised cartel organization as a response to the depression of the 1930's, but the United States backed away from the National Industrial Recovery Administration before wartime controls descended and the French have still not decided that they want to back away completely.

In the postwar period, the two countries seemed at first to be moving in radically different directions. Though the United States did accept government responsibility for maintaining employment, much more effort was devoted to improvement of antitrust enforcement than to changes in the scope of direct regulation. On the French side, the first move was a great increase in planning and control. But after the initial jump in this direction, policy began to curve back erratically toward acceptance of private market decisions. In fact, a low-key stir of interest in promotion of competition may be detected quite early in the 1950's, and a much stronger concern with it at the end of the decade.

It was evident to everyone that the immediate postwar creation of government monopolies through nationalization, the coordination of decisions through planning, and industry-wide negotiation in the process of controlling prices, all ran counter to any possibility of securing independent competition. Most American economists would have very nasty things to say if such moves were proposed here, for a number of reasons which might include the valid point that competition has often served American society well. Such protests in France were rare because few people indeed believed that competition had served French society well.

Some of the French distrust of competition was rooted in a simple identification of its consequences with the poor prewar performance. The breakdown of the economy in the 1930's, initiated by the American collapse and intensified by unhappy French policy, was widely regarded as a result of insufficient direction of private business choices. Keynes' message got through too slowly. Further, the long-accepted system of private cartel organization, unafflicted with any antitrust efforts, was widely taken to be the inevitable pattern of choice by private industry in France. Finally, French policy in the 1930's was infected by the same poison that weakened American policy at the time, and has done much to confuse both societies since: the meaning of competition was twisted into a system of protecting competitors from each other.

If it seems strange that the people trying to break away from the mistakes of the past emphasized concentration and control rather than decentralization and possible competition, it should be noted that they were reacting against a deadening system of thought that identified the welfare of existing institutions, specifically that of existing small business firms, with the welfare of the society as a whole. The attitude they were fighting has been well summarized by an economist who apparently sympathizes with the earlier emphasis on small business. "A large section of public opinion remains convinced that only the development of medium-sized and small firms is compatible with French traditions and with the conditions of economic progress. May I quote from a statement of the Radical and Radical-Socialist party: 'This party does not conceal its preference for small and middle sized undertakings, not only because with similar techniques they achieve lower costs than large companies, but principally because they are an indispensable stage enabling workers and employees to throw off the yoke of wage-earning and attain proprietorship, and the conditions which shall permit the full development of their personalities.' " [54, p. 42]

The attitude quoted does not differ radically from that of proponents of federal fair-trade legislation in the United States in the 1960's, or that of the opponents of technological change in France in the seventeenth century [33, pp. 146–87]. It is an eternal position, because it embodies one of society's multiple goals. It is a dangerous position when it is allowed to dominate economic policy, as it did in the 1930's. It provided the support for differential tax and regulatory policies adverse to larger-scale firms, helping to choke off recovery and economic advance prior to the war [37, p. 260]. It thereby added fuel to the postwar drive to force the economy by direct methods toward greater industrial concentration. This was not a deliberate effort to eliminate competition but an attempt to undo the effects of prolonged stress on protection against change. It ran parallel to a new note beginning about 1950, one of considering recourse to elements of competition as a possible aid in the same process of promoting structural change.

The first important step in the direction of using competition to promote change came from the same policy center that was simultaneously promoting mergers in the steel industry: the Planning Commission. The step consisted in opening up, by careful stages, limited international competition through the Coal-Steel community. This was one element in a complex policy aimed toward far-ranging political and economic goals, but it included conscious consideration of the possibility that competition would force the steel industry to carry out some of the reorganizational steps that the Commission could not secure by direct bargaining. It constituted an early recognition of an elusive policy thread which few French officials other than Monnet have ever accepted: that effective competition and intelligent planning are natural allies rather than enemies.

At almost the same time as the first major step was taken toward international competition, the French adopted their first modern antitrust legislation. More precisely, an administrative decree of 1953 established three new rules limiting enterprise behavior directly inimical to competition. The decree prohibited refusals of producers to supply retailers practicing price cutting, prohibited resale price maintenance, and established a commission for the investigation and control of agreements on pricing. As Jacques Houssiaux emphasized in his explanation of these measures, the approach is less one of forbidding collusion, in the sense of the American antitrust legislation, than it is one of introducing supervision of agreements

[59, pp. 201–07]. A Technical Commission established to investigate agreements was given the authority to establish the specific criteria of acceptable or unacceptable effects, guided only by the presumption that accords which act to raise costs or prices are probably, though not necessarily, undesirable. Nothing in this program resembles the Clayton Act or Kefauver legislation aimed at prevention of mergers reducing the number of competing firms. On the contrary, the Technical Commission has used its authority to promote combination as a solution to the difficulties of firms previously relying on collusive agreements [59, pp. 389–91].

It is possible to advance good reasons for doubting that this legislation in favor of competition does or ever will amount to much. As summarized by Warren Baum, "The legislation embodies a dubious distinction between 'good' and 'bad' cartels, and there is little record of enforcement against even so-called 'bad' cartels. . . . On balance, the net effect of government action appears to have been to strengthen the forces, formidable enough in their own right, that restrain the competitive process and reduce its effectiveness in allocating resources or promoting growth" [30, pp. 280–81]. This view is eminently defensible. But it may also be true that government actions have had many desirable effects in their own right, and that some lines of policy other than promotion of competition could be allied with that approach to achieve better results than would occur if reliance were placed on competition alone.

Businessmen who think that the American Government interferes in private markets to a point beyond endurance might conceivably alter that opinion if they had to live with French regulations for a year or two. And economists who think that extensions of government control provide the answer to problems of efficiency in market organization might also find new doubts rising if they observed closely the French methods of promotion and regulation. Some of the new experiments in the economic sphere are fairly awful, some good, and very few without interest to anyone who recognizes that our own economic system must keep evolving if it is to meet the problems of the future with the degree of success it has known in the past.

PART II | Industry Studies

4 | Aluminum: Duopoly Plus Price Control

The French aluminum industry is as thoroughly organized by the producers as the American industry was prior to the antitrust action against Alcoa. There are two companies engaged in producing primary aluminum, but they minimize possible difficulties by using a joint selling agency. New investment by the two firms is synchronized in a manner permitting expansion without greatly changed industry shares. This approach antedated the adoption of the postwar government planning system, and has been carried on without thorough government direction since the war. The industry has been under continuous supervision in its pricing. Its status is comparable to that of public utilities in the United States, but in a highly dynamic field combining extraction and manufacturing.

1. Organization

The leading producer, Pechiney, traces its history back to the very start of the industry. From 1859 to 1889 it had the only plant in the world continuously engaged in aluminum production [118] [123]. As the only producer, in 1886 it was offered the patent rights to the new electrolytic method of production developed independently by Paul Heroult in France. The company's reaction to this possibility, which provided the subsequent technical basis of the modern aluminum industry, neatly illustrated the advantages of monopoly. While recognizing that the innovation could lower costs, company officials considered the market to be unresponsive to possibly lower prices and decided that it was not worth the bother to adopt the new technique [123, p. 68]. As so often, new entry came to the rescue. The predecessor of Alcoa was soon in full swing in the United States, using the similar process developed by Charles Hall, and a new firm using Heroult's method drove Pechiney completely out of aluminum production in France.

For a short period following Heroult's innovation, the French industry possessed a fair number of independently competing small firms. But Pechiney, graced with a new management, came back with a steady policy of collecting patents and small firms. The remaining companies developed habits of reasonable consultation through the international Aluminum Association, led by Alcoa from 1895. This system fell apart in the 1908 depression, but was soon replaced in France with the present joint selling agency, *L'Aluminium Française.*

At the time of its establishment, *L'Aluminium Française* had to coordinate sales for four producers. Its task has been simplified since: Pechiney absorbed two of them during the interwar period, leaving Ugine as its only companion. As of the end of 1960, Pechiney owned 81 percent of total productive capacity in metropolitan France. Added plant then in construction by both firms was expected to raise capacity by one-sixth during 1961, and to leave Pechiney's share at 82 percent by the end of the year [119].

The two remaining aluminum producers, with their sales agency, are located at the strategic point between six bauxite producers and a dispersed set of aluminum product fabricators. Three of the other four bauxite producers normally export their supplies. The fourth produces its own alumina in France, but delivers it for aluminum smelting to an associated company in Switzerland. Pechiney and Ugine are the only two with facilities integrated all the way up to aluminum production in France, but they in turn stop at the boundary line of ingot deliveries to *L'Aluminium Française*. All the firms engaged in fabricating products come to that agency for their supplies. It even handles the aluminum imports made available to fabricators, and these in turn come chiefly from the African plants in which Pechiney and Ugine have major interests.

The fact that the two producers do not themselves cross over into fabrication of finished products is not to be ascribed to a desire for concentration on aluminum smelting. Both of them are highly diversified metal and chemical companies. For Pechiney, chemical products provide nearly half of total sales. And both have a host of partially or wholly owned subsidiaries in other fields. Pechiney's Annual Report for 1958 lists interests in 46 firms, one of which is in the aluminum fabricating industry.

In 1950, one-third of all bauxite and an equal proportion of alumina production were exported. By 1958 the production of bauxite had increased 2.3 times, but exports only 1.2, reducing the export ratio to 17 percent. Alumina production increased 2.6 times in this period, but again (except for a temporary jump in 1958), exports have risen less rapidly than production [118]. In this instance, the trend toward lower export ratios is a favorable sign: while output at all stages has risen rapidly, the balance has shifted toward higher-value aluminum.

Although the industry has been blessed with good supplies of high-quality bauxite, its expansion has been handicapped on the resource side by inadequate availability of low-cost power. Before the war, production was located in areas where the companies were able to develop their own hydroelectric facilities. Since the war, all these facilities have been nationalized. Their output has been sold to the firms at special rates intended to be comparable to costs the companies would have realized in the absence of nationalization. Special rates have also been negotiated for newer energy supplies, notably that derived from natural gas at Lacq. The rates involved apparently run from a minimum of .4 of a cent up to one cent per kilowatt-hour, averaging well below French power costs generally, though above those for major aluminum reduction operations in other countries.

The effort to utilize hydroelectric power sources and to locate near bauxite deposits led to a pattern of small plants, dispersing production in a manner that seems at first sight most inefficient. The industry's reduction capacity in 1959, of 171,000 tons, was almost exactly equal to that of the Reynolds Metals' plant at Listerhill, Alabama. The smallest plant in either Canada or the United States at the end of 1960 had a capacity of 35,000 tons. The French capacity of 1959 was distributed in 11 plants, only one of them above 20,000 tons. But two new plants over 20,000 tons came into operation in 1960–61, both based on the gas at Lacq. One of them has a capacity equal to 50 percent of that of the whole industry as of 1959 [118] [125, 1961, p. 60]. And one of the smallest plants, with only 3500 tons capacity, went out of operation at the end of 1959. The average size is creeping up, but remains out of touch with that in other producing countries.

It may be considered that the persistence of such small-scale operations is a mark of either poor planning or slow progress by the French producers. The former of the two criticisms may be partly valid. It does seem most doubtful that some of the smallest of these operations would have been undertaken if the pace of the industry's growth had been accurately foreseen. But industry officials insist that it would be a great mistake to consider these small plants as systematically high-cost operations. They state that the process of continuing modification of these plants has enabled them to achieve running costs closely comparable to the largest installations in the industry. When the basic facilities require replacement, the plants are likely to be closed down, as one was at the end of 1959. But in the meantime they have reasonably low operating costs and, because of their dispersion in close proximity to bauxite supplies, low transport costs. Perhaps the most convincing reason offered for the argument that these plants are not in fact evidence of inefficiency is the point discussed in section 2 below: the industry has operated profitably with prices below those in the United States or Canada.

Until the development of the Lacq natural gas field the energy problem rendered the prospect for major new aluminum installations in France decidedly poor. The producers directed their attention instead to development of two large-scale plants in Africa: Edea in the Camerouns and Fria in Guinea. The two French firms own eight-ninths of the former installation. This proportion corresponded to 40,000 tons capacity in 1960, adding 15 percent to the metropolitan total. Fria is owned by a more diversified group of international aluminum producers. Pechiney's share in this operation is slightly less than 18 percent. This plant, which will have a capacity exceeding that of the entire metropolitan French industry, began operations in 1960. Despite the important initial role and continuing voice of the French producers in Fria's development, the political antagonisms between Guinea and France make it somewhat doubtful that any part of this production can be counted on as a stable source of metropolitan supply.

Domestic bauxite supplies and possibilities of further energy development make it perfectly conceivable that the industry may continue to expand for some time in France itself. The critical question will be the availability of further low-cost power. The industry's past and future are closely bound up with natural resource problems. But factors of market organization and control have been by no means irrelevant in its development to date and provide some interesting comparisons with the evolution of the American industry under somewhat more competitive conditions.

2. Performance

As Donald Wallace explained with respect to the prewar performance of Alcoa in its monopoly position, market control in an industry for which demand is rapidly expanding may easily be consistent with effective growth choices by the firm [126]. Where the chief objective in a stagnant market may be to adjust supply to the optimum price indicated by the elasticity of demand, the more important goal in a swiftly moving market may become one of raising capacity fast enough to minimize the temptations for new entry. It is conceivable that a firm in this situation may lag in its expansion of supply in order to facilitate an effort to raise prices, but Alcoa did not choose to behave this way and the French firms have not done so either.

Output of aluminum in France rose more rapidly than that in the United States from 1920 to 1939, increasing from 20 to 35 percent of the American total. It kept pace with the other European producers in the 1920's, but fell behind the five-fold German expansion of the 1930's. By 1939, French output was slightly under half that in Germany [179].

The American industry produced only one-half as much primary aluminum as the combined European producers in 1939 but pulled far ahead of them during and immediately after the war. In 1946 its output was more than double the European total. French output oscillated around its 1939 peak, badly hampered by power shortages and the general disorganization of the economy, from 1946 through 1950. In the latter year it was only 9 percent of the American total. From that year, with output at 61 thousand tons as against the prewar peak of 53, the industry's expansion became steady and rapid. By 1960, output was 3.9 times as high as in 1950. This rate of expansion was slightly greater than that for all OEEC producers combined (3.4 times), and well above that in the United States (2.8 times). All three of these areas raised their output sharply relative to that of the Canadian industry during the 1950's. By 1960, French production was still only one-eighth of the American level, but it was 39 percent greater than that in Germany, the second largest European producer [178].

Two major difficulties with the preceding comparisons are that they consider expansion solely in terms of output, neglecting trends in the installation of new capacity, and they suggest an identification of the national area with the effective scope of industry decisions. Comparison in terms of production favors the French industry, because it operated at full capacity through the last half of the 1950's, while both Canada and the United States increased capacity faster than output. At the end of 1960 the American industry's annual capacity was 2.2 million tons [125, 1961, p. 60], against an output of 1.8 million tons in that year. The percentage of idle capacity in the Canadian industry was probably even higher. In both cases, the extra capacity represented an asset for the community that should be counted as part of the industry's growth in some degree. But even if growth from 1950 to 1960 were measured purely in terms of productive capacity, the expansion in France remains greater than that in the other two countries. Besides, they were able to use it.

The other difficulty in these comparisons is that all the major producers have devoted financial and managerial resources to production outside their national boundaries. The achievement of each of these groups has been greater than that measured by domestic capacity. The French do measure this aspect directly. In 1959 and in 1960 they considered 40,000 tons of output from their plant in the Camerouns as part of their production [119]. Since they provide the management and most of the capital, and did import the production into France, this does seem a legitimate inclusion for purposes of measuring the industry's expansionary effort. If this output were included in the industry's total, which it is not in the calculations given above, it would raise the 1960 production level by 15 percent. It is doubtful that the foreign interests of the American and Canadian producers would, if added to their domestic production, make a difference of that magnitude. All this does not prove that the expansion of the French industry has been at a pace optimal for its own economy. It only means that the industry's growth under conditions of monopoly and price control was superior during the 1950's to those achieved by the aluminum industries of the other western countries.

The ability of the French industry to maintain its capacity in full use has been aided by the important role of its exports. The latter have always accounted for a substantial share of total sales, ranging from 25 to 35 percent up to the war. Exports were negligible in the first years after the war, but picked up to a new high by 1950, slightly over one-fourth of total output. Since 1950, the pattern of exports reveals a pronounced inverse association with domestic economic activity. They fell in 1951–52 while production rose rapidly, quadrupled in 1953 during the domestic recession, returned to lower levels as the economy expanded swiftly from 1954 to 1957, then moved up to new record levels. Exports averaged 16 thousand tons in 1956–57 and 51 thousand in 1958–59, then reached 70 thousand in 1960.

It should be noted that the steep export increases of 1953 and 1958 were achieved in conditions of temporarily weakened world demand. The decreases in 1951 and 1954–57 occurred despite strong external markets. This pattern could conceivably have been caused by steeply rising prices in conditions of strong demand, choking off export possibilities and diverting production to the protected domestic market. But this was not in fact the case. Domestic prices did not rise at all from 1951 to 1957 while world trade prices were rising steadily. Exports were apparently treated as a marginal outlet, readily open whenever the industry had adequate supplies available but promptly neglected when domestic demand picked up. Domestic and world prices were out of line, but the domestic were the lower.

The situation seems to have been at once a tribute to low costs and an indictment of possibly inadequate expansion.

3. Domestic Prices and World Trade

The statement that French prices have been below world trading levels refers to an evolving situation that is not perfectly clear. The basic French price was until late in 1960 reported for a different grade of metal than that for American and Canadian prices, it refers to factory rather than delivered prices, and it is quoted free of the domestic tax on value added. Further, export prices seem to have varied from domestic prices, at least on occasion, in all these countries. Relying on industry explanations of the corrections necessary for comparability, French prices in October 1951 were roughly one-fourth above the Canadian and American level. The domestic price, ex tax, was then 1.81 NF per kilo. It was forced down by price controls to 1.74, then held at that level until early 1957. In the interval in which the French price was blocked, Canadian export prices increased 36 percent and American prices 37 percent [124, p. 20] [172, October 24, 1957]. In this period, French output rose faster than in Canada but only three-fourths as rapidly as in the United States.

In the course of 1957, government policy began to alter toward a reduction in the severity of administrative restraint on price increases. The aluminum industry was allowed three increases within a year, bringing a total rise of 14 percent—approximately one-third of that in the Canadian and American cases during the preceding five years. From 1958 through 1960, with controls further relaxed and with two devaluations opening up a wide gap between foreign prices and the foreign exchange equivalent of domestic French quotations, prices in France increased several times. By March 1961 the price of primary aluminum had reached 2.48 NF per kilo, equivalent to 23 American cents per pound [119].

Throughout the period of effective price control in France, prices of aluminum in the United States marched inexorably upward. In 1951, briefly in 1953, and again in 1955–56, premium prices for secondary aluminum indicated that demand exceeded supply for primary ingot. But the price moved up both when demand was greater than supply and when it was not. From .18 a pound in 1951 it moved to .26 by July 1957. The last increase was implemented by all producers in the midst of a sharp economic downturn, after nearly a year in which falling prices for secondary aluminum had indicated lessening demand pressure. All increases were impressively synchronized. Alcoa as the low-cost producer exerted a restraining influence and all the others were ready to jump as soon as permitted to do so by an increase in Alcoa's price [124, ch. 4].

Exactly when French controls were eased and the domestic price of ingot began to climb toward the external level, the previously invulnerable American price structure began to come under pressure. Aluminum Limited departed from its passive role, usually involving only polite acceptance of the going price in the American market, and initiated a decrease. This forced the first postwar cut in American prices. This step was taken in March 1958, following the entry of both American and Russian aluminum in some of the traditional markets of Aluminum Limited [124, pp. 46–51]. The North American producers soon got over the shock of incipient competition, and the price in the United States market moved back up to .26 per pound. But the pressure of excess capacity in the Canadian and American industries, and rising supply from other producers, reasserted itself in 1961. The Canadian firm cut its export price again, and the American price promptly fell back to .24 a pound—the level first established in 1956. At this point the gap between American and French prices, and indeed the differentials among quotations of all the leading western producers, were practically eliminated [119]. Market forces grind exceeding slow in this well organized field, but they do not go away.

From a sufficiently long-run view, private market control in North America and government price control in France might well seem irrelevant: everybody's prices came into line not long after supply caught up with demand. Alternatively, it might be considered that the producers with a commanding position in an industry giving important advantages to scale overestimated the degree to which they might widen margins without encouraging rapid expansion of capacity by others, and thus helped alter the world's production structure. At the same time, French producers who were utterly out of touch with external prices in 1951 were subsequently held under controls so well that export sales became more profitable than domestic, even prior to the 1957–58 currency devaluations. In the process, the industry prospered and grew to be a more important exporter than ever before.

The question of burning interest to the producers now is that of protection from foreign competition. The French producers have a clear position. Despite their competitive prices, they fought bitterly for a high level of tariff protection on imports into the Common Market. Their position, apparently accepted wholeheartedly by the French Government, resulted in placing aluminum on the "G list" of those for which establishment of the common external tariff was particularly difficult [185, February 12, 1960]. Opposite preferences by Germany and Italy as net importing countries led to a compromise tariff of 10 percent. (The American tariff, at 1.5 cents per pound, was equivalent to just over 6 percent of the domestic price at the end of 1961.) The reason that the French producers so strongly want protection is that they consider their own growth threatened by possible competition intended to put to work idle capacity in other countries. "Harmonious development of production and consumption is possible if the market on which the aluminum industry relies is not exposed to attacks from the exterior in periods of world or local economic crisis. . . . The stability of prices which the producers of the six countries have always sought serves the interests, properly understood, of the consumer. For this, it is indispensable that aluminum conserve a minimum of tariff protection" [122].

The arguments of the French producers for tariff protection blend self-interest and objectives of harmonized growth in classical style. They appear in a new light as a close approximation to the case for free trade when compared to the position taken by the American aluminum producers in 1961 [117]. The American firms have a larger vision: harmonizing expansion of aluminum trade in a coordinated system of import quotas to be established jointly by all western producers.

Both the American and the French producers look at the problem as one in which foreign firms, rashly expanding capacity beyond the confines of markets to which tradition has entitled them, may force prices down to unprofitable levels in an attempt to put their capacity to use. The ogre looks particularly nasty to the industry because marginal costs are far below average unit costs up to full capacity, hence far below going prices for many firms which have idle plant. Merton Peck estimates that variable costs are barely over half of total costs in the American industry, even at full capacity [124, ch. 6]. This need not (and has not) encouraged any firms to move prices below average costs for their whole market, but it might well tempt a firm with a protected domestic market to do so for export sales. The somewhat brutal reasoning of traditional economics—that such sales would constitute a gift of resources to purchasing countries—is small consolation to uneasy producers. And the reasoning may be faulty. Erratic sales below long-run average cost, in an industry which must expand, may distort the allocation of resources among producing countries. Further, the possibility raises the risk attached to new investment, and may thereby restrain expansion and raise the long-run supply price.

If the American industry's proposal of a quota system to limit imports were adopted, it would be difficult to resist the logic of the French case for tariff protection. The alternative is to go the other way around and allow free movement of trade in all directions. In such conditions, the external price becomes available to domestic buyers and dumping is practically precluded. And if dumping is thereby made impossible, no firm can hope to grow unless its sales, both external and domestic, are made at prices covering long-run average costs.

The foregoing does not provide an answer to the problem of possibly serious dumping by countries outside the western trading group. Peck makes clear that the Russian sales of aluminum which have so bothered the western producers have not yet been sufficient in volume to matter in a competitive western market [124, pp. 47–51]. They did have an impact on price in 1958, because the western firms were operating with prices well above average costs in conditions of excess supply, at least as indicated by continuing profits at the lower prices which resulted from Russian intervention in the market. This episode was a gain for all western countries because it brought prices closer into line with costs, apart from the fact that some consuming countries were in effect subsidized in small amount by Russia. High-volume sales below average costs coming erratically from a country not allowing freedom for imports could conceivably be undesirable, for the reasons indicated above, but this rather remote possibility might better be met if it occurs than accepted as a reason for permanently suboptimal arrangements among the western countries.

The relevance of the trading system to the problem of domestic market control is clear enough. If the Canadian producer had not feared a possible flight to higher American tariffs, it could have and might well have provided more aggressive competition and choked off the arbitrary price increases of the American firms in the latter half of the 1950's. It would have been difficult for the French price level to get so high above external prices prior to domestic price control, and difficult for North American prices to stay above European levels when the latter moved to the lower side. Absent international competition, recourse to price control seems to work better than reliance on unregulated domestic markets.

4. Market Power and Price Regulation

If the combination of monopoly and price control in this industry in France had any seriously adverse effects on performance, they are not easy to locate. The rate of expansion compares well with that in other European countries or in North America, the industry is eminently capable of competing in world export markets, and its prices have risen less rapidly than those of the dominant United States and Canadian producers. As measured by its revenue from patents, by use of its techniques in the newest installations in other countries, and by the reduction of input requirements for labor and energy at home, the major producer is very much alive technically.

It would be a great mistake to conclude that this case demonstrates any necessary superiority of monopoly in the French industry as compared to competition in the American. The American producers do compete in research, independent capacity expansion, and development of new products. In these areas their record has been decidedly good. They do not seem to compete with respect to pricing. In this area their record is not very good. The French industry does not compete at all in pricing, but it has been checked here by government control. The chief effect of this control was quite simply to hold down price increases. It accomplished a very considerable reduction in French prices relative to those in Canada and the United States during the 1950's, without any clearly harmful effects on expansion and technical progress. It may even have had the effect of fostering such progress, by an environment discouraging recourse to price increase.

Price control worked well in the case of aluminum for two reasons. On the administrative level, it was easy to apply because of the standardized nature of the product. More importantly, it could hold down prices without checking investment because increasing efficiency held down rises in unit costs. The French producers were faced with more rapidly rising wages than the American producers, but they seem to have had greater success in holding down cost repercussions by technical advance.

Working with electricity costs higher and wage rates lower than the American producers, the French companies have focused much of their research on efforts to reduce power requirements. From 1951 to 1959 the power requirements per ton of final product, for the integrated process from production of alumina through primary aluminum, were reduced 18 percent [121, p. 9].

Labor productivity is perhaps less important to the industry than efficiency in use of electricity. Power costs were estimated at 32 percent of total costs in 1959, while labor costs (judging crudely from Pechiney's annual report combining chemical and aluminum production), were on the order of one-fifth of all expenditures for goods and services. Still, improvements in labor efficiency have been decidedly helpful. Man-hours per ton of final aluminum required in alumina and aluminum production were reduced by 55 percent from 1929 to 1951, and a further 51 percent from 1951 to 1959 [121, p. 9]. The final operation of aluminum fusion required approximately eight hours per ton in Pechiney's largest plant as of 1959. The new plant placed in operation at Noguères in 1960 is expected to require about 4.5 man-hours per ton [175, February 14, 1960].

The increase in labor productivity between 1951 and 1959 took much of the sting out of a rate of wage increase about double that suffered by the American producers. Official data on wage rates are not given separately for this industry, but wages may be approximated from those for workers in all primary metals industries. Hourly wage rates for such workers rose 109 percent from June 1951 to September 1959. In this period, taxes and social security charges on employers rose from 38 to

48 percent of wages for workers in the mechanical and electrical equipment industries, and presumably in about the same degree in the metals industries [12, pp. 258, 260]. If all these approximations are linked to the improvement in labor productivity they indicate a rise in wage costs per ton of slightly less than 10 percent.

In the 1952–57 period of particularly rigid price control, Pechiney's pre-tax operating profit as a ratio to sales rose from 6.2 to 11.0 percent, while its net profits as a percentage of sales rose from 3.7 to 4.5. This may have been due to gains from chemical operations offsetting a squeeze in aluminum. But it is in any event clear that the reason price controls worked, without blocking expansion, was that gains in efficiency offsetting higher input prices left profit margins sufficient to encourage and facilitate steady new investment.

The fact that exports had to be reduced in years of vigorous domestic booms, while prices were competitive, suggests that a greater expansion of capacity would have been desirable. Industry officials seem to agree. The key obstacle cited has been domestic energy supply [120]. No cost data are available to prove it, but the situation seems to have been one in which average cost in existing plants has been well below world export price levels, while costs in added plants that would have been forced to use high-price energy would have gone above competitive levels. As noted, the producers did turn to development of new plants in Africa, and did quickly take advantage of the one major new possibility opened up at home by the discovery of natural gas at Lacq.

The monopoly situation in the French industry did reveal a serious drawback in the early stages of development, when Pechiney kicked away the chance to be the first firm in the world using modern techniques of production. Considering the company's stress on technical advance today, and its record of continuing improvements, repetition of such a mistake would seem properly incredible. But the case suggests a warning supported by similar instances in American industrial history. Where the question is one of reducing costs or improving quality with a fairly well-defined technology, a large enterprise run by a progressively oriented management may be unbeatable. When the question becomes one of radical departure to entirely new processes or products conceived outside the company's own range of research, the large organization is not always quick to see the possibilities and act on them.

The French aluminum producers have been in a strong position to bargain for favors in the pricing of their energy supplies, on tariffs, and on the prices allowed them for their products. When controls were tightly exercised, they went ahead anyway. When the controls were relaxed in a climate more favorable to business interests beginning in 1958, the industry's prices moved up rapidly. In the absence of competition, the society must depend on the progressive character and generosity of two cooperating managements, sometimes checked by government agencies and sometimes not.

The scale of the American industry permits actual or potential competition among a number of producers able to operate with efficient techniques. This is much better than the French situation because it offers a diversity of approaches to technical advance and less danger of general loss from costly mistakes by any single group. On the other hand, it has yielded an inferior pricing performance. The greater number of producers during the 1950's did not lead to any evident independence of pricing among them. The French industry does not engage in price cutting either, and is most unlikely ever to do so with its present organization. But if aluminum producers do not engage in pricing competition, and international competition cannot be secured, it would seem from the French experience that there may be something to be gained from applying external restraint on this aspect of their decisions.

5 | Steel: Planning in Practice

The postwar experience of the steel industry provides a tempting, if treacherous, test of the effectiveness of the French approach to planning and the relevance of competition. Steel has been more closely associated with the postwar plans than any other manufacturing industry. The planning process has included explicit pressure for increased concentration of ownership and extensive marketing agreements. The unusually well-organized trade association has cooperated on this program. Never very thoroughly competitive, the industry has possibly never been less so than in the postwar period. The results have been cited both as a vindication of planning and as a dismal disappointment. These two interpretations clearly leave room for a third, duly expressed by other qualified observers, that government interference has been for the most part unhelpful, but that the industry has made striking progress anyway [100, pp. 87, 166] [129] [133].

1. Industry Organization and Relationships with the Government

The steel industry never went through an early merger process comparable to that culminating in the organization of United States Steel. The mergers that did take place before the war left the industry in the same nonconcentrated state that characterized it in the latter half of the nineteenth century. Most firms remained under family control. One of the largest, de Wendel, was even split in two to facilitate apportionment of the property for inheritance within the family. The dispersion of ownership was counterbalanced to some extent by two factors: a multiplicity of cartel arrangements and a considerable development of inter-company interests. The latter were fostered by family alliances and personal associations rather than by direct combination or extensive use of holding companies.

Estimates of the significance of these interest links differ widely. One excellent study suggests that mutual distrust and frequent desire to outmaneuver associates led to considerable independence of behavior despite outwardly thorough agreements. In contrast to the ponderously organized German cartels, the French producers formed "a school of small sharks, swimming in a different medium and comporting well with one another" [143, p. 336]. They comported well enough together to stabilize a high level of prices collectively from 1933, in the midst of general economic collapse [180, p. 130]. On the other hand, their growth and modernization record compared very favorably with that of the British industry [130]. From 1913 to 1929, their production grew at the same rate as all European producers combined, despite the slower growth of French population and labor force [179]. The industry was able to provide 6 percent of all French export earnings in 1929, and 8 percent in 1938 [6, p. 13].

The major weakness of the style of competition practiced in France was that it did not provide great pressure for the elimination of inefficient facilities, nor for rapid adoption of technological improvements. Duncan Burn's indictment of the prewar British steel industry would be almost fully transferable to the French scene, except that the size distribution of plants in France was moderately more favorable for achievement of economies of scale [130, pp. 432–33]. He compares British and French production structures to the detriment of the former, but also notes that "with Germany the contrast was of course more striking . . ." [130, p. 432]. Indeed it was. In 1913, only one French firm possessed a productive capacity of over 400,000 tons per year. It provided only 10 percent of the total output in the major producing areas of the north and east. In the German Saar and Lorraine at the same time 77 percent of all production was provided by plants this size or larger [143, p. 311].

The dramatic improvement of efficiency made possible by the modern wide-strip mill was first demonstrated in the United States in 1924. The American industry installed 28 such units by 1939. The British industry installed 2 and the German one prior to the second world war [180, pp. 132–33]. The first such plant in the French industry was installed in the late 1940's under pressure from the government's Planning Commission.

When the first Monnet Plan was drawn up in 1946, the committee concerned with the steel industry prepared a thorough report on existing installations. Their census noted the existence of 177 plants, with a combined capacity on the order of 12 million tons—well short of that of the United States Steel Corporation. The committee concluded that the smallest-scale facilities appropriate for efficient production would leave room for no more than 12 basic producers and 12 specialty steel plants. They had little difficulty in picking out numerous instances of plants that could not hope to produce at or near world price levels, and were so out of date or poorly located that expenditures for modernization were deemed completely undesirable. In most instances the descriptions published make it difficult to understand how the firms had survived at all before the war [5, pp. 4–8, 26–28] [129, pp. 53–60].

The plan drawn up in 1946 was based on industry-government discussion of individual company projects submitted by practically all the producers. But the plan did not by any means constitute a simple acceptance of these proposals. The latter projected a piecemeal modernization and extension of existing facilities in line with the policies and financial possibilities of each firm separately: i.e., a continuation of the existing pattern of production. The plan retained many of these projects but stipulated major shifts in the direction of greater concentration and specialization. Basic crude production was to be largely reserved to the north and the Lorraine regions, production of most specialty steels to the center and south, and some high-carbon steels (too important in both sectors to be eliminated in either), were to be allocated by quota between regions. Firms whose facilities contradicted these divisions, or were ill-located or too archaic for low-cost modernization, were discouraged from any expansion and encouraged to close down entirely. The suggestion to shut down was ignored by some of the smaller producers. It was more difficult to ignore advice against expansion, because access to capital markets and permits for construction both required official approval.

New investment, centering in the north and the Lorraine on two modern wide-strip mills, was conceived on a scale calculated to yield maximum efficiency rather than to fit the financing and market possibilities of existing firms. Relocation and specialization within regions was outlined in terms of resource and transport facilities for the area as a whole. In the northern region the two major firms were converted into holding companies, supervising a regional monopoly. Their jointly owned subsidiary, Usinor, became and remains the largest single producer of crude. The Planning Commission obtained the bulk of the financing for Usinor's key new mill and for the relocation of many of the existing operations of the two original producers. It also provided most of the financing for the new mill in the Lorraine, as well as an accompanying reorganization of surrounding coke-preparation and steel finishing facilities. The Lorraine plant was set up as a new firm, Sollac, jointly owned by seven producers in that area. In this case the parent companies remained separate firms. The plan further specified four new groups for the center and the south, intended to foster concentration on the more efficient facilities within each group, while retaining the benefits of "competition, generator of progress" [5, pp. 52–182, quote from p. 79].

The 1946 plan constituted a detailed program for reshaping the industry through changes in ownership and in the direction of investment. The Planning Commission did not itself formulate the details. It did initiate the process of drawing up the program, select the industry and public officials who worked it out in group discussion, and provide guiding estimates of raw material supplies and steel markets. It did not have powers to force compliance and did not get agreement for cooperation by all producers. The plan was a product of government-industry coordination, not a unilateral order issued to the producers from the outside.

The largest producers agreed with the plan adopted in the first place, and in general acted in line with its objectives. Many of the smaller firms, in particular those called on to give up their independence or to convert to entirely new operations, did not [138, pp. 167–231]. The two key projects were quickly carried out, the recommendations for exchanges of plant and marketing agreements were to a large extent adopted, and productive facilities were concentrated to a degree markedly changing the traditional lines of the industry. By 1954, 86 percent of all workers were employed in plants with 1000 or more employees [14, table 1-5].

The reasons for which the major producers cooperated are not mysterious. Cooperation assured essential financing help on favorable terms in a very capital-tight period [6, pp. 48–51] [133, pp. 209–12]. It provided assistance in obtaining materials and equipment. And, perhaps not least, the plan was drawn up in order to strengthen the industry, by changes that the producers had not achieved themselves but agreed to be desirable.

The reorganization accomplished did not impress everyone [129, pp. 109–29, 304–10] [143, p. 346]. Some criticisms of the result relate to production and price performance, discussed below. In terms of structure, the negative judgments stress that the industry did not become any more competitive, and that the old families, the individuals and holding companies long celebrated by critics of the industry, all remained in place. All this is true. None of it contradicts the fact of a significant reorganization in the direction of greater productive efficiency. The question is the choice of goals. The method and objective chosen placed the premium on cooperation, practically ruling out any attack on positions of privilege. Acceptance of strengthened market control by the leading firms was implicit in the planning process.

The series of mergers and coalitions started in 1946 has created a higher degree of concentration than in either the English or the German industries, though not as high as in the United States. The four leading companies provided 57 percent of total output in 1957, compared to 51 in England, 45 in Germany, and 65 in the United States [140, p. 8]. Unlike the situation in the American industry, the four leading concerns are not widely separated in scale. The largest firm, Usinor, produced 13.5 percent of total crude in 1952 and 15 percent from 1956 through 1958. The output shares of the next three firms (Sidelor, Lorraine-Escaut and de Wendel) have been steadily within a range of 12 to 14 percent. The same scale is approached by the group of firms associated with Schneider. If the three principal producers controlled by that company were combined they would add a fifth share of about 11 percent [129, p. 79] [140, pp. 67–82]. With one important exception noted below, the merger process since 1953 has affected primarily the smaller companies. This may suggest that a competitive market structure has been established, with five nearly-equal leaders and strengthened secondary firms. But any contribution of this structure to possible competition is counteracted by strong influences acting to prevent it.

One of the factors which tends to encourage cooperation among the firms is a heightened degree of the traditional technique of ownership interconnections. The most important instance is that of Sollac, the postwar creation built around the new wide-strip mill specified for the Lorraine in the 1946 plan. This company produced 9 percent of total crude in 1959, while processing a much higher proportion of finished steel products for the account of its seven joint owners. De Wendel, the fourth largest crude producer, owns 45 percent of Sollac's stock. Both Sidelor and Lorraine-Escaut, the second and third largest firms, are among the other seven owners. The fifth largest producer of crude, U.C.P.M.I., is another one of the owners of Sollac. It is in turn partly owned by the holding company which controls Lorraine-Escaut. One of the three important subsidiaries of the Schneider group is owned jointly with de Wendel. Some of these connections are ancient. Others were added in the course of exchanging plants and joining in the financing of new facilities specified in the 1946 plan [129, pp. 73–85] [140, pp. 67–82] [141, pp. 422–24].

The numerous specialty producers in the Loire were also consolidated as suggested in the plan, forming one company for the whole area. The two firms which emerged as the principal owners of this company in turn announced their own fusion in 1960, adding their interests in the north and in Lorraine to the Loire group [175, February 7, 1960]. The producers here had resisted proposed changes during the first plan, but finally adopted them when brought under pressure from competition in the Coal-Steel Community. Similarly, four producers of high-grade steel in the Massif Central, who had refused to implement the consolidation proposed in the Monnet Plan, did carry it out in the mid-1950's as a result of the new force brought to bear on them through the Community [131, p. 461].

The degree of concentration will be raised through the most important project developed subsequent to the Monnet Plan, the complex of facilities nearing completion at Dunquerque. This was planned as a separate firm, to be owned jointly by four steel producers and an investment bank. The largest ownership share, 43 percent, belonged to Usinor. Continuing expansion of demand led to modifications of original plans, including the addition of a more modern strip mill of the type installed by Usinor in the same region in 1948. This decision implied the possibility of eventual conflicts of interest between the two sets of facilities. The result was a new agreement on financing, under which Usinor has obtained complete control of Dunquerque. In the process, marketing agreements and exchanges of stock were concluded with the other steel firms interested in the project [175, January 22 and 27, 1960].

The effects of ownership interrelations are reinforced by a set of industry-wide commercial, financing, and research organizations. The trade association, *La Chambre Syndicale de la Sidérurgie*, is generally considered to be one of the most active in all French industry. The planning process has relied heavily on cooperation through this association [5, pp. 206–07] [34, ch. 6]. Four other organizations active or envisaged in 1946 have had varying fates. A joint research institute has been operating very successfully. An intended system of pooled depreciation allowances, envisaged as a major source of financing to be allocated in cooperation with the Planning Commission, never gained acceptance [5, pp. 203–05]. An alternative system of common financing has worked well. All of the larger producers, and many secondary companies, are members of *Le Groupement De L'Industrie Sidérurgique*, which borrows from the public under its collective guarantee and allots the funds among members by agreement. Finally, a single selling agency was established for all the basic steel producers. Although this did not extend to specialty steels, it effectively controlled sales of crude and most finished products until the opening of the Coal-Steel Community. Since that time it has nominally restricted its activities to collecting and organizing data on sales, which are handled directly by the separate selling agencies of the major firms [5, p. 75] [129, pp. 91–94].

Group discussions of industry development through active professional associations have been accompanied by periodic confrontation of objectives under the auspices of the Planning Commission. The published reports concerned with the second and third plans differ fundamentally from that of 1946. Consideration of individual enterprise reorganization and investment has been confined to internal working group studies. The published documents report probable results of collected individual projects. There is little evidence to show that these projects are significantly altered by the process of group discussion, and some suggestion by people associated with the operation that they are not. In any event, the published documents include sector-by-sector confrontations of product markets and probable availabilities, with indications of expected areas of shortage or surplus, but little hint of any pressure for marked change in industry organization or behavior.

Those officials of the Planning Commission concerned with the industry do follow closely the evolution of markets, production, and investment. The flow of advice and inquiry is two-way: the Commission attempts to influence current industry decisions and the producers try to influence government action through the Commission. The latter's capacity to shape industry choices in fact depends heavily on its ability to cast an important vote within the government on such matters as loans from public funds, import licensing, tax legislation, and price control [100, pp. 166–69].

The crucial role of public funds in the early postwar period was noted above. It has become much less important since, though government loans still covered 7 percent of investment financing in 1959 [4, pp. 131–32]. Special depreciation provisions were secured in the early 1950's and are still in effect. They are based on the principle of allowing depreciation proportional to production. Maximum deductions allowed vary among the industry's products. For Bessemer steel, depreciation is allowed up to 8 percent of sales [87, p. 393]. The over-all average rate most often mentioned in industry discussions is 12 percent. But in fact the industry as a whole was not able until quite recently to earn the full allowances intended. The restraint on earnings derived from resistance to proposed price increases by the price control agency [5, pp. 200–02] [6, pp. 45–46] [7, pp. 48, 57] [133, pp. 209–26].

The Planning Commission has sided consistently with the producers' argument that price controls as exercised have restrained expansion. The fact that there has been such a conflict brings out one of the key aspects of government-business relationships. "Government," like "business," is a many-headed animal. The steel producers, the Planning Commission, and the Ministry of Industry can generally agree on the need of higher steel prices. Steel-consuming industries, the Ministry of Finance, and the price control agency often line up on the resisting side. It is easy to see how studies of the industry can arrive at differing conclusions on the question of whether government intervention has been helpful or harmful, depending on which aspect of that anomalous collection of conflicting interests is intended by the term government.

The Planning Commission can influence, but cannot always control, such critical areas of decision as price controls and taxation. The plans must be shaped to fit basic monetary, fiscal and regulatory decisions of other agencies, rather than those decisions fitted to the plans [100, pp. 49–56]. The Commission is one of many negotiating agencies within the government, and is at the same time a channel of two-way influence between the private economy and the other government agencies. On the industry side, the Commission can exercise the influence inherent in its role within government. It cannot force actions that the firms do not choose to adopt, but it can alter the factors affecting their choices. The natural result of the joint industry and Commission interest in expansion is that the two are allies rather than opponents. This does not mean that the Commission is in effect a subsidiary of the trade association.

It has in general pushed much more vigorously for the idea of continuing expansion than the industry preferred and has helped move the producers in this direction. Further, the strongest political move of the industry since the war, its attempt to block the Schuman Plan, was directly and successfully opposed by the Planning Commission [34, pp. 408–11]. Their interests usually coincide in such matters as pricing and taxation, but the Commission has wider objectives than the steel industry.

2. Factor Supply and Technological Improvement

Evaluation of performance requires review of the special input conditions of the industry. The producers themselves place considerable stress on the handicaps imposed by factor supply difficulties. Less charitable interpretations suggest rather that the supply situation has been highly favorable. The chief questions concern ore qualities, availability of coke, equipment supply, manpower shortages, and the social security costs charged to employers.*

The industry has long had at least one great natural asset in the form of an enormous supply of iron ore. Ore production has usually exceeded domestic requirements and provided substantial exports. While recourse to marginal imports of particular grades is now desirable for some purposes and will become increasingly important, reserves are estimated to be adequate for basic requirements for approximately another century. Over 90 percent of current supply is drawn from the Lorraine, in conditions favorable for low-cost extraction.

Lorraine ore has an unusually high phosphorous content, which posed a difficult problem until quite recently. The ore has long been usable through the Thomas conversion process,

* The following discussion is drawn from: [7, chs. 2–4] [31, pp. 95–100, 174–92, 217–18] [129, pp. 159–77] [133, pp. 41–69, 95–105] [143, chs. 7–10].

but the quality of the resulting product was always inferior to that of the open-hearth process. The latter, used for roughly 90 percent of steel production in the United States, is used for less than one-third of French production. This difficulty has been gradually resolved by generalized adoption of the process of adding oxygen to the air blown through the furnaces in the Thomas process. The asset of plentiful reserves has thus been improved to one of a high degree of qualitative adequacy.

The industry has long had to rely on imported supplies of coke and coking coal. The transport costs involved did not, in the prewar period, offset the producers' cost advantage from cheap ore. As of the 1920's the French industry operated profitably with domestic prices below those of both the English and German industries [130, pp. 426–34]. But in the early postwar years the costs of imported coke were aggravated by dual pricing on the part of exporting countries. In 1952 the price of coke in France was double that in Germany. Coke and energy costs were equal to 54 percent of total costs per ton of Thomas steel in France and 39 percent in Germany [31, p. 72]. These differences have been greatly narrowed since by the combined benefits of better organized trade through the Coal-Steel Community and the process of technical change focused on the coke problem.

The effect of the Coal-Steel Community on French resource costs was exactly in line with the objectives of international trade. Ore and scrap, previously cheaper in France, went up in price as they became available on equal terms to German users for whom they had been in short supply. Artificially high prices for German coke exports were simultaneously eliminated as this input became available on equal terms to French users. None of these resources can be moved without cost—the French industry would without doubt be better off if it possessed adequate supplies of coking coal within the country—but the specific difficulties of the coke supply were considerably eased by this improvement in international economic organization.

Technical progress in the same helpful direction has also been important in recent years. This has taken two forms: improvement of facilities for producing coke from French grades of coal, and reduction of coke requirements per ton of steel. These gains were achieved by cooperative research and investment by the steel producers and the nationalized coal industry. Consumption of French coking coal (excluding Saar supplies) rose from 23 percent of the total used in 1954 to 33 percent in 1958. Economies in the use of coke, as well as gains in the capacity of existing furnaces, have been secured by new methods of preparing inputs for the furnaces. The quantity of prepared inputs provided by postwar "agglomeration" facilities increased 80 percent between 1954 and 1958, permitting a 38 percent rise in steel output with a 26 percent increase in consumption of coking coal. The effect of the two forms of improvement combined was that the use of foreign supplies of coking coal increased only one-third as rapidly as the output of steel.*

One of the critical questions in the postwar modernization program was the supply of equipment. The absence of large-scale investment by the industry in the 1930's, followed by wartime isolation from technical advance elsewhere, left domestic equipment producers in a very poor position to supply modern plant. This problem was practically removed for the steel industry through its participation in the 1946 plan. It was given preferential access to imports for investment in line with the plan in the early postwar years, and maintained a relatively favorable position in this respect all through the 1950's. Since foreign currency availabilities were linked to export earnings for much of the postwar period and since the steel industry was consistently able to provide substantial exports, it did not suffer the handicap of restriction to domestic equipment suppliers to the same degree as French industry generally.

Manpower difficulties were severe in the years immediately

* [132, no. 325, September 1959]. The Saar is included here in foreign sources of supply.

after the war because of the persistence of excess aggregate demand. The ability to maintain the economy close to full employment has always meant that recruitment of labor has been less easy than in the United States, but labor availability was probably not an important limit on output except in the 1945–48 period and possibly in 1956–57. The industry has not found it necessary or desirable to raise wages above the average for all mechanical industries. This contrasts sharply with the situation in the United States, where steel industry wages are one-third higher than the average for mechanical industries generally [139, p. 3]. For better or worse, the French steel industry has not had to cope with the United Steelworkers of America.

Average hourly wage costs, including associated social charges, increased 69 percent in the French iron and steel industry between 1954 and 1959 [136, annex table 53]. The ratio of crude steel produced to hours worked rose 44 percent [137, pp. 201, 239]. The two indexes are not precisely comparable, but suggest an increase in wage costs per unit on the order of 12 percent for these five years. The American Iron and Steel Institute estimates that total employment costs per hour in the American steel industry increased 51 percent in this period [128, table 34a, p. 75]. This is one-fourth less than the increase incurred by the French industry, but it was made more painful by the absence of offsetting devaluation and by a distinctly slower improvement in output per man-hour. American productivity figures are tormented in this period by cyclical movements and strikes, but the five years ending in 1957 make an almost defensible basis of comparison. In those years, output per man-hour, for production workers only, increased just 16 percent [134, p. 21], less than half the rate of improvement in France.

An alternative measure of labor productivity in crude steel production in France has been provided by the OEEC. This measure excludes independent steel foundries, and does not take account of changes in hours worked per employee. The increase in production per man between 1954 and 1959 in the French industry is calculated at 33 percent [142, p. 59]. This is distinctly less than the estimate above, although still double the rate of improvement in the United States. It is much better than the gains shown for Germany or the United Kingdom, but inferior to those achieved by Italy and Sweden.

The French producers lose no chance to emphasize the exceptionally high ratio of social insurance and similar charges added to the basic wage rates they must pay. These charges did add approximately 67 percent to basic hourly wage rates in 1959 [16c, p. 226]. But even with all these charges taken into account, hourly costs of labor were only 28 percent of those in the American industry, and were 14 percent below those in the German industry, just after the 1957 devaluation. By March 1959, after the second successive devaluation, they were 22 percent below hourly wage costs in the German steel industry and only 24 percent of those in the American industry [16c, p. 238].

This difference in hourly labor costs between the French and American industries was considerably greater than that between output per man-hour in the two cases. The ratio of output per man-hour in the United States steel industry to that in France was about 2.4 in 1956 [141, p. 68].

3. Postwar Market Performance

Crude steel production in 1946 was 4.4 million tons. The plan issued in that year specified the objective of returning to the 1929 peak of 10 million within three years. That objective was to be sought within a framework of investment decisions guided toward production at competitive costs on successive levels of 10, 12 and 15 million tons. By 1949 the industry had more than doubled 1946 production but turned out only 9.2 rather than 10 million tons. A recession in the metals-using industries the next year led to a fall in steel production and some tendency to cut back investment plans. The 1949 target was not achieved until 1951. The basic modernization program proceeded with a wave of new installations from 1950 through 1953, largely completing the reorientation of the industry intended in the 1946 plan. Neither that plan nor the industry's response can be considered failures.

The investment bulge of 1951–53 was completed in conditions of recession. Domestic steel consumption fell 10 percent between 1952 and 1953. Current capacity became temporarily excessive just when moderate unemployment and idle resources for the economy as a whole improved the input situation for possible further expansion. The second modernization plan was prepared in this environment. The plan, published in 1954, suggested that capacity likely to be available by 1957 would be well above market requirements. With idle resources available, and cyclical recovery just beginning, the plan proposed a reduction of scheduled investment [6, esp. pp. 26–31].

The 1954 plan looks particularly unfortunate from the privileged position of hindsight because the recovery then beginning swept on to one of the most vigorous booms in French economic history. By 1956, steel demand exceeded capacity. Production in 1957 was at almost exactly the rate called for in the 1954 plan (14.1 million tons, as against the producers' original intentions of 15.4). This was so far short of being adequate that exports had to be restricted in the midst of a severe balance of payments crisis in order to alleviate domestic steel delivery delays [7, p. 4].

The third postwar plan was issued in 1957 in conditions of unquestionably inadequate supply. Although it accepted as appropriate the total investment projected by producers for 1957–61, it specified eight product categories in which the margin of capacity over anticipated demand was unduly thin [7, pp. 13–36]. A review of progress in late 1959 indicated that investment expenditures were running above expectations, but capacity in the fields stressed by the plan was expanding less rapidly than intended. The difficulty apparently related to an original underestimation of the costs of adding capacity rather than to any policy decision opposite to the sense of the 1957 plan.

The reorganization of the industry immediately after the war was thus reasonably rapid, but subsequent expansion was too slow to avoid the emergence of costly bottlenecks in 1956–57. The producers were geared to a rate of growth too low for that of the economy as a whole. The aggregative expansion was itself too rapid in 1956–57, in the sense that it gave rise to a serious balance of payments deficit and internal inflation. But the shortage of steel was one of the principal factors aggravating the external deficit and impeding domestic supply adjustments. Foreign demand would have permitted augmentation of steel exports if lack of capacity, traceable to preceding reductions of the industry's investment program encouraged by the Planning Commission, had not forced their contraction.

The industry's rate of expansion has been too slow when compared to its own opportunities, but does compare reasonably well to those in other countries. French production equalled 17 percent of the total for all OEEC member countries in 1950, and 16 percent in 1960. It was equal to 10 percent of American production in 1950 and 19 percent by 1960 [178]. The American output figures were far short of capacity in 1960, while the French were not. This may be taken to mean that the American producers have been bolder in their investment but handicapped by weak demand, while the French have been more cautious in investment despite excellent demand. Such an interpretation would be defensible but unduly simple. The producer attitudes did lean in different directions, but the output records of the two groups were not entirely determined by demand factors external to their own choices.

Between 1954 and 1959, the increase in exports of the French iron and steel industry equalled 37 percent of the concurrent rise in production (Table 9 below). In the same five-year period, the total value of American iron and steel exports decreased [181].

The other three-fifths of the increase in French steel production did depend heavily on the vigorous investment program of the French economy. This contrast to the American situation was largely, but not quite entirely, a matter external to industry behavior. One reason that it was not entirely external was the performance in exports itself, acting as a drag on aggregate demand in the American case and an important expansionary element in the French. A second reason is that the French industry financed a good share of its investment by credit drawn from outside the industry, raising aggregate monetary demand, in contrast to the American industry's method of financing investment by taking purchasing power out of the market through price increases. A third reason is that French steel prices did not take off skyward in the middle 1950's as did those of the American industry, and did not rise out of line with other domestic prices in the process of adjusting to the devaluations of 1957 and 1958. The difference encouraged the use of the product in one case and discouraged it in the other. Perhaps more importantly, the American steel industry's pricing stimulated recourse to overly deflationary aggregative policies by its potent effect on the behavior of American wholesale prices [134].

French iron and steel prices did go up at a dazzling pace, along with all other prices, from the end of the war until 1952. At that point they were hit by the imposition of strong price controls. This did not stop all increases, as in the aluminum industry, because the controls were adjusted in line with changes in costs and the industry did not succeed as well as the aluminum producers in holding costs down. From 1952 to 1957, in the period of most active control, the index of iron and steel prices rose 17 percent. In the following two years, with controls exercised less tightly and two devaluations helping to open up a gap below foreign prices, these prices went up another 17 percent, for a total increase of 37 percent in the period 1952–59. In these seven years, with hourly wage costs increasing less rapidly, with excess capacity rather than pressure of demand on supply, and with no mitigating devaluations, the index of American iron and steel prices rose 38 percent.

The French producers have persistently attacked the restraints exercised on their pricing, arguing that they check expansion by holding down internal funds and forcing reliance on unduly heavy borrowing. As compared to an average ratio of internal financing to investment expenditures on the order of two-thirds in both French and American industry, the ratio for the steel producers was only 42 percent from 1946 through 1952, and 51 percent from 1953 through 1956 [7, pp. 47–50]. The ratio of debt to sales reached 65 percent at the end of 1954. In the boom year of 1957, with operations at capacity, the leading firm in the industry reported a net loss.

It is probably correct that the industry's expansion was held back by price controls, at least during the attempt at rigid restrictions in the face of excess demand in 1956–57. On the other hand, the shortages in those years followed a period in which the steel industry had radically reduced its investment program, with an excessively cautious reaction to the temporary reduction of demand in 1952–53. And it is difficult to argue that the level of prices was the key factor restraining investment in 1957, when internally generated funds actually matched total investment expenditures. Much of the apparently weak profit data for the industry may be explained by its special depreciation system [87]. Usinor did report a loss in 1957, but its depreciation charges fully covered a record high level of investment expenditure, as they did for the whole six-year period from 1953 to 1958. All this is not to say that higher prices might not have led to higher investment, but to suggest that the actual rate of investment from 1957 on could have been higher even with controls. The context has become one of bargaining centered more on the question of the share of financing to be provided through the market than on the level of investment itself.

The upper limit for increases in French steel prices has been determined by those of other countries within the Coal-Steel Community. In May 1953, French domestic prices for basic products of both Thomas and Martin type steels were closely aligned with those in the other producing countries. Over the next four years, French prices rose least of all in the Community on Thomas steel products, though faster than German prices of Martin steel [131, pp. 439, 565]. French prices were thus the lowest in the community for Thomas steel even prior to the 1957–58 devaluations, and became the lowest for both types after the value of the franc was reduced. Converted into dollars at official exchange rates, French prices in January 1961 were still no higher than in May 1953 [136, p. 414]. Since 1957 they have been the lowest in the Coal-Steel Community.

The French controls, given treaty provisions prohibiting dual prices, have served as a braking factor on prices in all the Community. The German steel producers are among the more urgent proponents of a return to free market pricing in France. It is possible that the international competition within the group might provide an effective ceiling in the absence of controls. It is also possible that it would not, and it is quite certain that internal competition in France would not.

4. The Effects of Planning

The fundamental reorganization of the industry after the war, concentrating investment on lines selected to provide a firm base for efficient expansion, was conceived and implemented through the first modernization plan. In the absence of strong competition forcing such moves, they might have been very slow indeed. The information collected in 1946 on individual projects for the planning discussions suggests rather that the pattern of poor location, inadequate scale, and excessive diversification within firms would have been perpetuated if they had not been attacked through the plan. It is difficult to believe that the spontaneous individual decisions of so many firms operating with outdated basic plant, each handicapped by limited financing capacity and haunted by a background of prolonged demand inadequacy, could have accomplished any reorganization comparable to that actually achieved by the early 1950's.

Compliance with the reorganization efforts of the Planning Commission in this period did owe something to the threat of new competition through the Coal-Steel Community. This promoted reconversion efforts once it was accepted as a likely possibility, and the actual effect of trade in raising the extremely low level of French scrap prices forced the smaller producers of the west and center, previously hanging on to existence on the basis of cheap scrap, to convert to the production of special steels along the lines recommended by the Commission [131, pp. 461–62] [138, p. 341]. Credit cannot be assigned either to planning or to competition separately: the propulsion for action came from international competition, but the guidance on how to act and assistance in doing it came from planning. Further, the possibility of such competition was itself secured primarily by the Planning Commission, as the main proponent of the Coal-Steel Community. In this instance, in marked contrast to the succeeding policies of the Commission, recourse to competitive pressure was used to promote implementation of plans.

The results did not flow automatically from the fact that there was a plan for the steel industry, nor from the existence of a national plan with which that for the steel industry was at least nominally connected. They were brought about by the way in which planning was implemented, combining independent pressure from outside the industry itself with early recourse to international competition. The contrast with the English industry in this period is of particular interest. The

English producers were apparently even less concentrated and at least as uneven in efficiency as the French [131]. They were brought under planning at almost the same time, for almost identical objectives. But the results of the English plan, though by no means negligible, were a good deal less impressive. According to Duncan Burn, the difference in France was that planning there "showed a purposive direct and continuous participation of the state from the start, and was an integrated process, not planning within industry followed by state intervention or supervision as in Britain" [131, p. 392].

The reverse side of the planning process has been its effect of reducing the number of independent centers of initiative, increasing the importance of inter-firm connections, and strengthening the pattern of cooperation at the expense of possible competition. Neither the ownership connections nor group discussions originated with the 1946 plan, but the plan certainly had the effect of re-enforcing both. This result was not accidental. It was inherent in the process of implementing the plans through voluntary cooperation by the major firms and trade association.

The conclusion that planning reduced the possibility of competition only leads to the further question of the significance of the loss. The history of this industry in France, and contemporary practice in the United States, does not suggest that open price competition would have been strong in any case. Elements of partially hidden price competition in depression have continued in France as in the United States [19, pp. 360, 366]. Ability to exert a general upward pressure through simultaneous increases in list prices by all firms is not confined to the French industry. The operation of price control in France has been a stronger check in this respect than the market has been in the United States.

Planning has permitted an active government agency to enter within the counsels of the industry and to push for more vigorous expansion than might otherwise have been accomplished. But it has simultaneously discouraged conceivably duplicating projects and failed to counteract the firms' tendency to cut back investment programs in recession. The Planning Commission has shared the producers' reluctance to go out on a limb with expansion ahead of markets. The moderate pace of the industry's growth is partly attributable to excessively tight price control in boom periods, but also to hesitation in recessions and a pronounced tendency to stay very close to conservatively forecast rates of market growth.

The first plan achieved a vital improvement over a situation which a competitive industry probably would have prevented in the first place. The reorganization following left a structure that would appear reasonably well adapted to competition: five nearly equal groups of crude producers plus a fringe of largely modernized and specialized smaller firms. The growth of demand has since led to one new complex of facilities not originally subject to complete control by any of the dominant firms. The reaction to this latter situation, establishing full control by the largest existing firm, does not auger well for the emergence of increasing competition as a natural consequence of an expanding market. The industry's inability to provide active competition opened the way to a considerable gain from government intervention in 1946, and weakens any case for eliminating it now.

Since the early 1950's, the process of planning has done little to change the fundamental path of the industry and has probably served to reduce independent initiative, but it has still been consistent with a reasonably effective performance. The French industry has expanded too slowly, but has done far better than the American industry in practically all other respects. This has not been a triumph of planning over competition but rather an indication that, in the absence of strong competition, public participation in the decision processes of a cooperating industry group may be the next best alternative.

6 Industrial Equipment: An Attempt at Balanced Growth

Perhaps the most troublesome structural weakness in French industry from the end of the war until the end of the 1950's was the relatively high costs and slow improvement of the producers of machinery and equipment. As noted in Chapter 2, the ratio of prices for producers' durable goods to prices for consumer goods was much higher in France than in other industrialized nations in both 1950 and 1955. The following considerations are directed toward a possible explanation of this situation, and of its evolution in recent years.

Accurate description and analysis are rendered difficult in this case by the extreme heterogeneity of the producing group concerned. The broad meaning of industrial equipment intended here is not matched by any well-bounded definition of products which can be linked with published data. It is meant to include both electrical and nonelectrical machinery and equipment, which separately include many distinct industries and collectively include some 19,000 different plants [15, table 1]. Not very many of the specifically included industries have been investigated in detail by economists, either previous to or in connection with the present study. This means that the general discussion here falls in between aggregative sector analysis taking market factors as given, and the more precise techniques of inquiry suited to particular industries. The attempt relies on two unifying aspects of the equipment field. The first is the widespread dissatisfaction with its aggregative performance among government officials and students of French industry [16f] [28] [29, pp. 15–16, 44–46]. The second is the fact that many of the producing groups included are somewhat similarly organized. The characteristic organization is one of low concentration, with a large number of relatively small firms producing closely similar products. Granting the importance of some of the exceptions to this description, the troublesome general fact remains to be explained: this broad sector is organized on lines that should facilitate effective competition, but its performance has in most respects been inferior to that of the more concentrated sectors of the economy.

1. Organization of the Sector

One important clue to the difficulties of the French producers of capital equipment is that they entered the postwar period with a more severe handicap of preceding stagnation than that experienced by any of their major rivals. Even prior to 1930, demand for capital equipment was relatively restrained by the slow growth of aggregate demand and population. Equipment production was then blighted from 1929 to 1938 by the fact that the depression was more severe in France than elsewhere in Europe. The only important instance of a deeper depression was that in the United States, but here the equipment producers were more nearly able to rebuild their organizations and productive capacity during the war.

The long gap in equipment purchases in France was revealed clearly by a census of the machine-tool stocks of the engineering industries in December 1955. At that time, 38 percent of the total stock of machine tools was of postwar vintage, not greatly inferior to the ratio of 45 percent for American industry. But the age distribution of the rest of the inventories differed markedly. In France, only 18 percent of the total was between 10 and 20 years old (i.e., purchased between 1935 and

1945), as against 35 percent in the United States; 44 percent of the French stock, and only 20 percent of the American, was over 20 years old [147].

The sluggish character of domestic demand generated an understandably defensive set of producer reactions. The leading characteristic of producer choices seems to have been an orientation toward conservation of existing customers by a diversification of output to meet as fully as possible all the requirements of the firms with which they could maintain contact. Weak aggregate demand not only discouraged expansion of scale, it also led to excess product diversification and high costs within plants [28] [145] [147] [149]. High costs tended to close the possibility of developing exports, and led the government to accept the necessity of an unusual degree of tariff protection to keep the domestic firms alive.

The frequent assertion that possibilities of gains from specialization have been neglected is difficult to control. People within the industry itself seem in agreement with the proposition, and it is certainly consistent with the result in terms of relative costs, but it remains a question of degree for which no direct quantitative test has been established. An examination of the British machine-tool industry, frequently subject to much the same domestic criticism as the French, emphasizes that the extreme variety of special-purpose tools required by consuming industries greatly limits the possibilities of gain from greater concentration and scale in this field [144]. But the necessity of a great variety of end products does not preclude gain from reducing the range attempted within individual small plants. It may be that the impossibility of a major break-through by any particularly well-organized specialist producer, an impossibility resting on the necessary variety of end products, itself allows the indefinite prolongation of overly fragmented, unhelpfully diversified production in habit-bound small plants. Direct inquiry for machine tools and for electrical engineering equipment in France is at least consistent in the finding that the French industries have been less well organized than their European or American rivals [147] [149].

The point concerning excessive diversification within plants remains a matter of judgment, but the accompanying suggestion that plant scale has been unusually small is more readily verifiable. Planning Commission data, derived from an OEEC study, give the following comparison for 1954–55.

Table 4. Distribution of Employment in the Engineering Industries by size of Plant, 1954–55

	(Percentage distribution of all workers employed in plants with 10 or more employees)		
	10 to 100 workers	101–1000 workers	Over 1000 workers
France	28	41	31
Germany	12.5	38.5	49
United Kingdom	11	36	53
United States	14	36	50

Source: Commissariat du Plan, IIIe Plan, *Rapport Général de la Commission des Industries de Transformation,* Paris, 1958, p. 121.

Comparisons of plant size among countries such as the preceding are so full of difficulties that they have been cited as exemplifying the statistically impossible [16b]. In fact there are many valid reasons for reserving judgment on such data, especially as concerns differences in national systems of counting the very small "artisanal" firms which abound in these industries. But, from any feasible cutoff point leaving the smallest firms out of the picture, the distribution of employment in the French engineering industries has been oriented toward smaller plants than has been true in the other highly industrialized countries [62]. The data on comparative plant size definitely suggest that competitive pressure from the more efficient producers has not been strong enough. The plants which did operate on an inefficient scale, or with excessive product diversification keeping average costs high, survived in great numbers along with the more efficient.

The structural difficulties of the steel and the equipment industries bore certain similarities at the end of the second world war. Both were afflicted with out-of-date plant, small-scale, excessive diversification within plants, and entrenched memories of weak markets. And both were faced with a radically new situation of strong postwar demand. But their supply reactions were sharply different. In the case of steel, the Planning Commission went to work with all its initial fervor, contributing enormous financial help and aiding the industry to obtain required imports, while promoting a general reorganization of the productive structure. Led by the major firms, and spurred within a few years by international competition, the steel industry changed rapidly. But the resources and effort of the Commission did not extend to the equipment industries. They were left to fend for themselves in an environment in which credit, man power, and necessary imports were nearly impossible to secure without official help. Those producers who wished only to enjoy the fruits of a strong domestic market, without expanding beyond earlier capacity limits or changing their techniques of production, were in a good position to do just that. Those producers who attempted to expand and modernize found themselves checked by stringent scarcities of all necessary inputs, a condition worsened to some degree by the very success of the Planning Commission's efforts to generate expansion of the basic power-producing, transport and metals industries.

The equipment producers were more fortunate than the steel and aluminum firms in one respect. They were not subject to as close supervision in their pricing. This was less a matter of principle than one of practical difficulties, inherent in their dispersed structures and multitude of products. But controls were brought to bear on this sector too in the 1956–57 period of particularly intense effort to keep general excess demand from showing up in the price indices. In these years, some of the equipment firms were tightly squeezed between a fairly rigid block on their prices and a rapid rise in the costs of their labor-intensive operations.* In the 1957 boom year, profits were held to 4.1 percent of sales for nonelectrical machinery, compared to 5.9 percent in the 1952 recession; they were reduced to 3.5 percent for electrical equipment, compared to 5.3 in 1952 [25].

The one important form of direct governmental "assistance" to the equipment producers consisted of a strong set of protective barriers around their domestic market. The normal objections of equipment purchasing industries seem to have been subdued, perhaps because the overvalued currency encouraged a general acceptance of import protection for everyone. Active debate on this policy within the working groups sponsored by the Planning Commission was apparently limited to the question of keeping high tariffs on the equipment items not manufactured in France. The decision on this point was unambiguous: if imports were allowed without tariffs on items not produced domestically, the French producers would never want to go into these fields, so they too had to be protected [147, p. 19, n. 1].

The policy followed with respect to capital equipment in the 1950's might be summarized as an attempt to promote the diversity and the capacity necessary to meet domestic requirements from national sources of supply. Both the level of protection chosen and the emphasis on diversification to eliminate gaps in the types of equipment produced domestically support this interpretation [8] [28]. It is most doubtful that any responsible agency ever contemplated elimination of imports. What they did choose to do was to handicap imports severely, while maintaining strong demand, so that domestic producers

* The ratios of labor to materials costs in 1951 were 46 percent for the mechanical equipment and 44 for the electrical equipment industries, compared to 35 percent for metallurgical firms [26, p. 453, table 20a].

would expand and redirect production as necessary to fill in most of the gaps. The expectation was not that all the gaps would be eliminated, but that they would be significantly reduced, and that the equipment sector would develop a new dynamism and export capacity in the process. The results of this policy were not brilliant.

2. Aspects of Performance

Discussions of the equipment sector almost invariably center on its persistent import surplus. The fact that this can be cited as an instance of comparative disadvantage, balanced by net exports of semiprocessed materials and finished consumer goods, is not often considered to be a great consolation. It is as if the hallmark of any self-respecting industrial economy must be an approximation to self-sufficiency in the specific domain of machinery. The objective has in fact been confused between the costly goal of self-sufficiency and the very different one of seeking competitive superiority permitting greater exports of particular lines. But the dissatisfaction was understandable. The leading aspect of performance, at least through 1958, was precisely the inability to achieve a satisfactory competitive position. For no reason easily explicable in terms of resource endowment or market requirements, investment goods remained for the most part unduly expensive, particularly deficient in alternatives of the more "modern" types, and relatively inelastic in supply when demand moved ahead rapidly.

The most important handicap of the equipment industry in international trade was its high price level. Rapidly improving international competition in this field made the elasticity of demand too high to permit significant exports given the industry's high relative costs. For 1950, Gilbert and Kravis have provided data showing the purchasing power of one dollar's worth of domestic currency used to buy machinery and equipment, relative to its purchasing power when used for consumption. Taking the ratio in the United States as 100, and using American quantity weights for all countries, the ratio for the United Kingdom was .90, that for Germany .84, and that for France .75 [115, pp. 40, 56].

From 1950 to 1955, with the two economies expanding at similar rates, the relative prices of equipment and consumer goods moved in close parallel in France and the United States. From 1955, the French economy continued to move ahead rapidly while the American did not. A rough indication of the changes in producers' goods prices relative to consumers' goods from 1955 to 1960 can be deduced from the price deflators calculated by the OEEC. French machinery and equipment prices increased 27 percent, against 18 in the United States and 7 percent for all OEEC member countries combined. But the French increase, through conditions of general inflation in 1956–57 and a pair of devaluations, was slightly less than that of consumer goods prices. The ratio of machinery and equipment to consumer goods prices fell 6 percent, while falling one percent for all OEEC member countries and rising 7 percent in the United States. The period was one in which the American economy lost a good deal of its comparative advantage in industrial equipment to other European producers as well as to the French.

Although the French equipment firms did begin to bring their prices down relative to consumer goods in the latter 1950's, they were so high through most of the decade that the industry had very limited success in exporting or in competing with imports. From whatever angle the competitive position of capital goods is considered, it was not outstanding. One interesting study organized trade data to show the share of imports from France in the total imports of thirteen leading industrial nations: for all industrial products combined the French share in 1958 was 6 percent; for equipment goods separately it was barely 3 percent [16g, p. 470]. The share of exports in total deliveries of the engineering industries in that year was 14 percent for France, as against 31 percent for all OEEC members combined. The country's share of total engineering product exports by OEEC members dropped from 13.2 percent in 1952 to 9.7 by 1956, but did come back up to 11.8 percent by 1958 [148, pp. 40, 64]. In 1958, the share of equipment exports in total exports equalled 11 percent for France, compared to 15 for Italy, 22 for the United States, and 29 for Germany [16f, p. 436].

The general picture of relative weakness through 1958 was true enough, but it may easily be given different hues by focusing on different periods. Exports were definitely held back in the period 1954–57 by the pressure of extremely strong domestic demand. The ratio of equipment exports to total production fell to its lowest point in 1957, and moved back up promptly in 1958 when domestic expansion slowed. But this temporary downswing in exports cannot be explained wholly in terms of domestic claims on output: it was also a function of the equipment industries' ability to expand supply. In that period, the German economy expanded faster than the French, and the Italian economy at approximately the same pace, but the equipment industries of both Germany and Italy nevertheless achieved steadily rising ratios of exports to total production [16f, p. 428]. The supply elasticity of the French equipment producers was not adequate to cope with the fast pace of the economy's growth. This may well be considered a weakness on their part rather than a necessary result of the pace of the general expansion.

As might be expected with such a diverse group of industries, some did manage to meet the growth of demand while others fell far behind. From 1953 to 1957, production of all metals transformation industries rose 56 percent. Equipment producers achieved such varied increases as 69 percent for printing and paper machinery, 59 for internal combustion engines, 22 for machine tools, and 9 for steam engines and thermal powered turbines [3, pp. 5, 7, 193, 200–04]. These groups do have to cope with longer production cycles than do most consumer goods industries, but the degree to which some of them fell behind in an expansion sustained for four years can hardly be explained completely by this factor. Rather, the same organizational weaknesses which accounted for the unusually high ratio of equipment to consumer goods prices in 1950 probably acted to handicap the expansion of supply through the later boom period. The hopeful side of this negative judgment is that some of the main sources of weakness seem to be in the process of being corrected.

The initial competitive difficulty of the equipment producers in 1950 may be attributed to the long history of investment stagnation, leading to the problems of organization discussed above. As the 1950's advanced, a number of producers were reoriented toward expansion, in some cases specializing in relatively narrow ranges of new equipment for which demand growth was particularly strong. Two excellent examples are those of the *Cie. des Machines Bull* in office equipment and Renault in automatic transfer equipment. It is easy to find other examples of the good side [146] [146a], but the point is rather that they were special cases in a sector generally somewhat reluctant to move out in new directions. Most of the equipment producers, dealing with excellent demand conditions at home, behind substantial protection from imports, found it possible to do reasonably well without abandoning the scale and degree of diversification that they had evolved as a means of self-defense in a slower world. They were not impelled toward specialization for efficiency, and did not all leap toward it as the expanding market increased its feasibility. They simply rode up the wave of the general expansion, but at a pace so slow as to handicap the growth of the equipment using sectors.

The 1954–57 boom thus had mixed effects on efficiency. It

gave great scope for progress by the more dynamic firms, but kept alive inefficient techniques within many branches of the equipment sector. A simple cessation of growth would have been brutally unhelpful. It would have convinced the non-progressive firms that they were right all along to cling to defensive techniques, and might have put some of the more expansionary producers in serious trouble. Fortunately, the 1958 recession was not allowed to become more than a mild period of greatly slowed expansion, and its effects were supplemented by two useful policy changes. The first was that the exchange rate was corrected, making it possible for the more efficient producers to compete profitably in export markets. The second was that all branches of the equipment sector were warned that restrictions on imports would be progressively reduced to allow greater competition within the Common Market. This went beyond ever-useless exhortation or admonition. The producers were confronted with an early time limit on all quantitative restrictions and a schedule of impending tariff reductions. It was a clear signal, for the first time, that older techniques of production could no longer be considered safe.

According to people within the equipment industries, devaluation plus the Common Market—coupled with a growing conviction that reasonably well sustained expansion is likely to be the normal characteristic of the future—has encouraged a pronounced shift toward greater specialization within firms, linked in many cases to a conscious effort to enter export markets never seriously considered in the past. According to foreign trade data, the renewal of domestic expansion in 1959–60 has not handicapped the development of exports at all. The volume of export of industrial equipment outside the franc zone picked up 16 percent between 1958 and 1959 and their dollar value rose 4 percent [24] [177]. In 1960, with more time for the devaluations to take effect, exports of industrial equipment increased fully 47 percent over 1959 [82, p. 631].

3. Relationships of Organization to Performance

The equipment industries were not readily amenable to the forms of direction and control exercised in the cases of the aluminum and steel industries, because of their dispersed production structure and heterogeneous products. The structure was more dispersed than it should have been for optimum efficiency, because of the lack of competitive pressure, but it was probably a mistake to consider the problem as one of creating another set of concentrated producers along the lines of the steel industry. The two main choices open were either to organize more potent supervision by the Planning Commission, with greater powers of direct intervention, or to reach for possible means of stimulating competitive pressure to reshape the industry's behavior. French policy failed to do either. The Commission provided good advice and offered financial assistance for those firms wanting to reorganize, but too few did. Nothing pushed them, and the expanding market sheltered by import protection allowed them to stay put.

The reversal of policy at the end of 1958, correcting the value of the currency and placing the equipment producers squarely in front of the possibility of destruction by foreign competition, seems to have worked wonders. It should be noted that this change did not involve abandoning direct assistance or deflating domestic demand to force producer attention toward exports. Domestic expansion resumed in 1959–60, and the arsenal of special techniques for facilitating reconversion and expansion in line with the over-all plans has if anything been increased. In this instance again, as in the introduction of the Coal-Steel Community, a combination of competitive pressure and direct help has proven successful.

The changes since 1958 came later than they could have. Instead of channelling productive effort toward the more dynamic sectors, allowing international trade either to push this lagging group forward or to alleviate the cost burden of its weakness, the policies chosen handicapped industry generally in order to secure a more nearly balanced domestic expansion. For the postwar period as a whole, the sector has been a drag on the economy because public policies were not suited to its actual or possible organization. They have now been changed in a vastly more helpful direction.

7 | Automobiles: Government Competition

In 1950 the French automobile industry produced one passenger car for every twenty-six turned out in the United States. In 1960 the ratio was one for every six. This divergence in rates of expansion is primarily attributable to differences in domestic demand conditions. The French producers have been enjoying the benefits of a transition toward the mass automobile ownership achieved long ago in the United States. But differences in demand cannot be the whole story, since a significant proportion of the rise in French production has been exported, notably into the American market itself. Beyond this surface observation lie a number of interesting differences in the supply reactions of the two industries.

1. The Performance of the Industry

The automobile industry in France had a reasonably successful record of technical advance and commercial growth in the 1920's, but lost ground relative to other producers in the following decade. In 1929 its output of passenger cars was equal to 42 percent of the total for the present member countries of the OEEC. That share decreased to 23 percent by 1938.* A careful review of performance in the interwar period indicated

* Industry totals from [178] and [179]. All production, export and price information for individual firms are from annual review numbers of the automobile trade journal, *L'Argus*. Figures refer to passenger cars only, except where otherwise stated.

that, with the exception of Citroën's efforts until its ownership change in 1934, the producers were unnecessarily slow in realizing opportunities for gains in efficiency, little inclined to the exercise of competitive pressure, and overly reluctant to invest [150].

In the immediate postwar period the industry was not able to restore prewar production levels as rapidly as was done in the United States or England. The output total of 1938 was not passed until 1949, and the peak of 1929 not until 1950. The significant break with prewar capacities may perhaps be dated from 1950, when production reached a new record of 257,080 units. Output grew at an annual rate of 14 percent in the period 1950–54, then 21 percent from 1954 to 1958. It rose a further 17 percent the next year, but then ran head on into belated competition from the new compact cars in the American market and the beginnings of imports into France from other Common Market Countries. The increase in production in 1960 was only 3 percent. Output in that year, at 1.1 million units, was 4.3 times as high as in 1950.

The growth rate of this industry since 1950 has been outstanding. But a high rate of expansion is not necessarily a tribute to extraordinarily dynamic choices by the companies involved. In a group of studies of the industry, Eliane Mossé came to the conclusion that the dominant expansionary force was an autonomous shift of consumer preferences, strengthened by rising incomes but not significantly promoted by entrepreneurial action. The growth of sales in the period studied, 1947–55, followed a nearly linear logarithmic path, with moderate variations from this trend as income fluctuated but with no clear response to price changes. An excellent fit to sales data was secured by a multiple correlation model including only time and national income as independent variables. Further, the producers did little to stimulate demand growth by advertising or provision of new credit facilities. Finally, the expansion of production was not sufficient to keep up with demand. "In a particularly concentrated sector of production, where it would have been normal to expect action by firms to dominate the market through pricing or advertising, supply has been nearly always for 10 years—and is still—behind demand, the latter serving as the prime mover of the development of production" [158, p. 101] [157] [159].

The central point of Miss Mossé's results, the primary role of changing consumer preferences, is surely correct. The secondary implication, that the producers did little to promote growth, needs further examination. Some of the most important questions relate to prices and their effects, investment decisions and the fact that supply lagged behind demand, innovation and demand growth, and the development of exports.

The industry did succeed in providing greatly increased output with a decline in relative prices for its products. From 1949 to 1959 passenger car prices rose 59 percent, while retail prices for all consumer goods increased 85 percent. The superiority actually related only to prices of food and services: the retail index of all manufactured goods rose slightly less (56 percent) than that for automobiles [13]. These comparisons must be regarded with some reserve, in view of the logical problems involved in any index for which both the weights and the nature of the component items were changing rapidly. But the basic pattern is clear, and must have contributed to the factors favoring substitution of automobiles for other consumer goods. A thorough study of the demand characteristics of the French market concluded that the price elasticity of demand was approximately unity in the interwar period [156, pp. 62–63, 66–69]. Consumer reactions may well have altered since the war, but it remains probable that the growth of demand could have been restricted if the firms had been less able to restrain price increases.

The reduction in relative prices of automobiles was achieved in a period of highly favorable demand conditions, characterized by nearly continuous production at capacity and significant order backlogs for some major models. The absolute rise in prices which did occur was less than that which would have cleared the market. The points established by Miss Mossé about the statistical irrelevance of price variation and the low level of sales promotion activity become readily comprehensible in this context. But the lack of any systematic relationship between price changes and sales changes in the same year does not invalidate the presumption that the relative fall in automobile prices for the whole period contributed to the basic shift in demand.

The restraint on price increases while demand exceeded supply poses an interesting question: the situation persisted too long to be explained in terms of oligopolistic reluctance to make frequent price changes. It should in part be credited to the existence of government authority for regulation of prices. But it is clear from discussions with industry and government officials that the controls have not been exercised rigidly. In fact an industry-government accord specifically provides for a high degree of freedom in domestic pricing in return for successful effort to export. Estimated future cost changes, other than wage increases, have been accepted readily as justifying price increases even when profits were rising. In some cases, blanket percentage increases allowed for the whole industry have not been taken by all firms, and (exceptionally) some companies have actually reduced prices on their own volition. Granted that the existence of a review authority exercises some restraint, in the sense that proposed increases must be "explained," the crucial factors must be sought within the industry itself.

Restraint on prices from the side of the producers seems to have been real and to have derived from a combination of improving efficiency with moderate competitive pressure. The gains in efficiency have varied among firms, but in general have served to permit rising profits despite the relative decline in prices. Since all producers had fairly good profits, and some were doing very well, it was difficult for the less successful to fight the control commission for permission to raise prices faster. Since some firms did deviate downward in their pricing, it became dangerous for the others to push increases, even when the control authority would have approved further requests. A modest degree of price competition was present and was probably not irrelevant to the industry's expansion.

Restraint on price increases has been greatly aided by rapid improvement of labor productivity. A study by the Planning Commission estimated that average man-hours required per vehicle were reduced from 400 in 1953 to about 300 in 1956 [9, p. A-31]. Alternative data for 1954–59, applying to the whole branch of automobiles and cycles, show that their output per man-hour rose 54 percent in this period [27].

An imprecise but suggestive comparison with English and American gains in labor productivity indicates that the French industry has been improving faster than the other two. From 1950 to 1955, unit output per man-year rose 25 percent in the United Kingdom and 8 percent in the United States [155, p. 211]. These figures relate to employment in firms supplying parts as well as final construction. French data for construction only, and hence subject to distortion through changes in vertical integration, show an improvement of 71 percent between these two years [159]. More complete figures for the whole sector for 1955 permit the calculation that unit output per man-year was then 3.6 in France, as against 4.5 in England and 11.2 in the United States. The French industry has been raising labor productivity faster than the other two, but was apparently still behind them in 1955. Vehicles produced per man-year rose subsequently to 4.7 in 1958 and 5.6 in 1959 [27].

Information on efficiency in the use of capital is not clear. The faint clues discovered suggest that the capital requirements per unit output have remained approximately constant. The ratio of fixed investment to sales averaged 6.5 percent for the period 1952–56 [9, pp. A-6, A-33]. In 1956 value added was equal to 48 percent of sales, so investment was equivalent to about 13.5 percent of value added [22, p. 129]. Since production of all vehicles increased 13.5 percent per year in this period, the incremental capital-output ratio seems to have been unity. The period here is too short, and the data too weak, for any definitive conclusion about comparative progress. It does seem safe to conclude that the French industry, like those in other countries, has achieved its gains in labor productivity through transformation of productive techniques rather than through a costly substitution of capital for labor.

The report of the Planning Commission in preparation of the third plan states that investment by the industry has been too low, in the sense of falling short of the investment-sales ratios of the German and Italian industries. The absence of dependable data on vertical integration makes this comparison most difficult to evaluate. But investment was less than optimal in the simple sense that, for more than a decade, output lagged behind the growth of quantity demanded at profitable selling prices. On the ability to provide sufficient capacity, the French industry has been definitely inferior to the American. The weak record of the French firms in this respect is not equally applicable to all of them, and may best be considered in the discussion of the individual companies in section 2 below.

The industry has made very different choices from those of its American counterpart in a most important aspect of performance, that of product competition. As students of the industry have often noted, price competition tends to be eliminated over time, leaving product competition as the main form of independent behavior. But the nature of such rivalry can vary considerably, from forms serving interests of consumers quite well to forms which do not. One type is that described by George Maxcy and Aubrey Silberston with reference to the English industry: several key prices are gradually adopted and firms compete by introducing distinctly different models at the established prices. This can provide meaningful choices for buyers, and need not prevent considerable standardization for productive efficiency. But consumer interests would be even better served if one or more firms combined product change with a form of price competition by directing innovation to new price areas. This second type of competition could offer the consumer significantly different products through a wide range of prices. It may also be consistent with standardization on the more successful models, combining a healthy set of choices with low average costs.

A third type of performance may be envisaged in which the results are much less satisfactory. Instead of seeking to introduce different products, the producers may closely match the offers of their rivals, clustering a group of nearly identical products around a few key prices, offering little real consumer choice. Such a situation would be most dubiously improved if the producers resorted to frequent variations in external vehicle characteristics, again in close parallel with each other, raising costs without increasing variety. Product competition may become as atrophied as price competition.

Contrasting the performances of the French and the American industries with respect to product competition suggests that, prior to the war, the former should be placed nearer to the "negative" form of such competition. The French producers then proliferated duplicating models, limiting possible gains from scale, while the American industry combined independent innovation with considerable price competition to serve consumer interests more effectively. In the last decade, the shoes have been on the other feet. The French industry has avoided frequent model changes and at the same time provided a greater variety of consumer choice [152, pp. 33–34] [155, pp. 119–23, 139–41].

The ability of the French industry to minimize model change and excessive duplication since the war should be credited mostly to the nature of the domestic market. The producers have had the good fortune to be dealing with original rather than replacement demand. A special planning group concerned with the automobile industry recommended such model specialization in 1945 [31, pp. 216–17]. This may have had some effect on behavior in the years immediately following, though the character of demand at the time is perhaps a sufficient explanation.

The initial concentration on a small number of models has in any event been diminishing. One firm has offered considerable variety since about 1950, departing from previous standardization, and the others have been moving in this direction recently. Differences in the organization of the industry were not of great relevance in this respect, but they may well have been in one crucial set of decisions: the early introduction of new and very successful economy models.

If any decision may be singled out as having a key impact on expansion through the 1950's, it is surely that of the departure from the existing model range downward to new low-cost models. The two concerned were the Renault 4 CV and the Citroën 2 CV (the "quatre chevaux" and the "deux chevaux"). In the same period in which the American industry chose to move its models upward in cost and in gasoline consumption, with each major producer matching the style and price changes of the other two throughout the accepted range, the French industry offered genuinely new choices at much lower price levels.

A number of external factors make it natural that, apart from market organization, the French industry should produce smaller, less powerful cars than the American. Among these factors are the higher price of gasoline, lower average income, narrower streets and greater population density. Such considerations explain why the leading prewar and early postwar models were smaller in France than in the United States. But they do not explain why the subsequent directions of change should be exactly opposite to each other in the two cases. Differences in tastes between the two countries have certainly been relevant, but differences in the vitality of competition seem to have been present too. The leading American producers followed majority preferences upward, each matching the others and avoiding any independent offer appealing to markets where incomes or tastes would have dictated different products. The successive experiences of Volkswagen and Renault at the level of four-passenger economy models, plus American Motors and a host of foreign producers in the intermediate "compact" range, certainly indicated that significant consumer interests were being neglected by the larger firms. Their eventual—and simultaneous—decision to move back into the medium-price range in 1959 indicated that production for this market was not expected to be unprofitable in itself, suggesting that protection of the market for more expensive models was a basic factor in the preceding delay.

The argument here is not that the French producers were brighter than the Americans in assessing consumer preference, or that the latter made a mistake in terms of profit maximization. It is rather that the French firms have been less reluctant to make important deviations from the products offered by each other, and that their course of action has been more nearly in line with promotion of consumer welfare.

French production would probably have expanded at about the same rate up until at least 1950 even if the range of consumer choice had not included the new economy models. Sales of medium- and higher-powered automobiles continued to rise well after the introduction of the 4 CV and the 2 CV. But these and following models classified as less than 6 CV have not yet ceased to grow relative to total production. They constituted 49 percent of total output by 1956 and 64 percent by 1960. Further, they have provided the majority of sales outside the franc zone: automobiles with motors rated under 1000 CC provided 64 percent of such exports in 1960. The industry's phenomenal expansion from 1950 to 1960 could not possibly have been duplicated without the introduction of economy models significantly reducing the ratio of minimum automobile prices to average income and providing a very successful export product.

The industry did not anticipate or promptly exploit the export possibilities shown by Volkswagen. French exports outside the franc zone showed little progress until 1953. But from that time through 1959 their growth was most impressive. Exports outside the franc zone reached 474,000 units in 1959, nine times the 1953 figure. They then fell to 415,000 in 1960. But even then they were equal to 37 percent of production, against 14 percent in 1953.

Unit exports of the French industry were equal to 52 percent of those of the American industry in 1953, but passed the slowly declining United States total in 1957. The relationship of this result to changes in labor productivity would have pleased Ricardo: the ratio of gains in output per man in the automobile industry, relative to output per capita in the whole economy, has been higher in recent years in France than in the United States. American producers certainly face greater artificial barriers to their exports than do foreign producers. In the 1950's the differences were nowhere more extreme than between the insulated French and the low-tariff, quota-free American markets. But American exports have been decreasing for several years, without any notable increase in the artificial barriers against them, and French sales have increased particularly well in the American market itself. The key explanation of the greater progress of French exports would seem to lie in the industries' relative ability to respond quickly with competitive products to evolutions in world demand.

The French industry raised its own demand horizon in the 1950's by the development of exports, enabling output to grow faster than the domestic market. The growth of demand at home, primarily a result of rising incomes and changing consumer preferences, was encouraged by gradual reduction of automobile prices relative to other consumer goods and, most importantly, by the provision of new economy models effectively broadening the market. The industry has been much more than a passive beneficiary of a favorable economic environment. Section 2 examines the respective roles of the private and the government-owned firms in this expansionary process.

2. The Firms

As in the United States, the automobile industry in France has shown a definite long-run tendency toward increasing concentration. The three largest firms in the interwar period, Citroën, Renault and Peugeot, accounted for 48 percent of total output of automobiles and trucks in 1918, 56 percent in 1925, and 70 percent in 1930 [159, p. 9]. Simca entered the industry with substantial Italian backing in 1934, merged with Ford of France in 1954, and has changed the big three into a big four. In 1960 these four firms produced 96 percent of French automobiles and 95 percent of the combined output of automobiles and trucks.

The three major private firms have illustrated by the diversity of their performances the wide range of discretion possible for the larger companies in this most imperfect market. In fact Citroën has demonstrated the point all by itself: it has been at opposite poles of the leading group of producers in the industry's two best expansion periods, the 1920's and the 1950's.

Citroën was founded much later than Renault and Peugeot, on the eve of the first World War. But it was able to establish a firm position during the war, and rapidly outpaced the two older firms in the following decade. Under the lively management of its founder, the company pioneered adoption of mass production techniques and systematic industrial research, combining these efforts with an aggressive investment policy to secure leadership of the industry. The depression of the 1930's changed this most effectively. Citroën tried to move ahead with a major investment program against the preferences of the French banking community, and found it impossible to obtain financial help when squeezed by the collapsing automobile market.

The Michelin Tire Company, as the firm's leading creditor, acquired 66 percent of Citroën's stock in the resulting liquidation. It has maintained control ever since. The management's understandably conservative policy in the latter part of the depression still left the firm as the largest automobile producer immediately before and after the second World War, but the same policies persisting in the postwar period brought the company steadily downward in relative position.

Its share of total automobile production fell from 34 percent in 1948 to 19 in 1958, bringing the company down from first to third place. In 1959–60 its share did rise again slightly, to 20 percent in both years.

A possible explanation for the company's relative loss in the automobile market is that this field has proved too dynamic for a conservatively oriented commercial policy. The difficulty is certainly not attributable to lack of technical achievements. The company entered the postwar period with the best-selling model in the industry, replied to Renault's introduction of a small car with the then even more economical and spectacularly popular 2 CV, introduced in 1956 the fascinating DS-19 series at the more expensive end of the range, and went back to the economy side with the first 3 CV model in 1961.

Citroën's trouble was clearest with respect to the 2 CV. Introduced on a very small scale, as a genuinely different experimental car, it found enormous and deserved demand. It was inexpensive as an original purchase, and almost unbelievable in its economy of maintenance and fuel consumption. Some fanatical admirers even dispute the fact that it is aesthetically objectionable. It was immediately clear that the planned rate of output was totally insufficient. The management reacted by waiting to make sure that this was so, then added an inadequate increment to capacity. It continued this policy for a decade, squeezing out more production by cautious and increasingly costly small steps. The Planning Commission estimated the company's costs of transporting parts among its scattered small operations in the Paris region at 13 percent of total cost [159, p. 9].

As compared with its closest rival, the Renault 4 CV, the 2 CV has shown a consistent upward price trend, reflecting this basic production disability. The ratio of the price of the 2 CV to that of the 4 CV "Affaires" was 0.7 in 1952, 0.9 in 1955, and 1.1 in early 1958. Modest changes of style over this period may have increased the relative comfort of the 2 CV, but hardly to an extent invalidating the sense of this comparison.

More generally, Citroën was relatively slow in recognizing the strength of postwar demand. Investment policy was decidedly restrained until the latter half of the 1950's. By 1960 the company began to pull together its operations in a thoroughly modern plant, financed with help from the government. The company has never been greatly interested in exporting, except to traditional markets in adjacent countries. A French business journal commented in 1958 that the company lacked the flexibility necessary to compete in foreign markets: management thinking was geared too completely to production within a context of excess demand to cope with the special problems of export competition [154]. The company was penalized in 1958 by selective restraint on its prices because it failed to fulfill the terms of the government-industry export agreement of 1957, an agreement under which each firm undertook to export two-thirds of increases in production during the following year. Its exports then more than doubled between 1958 and 1960.

Peugeot, the fourth largest automobile producer, is the only important family-run firm in the industry. Its automobiles are renowned for dependability, respectable appearance, and absence of radical innovation. They breathe the *mesure* sometimes thought to be characteristic of the French. The company abstains almost completely from the temptations of borrowing, or diluting equity, to obtain funds for investment. Its ability to expand from retained earnings is aided by what is generally regarded as the highest rate of return in the industry [153, pp. 34–36]. Its expansion has not been quite fast enough to keep up with the industry as a whole: its share of total automobile production fell from 19 percent in 1948 to 15 in 1960.

Peugeot embodies the strengths and the inevitable strains of a traditional family firm in a newly dynamic economy. Like Citroën, it always leans to the careful side. This has not involved major blunders, unless an unfortunate decision to cut back its own investment program at the first sign of Simca's short-lived sales difficulties in 1952–53 be so considered. It has involved a consistent tendency to underestimate probable unit sales during the life of any given model, thus probably causing unnecessarily high costs as efforts are made to increase production beyond original plans, and possibly making the company's expansion a little slower than warranted by the strength of demand.

Peugeot's commercial policy is apparently subject to considerable internal debate, with a younger management group trying to pull the firm toward more expansionary decisions [154a]. From 1957, the company turned with increasing success to the development of exports outside the franc zone; such exports rose 163 percent from 1957 to 1960. This progress was aided by an agreement with Renault, providing for joint use of the latter's distribution system in the United States. Like Citroën, the firm gives signs of adjusting policies in directions more favorable for economic expansion, possibly in response to the continuing relative success of the more aggressive firms, Simca and Renault.

Simca has always followed American-style policies, with a

vigorous investment program and considerable stress on model variation. Associated with Fiat at first, then with Ford, the company became affiliated with Chrysler in 1958. Its rapid expansion of capacity has paid off with growth much faster than that of the industry as a whole. Its share of automobile production rose from 9 percent in 1948 to 19 percent in 1952. By 1955, the first year following its merger with Ford of France, the combined company's share was 26 percent. But the company's sales decreased in 1957, when those of all the others were increasing, and its later expansion failed to keep its share of production from falling to 18 percent in 1960.

Simca's mild sales difficulties have been in part a tribute to its relatively rapid expansion of capacity. Unlike Citroën and Peugeot it cleared up waiting lists rapidly. When it did slip temporarily it held a lead over both of them. But its heavy investment and imaginative design have been directed toward a great variety of relatively costly models with shiny trimmings and above-average gasoline consumption and have been subject to relatively early sales resistance in recessions. Against the two more cautious producers, it has done very well. Against the industry's nationalized firm, Renault, combining active investment policy with emphasis on more economical models, it has been losing ground.

Renault was established as a private firm in the early days of the industry, and remained under close control by its founder until 1944. It was the leading firm in the industry early in the 1920's, but then fell well behind Citroën. Its slower progress has been explained as due to excessive vertical integration and to avoidance of external financing at the price of inadequate investment in new equipment. By 1938 the firm had 15 percent of the automobile market, as against 30 percent for Citroën and 22 percent for Peugeot [150, pp. 384, 393–94].

The company was nationalized by executive decree in 1944, on the ground that its owner's wartime activities had been detrimental to the country. It was taken over with a minimum of public discussion or specific guidance to management. The Minister of Finance was given authority to nominate and to replace the firm's chief executive officer. The official chosen was an industrialist then serving as an economic planning official in the provisional government. A public review board was established and the new director was given free rein. No further legislation or more specific governmental control has been instituted since. Both the review board and the Parliamentary commission charged with supervising state-owned industry confine their "intervention" to informative but noncontroversial annual reports. The director originally appointed remained in charge until his death in 1955. The next and present director had also been a government official concerned with economic planning. Apart from this (decidedly important) choice of the firm's director, no government agency has intervened in the company's operations. An industry-approved booklet concludes that the only "essential difference between Renault and its competitors lies in the way in which profits are distributed" [160].*

Industry officials and outsiders seem to be in agreement on one central point: the fact that Renault belongs to the government has not significantly affected its market behavior. This is said by some in terms of praise, by others with distinct displeasure. They mean that Renault is not subject in its market policy to government control, is not aided or hampered by fiscal or regulatory activity differentiating it from other firms in the industry, and pursues profit in much the same ways and with roughly the same degree of success as the rival private firms. All this is true, as are the facts that Renault lobbies through the same trade associations for much the same objectives as the private firms and, of late, complains as bitterly in

* Renault pays taxes on the same basis as a private firm. It then divides profits after taxes three ways: one-third additional payment to the government as a dividend, one-third to workers as a bonus, and one-third retained for investment. This division is approximative only. It is a custom established by the firm, not a specific legal requirement.

equally glossy annual reports about the crushing burden of taxes. But it may be suggested that, beneath the broad lines of outward uniformity, actions of the company exhibit distinctive nuances of some importance.

One of the distinctive aspects of Renault's performance relates to model innovation. Immediately after the war, when all firms were still relying on prewar models for which they were unable to meet demand, Renault's management decided to introduce a new low-cost car, the 4 CV, and to concentrate on a restricted model range for production economy. As argued above, this policy and Citroën's reply with the 2 CV had a great deal to do with the industry's sustained postwar expansion. Renault's early postwar annual reports state that concentration on an economy model was conceived as a means of making it possible for workers and lower-income groups generally to own automobiles. In any event, the action did improve the choices available at the lower-price end of the market. That the move was an enormous commercial success does not detract from the welfare implications of the basic decision.

It is possible to view the introduction of the 4 CV either as an example of effective business management or of the use of a state firm to provide a lower-cost product. The next model innovation by the firm fitted neither category. This was a more expensive five-passenger car, the "Fregate." Introduced in 1951, and still in production after considerable transformation, this model has not proved a scintillating success.

Since 1955, the company has re-established its record for effective product innovation. The "Dauphine" was beautifully calculated to fit into the market opening between the cheapest economy models, then around 4000 NF, and the medium-power models beginning around 6000 NF. Whether or not this was the key price range in advance of the Dauphine's arrival, the new model took hold promptly and pulled away from all others for the next five years.

One of the rewards, or perhaps the ultimate test, of the

company's effective model innovation is the improvement in its share of the market: from 30 percent in 1948 to 39 in 1958 and 40 in 1960.

A second distinctive aspect of Renault's performance was its early stress on exports. It was the first company in the industry to devote serious effort to development of a sales organization in the United States, and consistently led in the rapid expansion of exports beginning in 1954. Renault provided 37 percent of automobile exports outside the franc zone in 1953 and 61 percent in 1960. As compared to Volkswagen, it got under way slowly. As compared to any other members of the French industry it has done very well.

The penalty of moving beyond domestic markets for a significant proportion of sales during the period that American producers were religiously avoiding any infringement of the market for compact cars was that Renault got hit more sharply than the other French companies when American competition came back to life. The company's export sales outside the franc zone fell 9 percent in 1960 and continued on down in the first half of 1961. Peugeot and Citroën began to gain on its rate of production. The company's reactions were in promising directions: the price of the Dauphine in the American market was sharply reduced, a new variant of the model with greater power was introduced, and the firm was the only one of the four major producers to stay out of the 1961 round of automobile price increases in France [175, April 11 and 16, June 7, 1961].

A third, and more debatable, difference in behavior concerns price policy. Those who imply criticism in identifying the company's performance with privately owned firms usually have in mind its systematic pursuit of profit, allied with pricing practices considered typical of oligopoly [90, pp. 76–78] [99, pp. 109–12]. It is beyond doubt that the management abhors the idea of operating at a loss. This did happen once, in 1946. The firm was squeezed in that year between rising costs and controlled selling prices, but it immediately became obvious to critics that a government-owned company is inherently inefficient. Officials of the firm seem exceedingly sensitive to such criticism. They place particular stress on the possibility that the apparatus of government supervision, purely formal in character as long as Renault continues to pay taxes and dividends to the state, could lead quickly to positive control if the company were unable to earn any net income. The management regards profit as the necessary condition of its own independence.

The fact that Renault aims at profits means that its choices must in many respects parallel those of its private rivals. It cannot upset the market with any price policy completely out of their reach, nor risk any major model changes not limited by much the same commercial considerations as those of the other firms. When steel costs go up, the company's prices advance at about the same time as those of its rivals. But within such limits, much room for discretion remains. Industry-wide price increases approved by the government are not uniformly taken by all producers, and Renault is usually on the low side in cases of divergent moves. Its pricing is indeed as "inflexible" as that of General Motors in the sense of frequency of change, but quite different in one respect—the infrequent changes are sometimes downward. E.g., the price of the 4 CV was reduced in 1953, 1954 and 1955. The decline in this model's price relative to the 2 CV was noted above. The possibility of making the change was opened up by more efficient production on Renault's part, and the public was given the benefit by reductions even though prices were rising for the most directly competitive product.

The pricing practices of Renault certainly do not constitute aggressive competition. The company acts within the traditional boundaries of oligopolistic performance. Its prices did move gradually downward relative to the average for the industry until the middle 1950's, then moved in close parallel to the others up to 1961.

A fourth difference in Renault's performance concerns the timing of investment. Like Simca, the company reduced delivery delays relatively early through rapid expansion of capacity. An estimate of investment by the four leading firms for 1947–55, adjusted to constant prices, indicates that the company accounted for 41 percent of the total [158, pp. 91–94]. This exceeded its share of automobile-plus-truck production by the four, but the excess may be accounted for by its expansion of facilities for tractor production in the same period. The major difference lay in timing. Renault expanded facilities rapidly in the early postwar years, and the rest of the producers joined in increasingly in the course of the 1950's as they more fully accepted the reality of the postwar expansion possibilities.

Renault's investment has been directed in two ways that would seem to have particularly high ratios of external benefit to company return: a great expansion of export selling and service facilities, and the development of an important new branch of machine-tool and automatic transfer equipment. As most of the rest of French industry, the automobile producers were handicapped by the technological lag and high costs of the domestic equipment producers, prolonged by the policy of import protection described in the preceding chapter. Instead of passively accepting this handicap, Renault followed the lead of several of the American and English automobile producers and itself engineered the transfer machinery needed to bring down its costs. The machinery proved so successfully adapted to the production scale of European industry that the company began to supply both other domestic firms and exports of such equipment. This has been highly strategic for the firm, and helpful for the whole economy, directly reducing costs and demonstrating a new technique of potentially wide applicability in the somewhat unprogressive machine-tool industry [155, pp. 59–60, 91–92].

As are all its domestic rivals, Renault is now moving into much rougher competitive waters. The introduction of the

American compacts in 1959, the beginnings of European-wide competition in previously closed national markets, and the expansion of capacity by automobile producers all over the world, promise, according to an official of Renault, "a rather serious battle" [151, p. 106]. The companies have been energetic in building distribution systems in other countries, usually by establishing alliances with foreign producers. This does not mean that all are aiming at an international cartel system. As Monnet pointed out, the accord by which Alfa Romeo began to handle sales of the Dauphine in Italy promptly provoked a round of price cuts by Fiat, Volkswagen, and in turn Renault [161, p. 56]. These skirmishes could lead to a continuing struggle among producers, to the benefit of consumers and to that smaller number of firms which would survive, or it could lead to an organized group program for orderly limitation of expansion. Officials of the French Government have been foremost among those urging the latter course, advocating planning for the industry on a European scale [175, May 3, 1961].

It is easy to sympathize with those French economists who believe that such a large-scale experiment in government competition should yield more dramatic results. Renault could have engaged in rigorous price competition, led Volkswagen in developing exports, possibly achieved a lower-cost model than the 4 CV, or perhaps penetrated boldly into such fields as construction or materials handling equipment. Its actual performance could conceivably have been duplicated or bettered by any one of its private rivals, without departing from a realistic pursuit of profitable long-run expansion. It has simply been, so far, the most successful growth firm within the industry. Its path to new markets—in lower-income groups at home and through exporting—has been effectively served by innovation directed to those markets, backed by a combination of moderately low unit margins and vigorous investment. Its choices led the industry in directions consistent with the public interest, and have reduced the country's dependence on the decisions of firms less oriented toward expansion. But it need not have been a nationalized firm to do this. The remaining question is whether the results should be considered an accident of management preferences in the particular case, or a general result to be expected from government competition.

3. Factors Determining Performance

An oligopoly selling differentiated products and enjoying reasonably satisfactory demand conditions offers many behavioral possibilities consistent with survival. Serious mistakes mean extinction for the fringe companies, but managements of the larger firms are not subject to the narrow limits of tolerance for error that can be expected in a highly competitive market. Each is free to seek profit through its own combination of pricing, product variation, investment and production techniques, subject at worst to gradual loss in relative position if it is slow in adapting to more successful alternatives chosen by its rivals. If all the major firms in the automobile industry were to follow a common policy of high margins and closely matched model variation, they could conceivably all expand quite profitably at approximately equal rates. On the other hand, if one of them chooses a more constructive course, it puts pressure on the rest to follow, and gradually reduces their influence in the market if they fail to do so. The government firm has provided such a constructive influence in the French industry since the war. It is impossible to prove that the industry has performed better than it would have if Renault had remained under private ownership, but those respects in which the firm's choices differed from the private companies were consistently in directions favorable to consumers and to the expansion of the French economy.

The beneficial results of government competition were probably more than accidental. Where management possesses considerable discretion, the relative weights attached to each of the multitude of factors entering into any major decision become extremely important. The presence of a group chosen for its interest in such goals as aggregative expansion, low prices, and the development of exports is very likely to alter decisions in useful directions.

Apart from pressures on the other firms resulting directly from the performance of a government-owned firm, the coexistence of diverse interests may make it difficult to achieve tacit policy coordination limiting competition. The gains to consumers might actually be raised by an overtly antagonistic situation among the producers, leading to attempts to cut into each other's markets even by such dangerous techniques as price competition. But this is probably asking too much. Citroën and Peugeot did withdraw for a time from the central trade association harboring Simca and Renault, but conflicts among the four do not now seem to have any ideological edge.

It may be that the Planning Commission contributed helpful advice on restricting model variation and on expansion in the early postwar years, but it played no important role in controlling performance in this industry in the course of the 1950's. The director of Renault was himself one of the most aggressively independent of all the managers of the state firms, and the company went its own way in all major respects [95, chs. 9, 10]. By the middle 1950's, it was a rare year in which the industry's production figures did not drastically exceed those indicated by the current plan. This pleased some of the officials of the Commission as a demonstration of the growth policy they were trying to promote, and disturbed others because it made clear that the industry was paying no attention at all to the idea of a nationally balanced program.

Primary credit for the industry's expansion certainly belongs less to planning or any other aspect of market organization than to the strength of demand, opening new opportunities for gains from economies of scale and for major improvements in market share by the more aggressive firms. As E. S. Mason pointed out with respect to the prewar American automobile industry, vigorous demand growth favors effective competitive responses [63, p. 67]. The real test here may lie ahead, when industry growth slows down. It should be interesting to review performance at the end of the 1960's.

Another special consideration is the fact that two important management groups were relatively new to the industry at the start of the postwar period. The industry's record suggests that well-established managements tend to become relatively inert. Citroën, new and much smaller than Renault and Peugeot on the eve of the first World War, outpaced them both in the interwar period. Simca, the newest firm in the 1930's, gained rapidly on the old leaders then and on Citroën and Peugeot after the war. Greater size may confer important economies of scale, but it does not ensure continuing initiative.* The introduction of a new group to direct Renault might have had helpful effects totally independent of the fact that the firm was placed under government ownership. In this respect, too, it should be of interest to reconsider Renault's performance at the end of another decade.

The ability of the industry to improve on the possibilities opened up by favorable domestic demand should be attributed to competition among the major firms rather than to any direction or control by the government. But the most effective competitor was in fact the state-owned firm. This was more than a coincidence. Management chosen for its interest and judged by its success in promoting economic expansion adopted policies more fully consistent with that objective than those followed by the firms which had previously dominated the industry. The leadership exercised by the government firm was

* This suggestion intentionally differs from the emphasis of Maxcy and Silberston on advantages of size [155, ch. vi–vii]. Their conclusions might usefully be checked against their own discussion of the fact that the two English leaders in 1929, Nuffield and Austin, with combined market shares of 88 percent in that year, exhibited the advantages of greater size by marching resolutely to a joint share of 51 percent in 1939.

effectively seconded by the newest of the three major private producers. Both of them departed from established behavioral patterns in directions enlarging the market, increasing competition, and leading the whole group toward policies favoring sustained growth by the industry and the French economy.

8 Cotton Textiles: Dispersion with Protection

The textile industries have been left largely to their own devices in the postwar period. Cloth does not ring, as do steel and automobiles, with the sound of control over the destinies of nations. More fundamentally, most of the textile fields are so dispersed that external control is difficult to envisage. In this sense, they resemble somewhat the machinery and equipment industries, and, like the latter, they present an unencouraging test of the relative effectiveness of dispersed private enterprise as against concentration and organized intervention. The cotton textile industry fits this general picture in terms of dispersion and of relatively weak long-term performance, but it does differ from the machinery case in two structural aspects. One is that its products are more homogeneous, permitting greater group promotion through the industry's trade association. The other is that it has not been favored by the strong demand conditions of the machinery producers. But with more difficult demand conditions, and with a stronger trade association role, it did make greater relative progress in the 1950's.

1. Performance

From 1901 to 1950, textile production increased 51 percent for all OEEC members combined. In France, it fell one percent [179]. The effect of much slower population growth was compounded by the fact that the share of textile products in total private consumption expenditures fell lower in France than in other European countries, both where per capita income is lower and where it is higher than in France. Further, one of the major adverse demand factors for all producers, and especially for the French cotton textile firms, has been the deterioration of sales in export markets open to international competition.

In 1950, per capita consumption of clothing and household textiles in France was approximately one-third as high as in the United States, one-half the levels in Belgium and Norway, three-fourths that in England, and approximately 10 percent above that in Germany. Gilbert and Kravis compared the structures of domestic consumption in eight European countries for that year, three of which had lower real income per capita than France. In every case, textile consumption was a greater share of total consumption than in France [115, pp. 60, 78].

The relatively depressed level of textile consumption seems traceable to a classic difficulty: prices have been unusually high. In 1950, approximately 30 percent more francs were required to buy the clothing and household textiles that could have been purchased for one dollar in the United States than to buy one dollar's worth of all consumer goods and services.* The absence of population growth held back the industry's growth at home, but relatively high prices also played a role in holding down any favorable effects of rising incomes [cf. 18, pp. 80, 173]. A second inevitable consequence of the price problem, here a matter of high production costs rather than any significant degree of market control, was a singularly poor record in export competition.

Textile production in all industrialized countries has long

* The calculation here is based on United States' quantity weights. On French weights the difference in cost would be 60 percent [115, pp. 79–80].

been under a double handicap. Domestic income elasticity of demand has been low and export sales have been subject to continuous attrition by the emergence of new centers of production in countries that had previously been importers. The technological leadership that made it possible for the European countries to import raw cotton and wool and then to export finished products made from these materials has greatly lessened during the twentieth century. This leadership used to be sufficient to compensate for the transportation costs and higher wages involved in European production, but the older producing centers have not been able to improve techniques sufficiently to stay ahead. The newer producing areas have been able to come close to European productivity levels with more abundant man power and often with less costly raw materials [162, pp. 59–60, 114–20].

The share of textiles in total exports of manufactured goods of seven European countries and the United States fell from 33 percent in 1913 to 18 percent in 1950. The French proportion of these textile exports did increase, from 15 to 17 percent [180, tables 53 and 54, pp. 180, 187]. But the apparent success of French exporters in this respect depended on a special factor which weakens its meaning: the distribution of exports, notably those for cottons, shifted away from open international markets to those of protected colonial territories. Two-fifths of all textile exports in 1950 went to countries within the franc zone [18, p. 245]. For cotton yarns, the share of export sales going to the franc zone increased from 9 percent in 1929 to 60 percent in 1951. For cotton tissues, the proportion rose from 60 to 90 percent [162, p. 282].

In the course of the 1950's, the French industry's performance improved in the sense that prices were reduced relative to other domestic goods, and that export sales did not decline significantly more than those of the other European countries, despite the loss of previously protected colonial markets. At the end of the decade, the cotton producers' exports rose particularly well in response to the currency devaluation of 1958 and the accompanying reduction of trade barriers.

From 1950 to 1959, the wholesale price index for all industrial products rose 58 percent in France, and that of textiles only 4 percent. All of the increase in textile prices came in the Korean War period. They decreased 6 percent from 1952 to 1959, while prices of other industrial products kept going up [13]. No separate index is available for cotton textiles, but a sample of two standard items indicates a parallel decrease, with sharply marked cyclical variations [166, p. 12]. Compared to the American index of textile prices, that in France went up much more steeply to 1952, then fell slightly more rapidly from 1952 to 1959. The fact that the French industry was able to bring down prices more rapidly than the American industry after 1952 was a decidedly creditable achievement, considering the competitive character of the American industry and the much sharper advance of wages and other prices in France during this period.

The cotton textile industry did not achieve any overwhelming export success in the course of the 1950's, although it ended the decade on a very promising note. For the period 1950–59 as a whole, it lost ground somewhat faster than did the industry in the other OEEC countries or in the United States. The French share of total exports of cotton fabrics by all OEEC members fell from 23 to 20 percent. The volume of French exports of cotton fabrics fell one-fourth, while that of American cotton cloth fell only 15 percent [179] [184, p. 190]. But the decline in French exports was entirely in sales to the franc zone, which were cut in half by the loss of protected markets. Although exports of cotton fabrics outside the franc zone remained less than 5 percent of domestic production, or of total OEEC exports, they did rise slowly and persistently up to 1958, then more than doubled in volume between 1958 and 1959 [168, p. 46] [177]. As in the case of the machinery and equipment producers, the firms had been unable to hurdle the barrier of an overvalued currency, but reacted vigorously when its value was corrected. The prompt reaction, as well as the achievement of decreasing relative prices after 1952, indicates that the organizational factors inhibiting performance must have been improving in the course of the decade.

2. Organization and Costs

Prior to the opening of the Common Market, all industry comment agreed that production costs were too high to permit open international competition. The experience of operating with an equilibrium exchange rate and lower import barriers in 1959–60 has led to the beginnings of a belief that the producers are not after all going to be annihilated by competition from other European firms, but the industry is no more eager than its American counterpart to take on world-wide competition. They too are unhappy about firms operating with cheap foreign labor. In many of the French industry's statements this seems to include, somewhat surprisingly, all the cotton textile firms outside of Europe. The reasons given for urging protection have concerned two sets of problems: factor costs and the organization of production. Factor price problems specific to the industry have centered on raw materials, wages of women employees, and textile machinery.

Producers point out frequently that they have been handicapped in competition with other domestic textiles by the cost-raising effects of American price supports for cotton, and, less frequently, that they have gained from subsidized exports by the United States. Producers were subject in the early postwar years to administrative interferences with efficient purchasing. An inflexible exchange control system held them to an unusually low proportion of American cotton when that source was cheapest, and then restricted their ability to shift to new sources when alternatives improved [162, pp. 371–88] [164, pp. 120–29]. In addition to the handicap of raw material prices running above those in competing countries, they suffered higher handling costs because of inability to obtain systematically the qualities best suited to each production process. On the other hand, they were in effect subsidized on the input side by the maintenance of an overvalued currency, keeping the franc prices of imported materials below the levels that would have been consistent with aggregate foreign exchange equilibrium.

The effort of French legislation to require equal wages for men and women workers has particularly bothered the industry, because this is not the practice in competing countries, and women make up two thirds of its labor force [165, pp. 64–66] [169, p. 8]. But the legal stipulation has been partially evaded by arranging job classification in such a way as to keep average wages for women below those for men, even when they occupy substantially equivalent positions. The actual ratio of women's wages to those of men in the French cotton textile industry is almost exactly the same as in Germany, but in both of these two countries it is much higher than in the rest of the Common Market [149, p. 188].

The French textile producers do have to pay wages somewhat closer to other fields of manufacturing than is true of their American counterparts. In 1958, wages in the French textile industry were 23 percent below the average for all manufacturing, while those of American textile workers were 29 percent below average [17a, p. 331] [182]. From 1954 to 1959, wages in the American textile industry increased 15 percent, equal to 65 percent of the increase for all manufacturing. Those in the French industry increased 44 percent, equal to 80 percent of the increase in the country's mechanical and electrical equipment industries (table 7 below). The difference in trends, during a period in which American textile production increased more than twice as rapidly as that in France, is probably attributable to the much better employment opportunities open in France, a situation which acted to equalize earnings a little more effectively. In both textile industries, but more particularly in the American, payment of wages below the average for all industry acted as a subsidy permitting the survival of marginal firms. The French producers have been somewhat more directly exposed than the Americans to the consequences of trying to maintain labor-intensive operations in an economy in which the factor balance is altering toward increased labor scarcity.

Labor cost difficulties have been aggravated by the equipment supply situation facing French producers. Textile machinery is one of the more important examples of high-cost industrial equipment discussed in Chapter 6. Some modern machinery has not been made available by domestic producers. Until 1959, the textile firms were impeded in efforts to turn to foreign sources of supply for part of the time by quantitative restriction and all of the time by high tariffs [162, p. 217] [169, p. 42]. The cotton textile producers have been among those seriously handicapped by the general policy of protection for producers of industrial equipment.

Apart from these special cost difficulties arising from economic policy choices external to the industry, it remains apparent that many of their problems have been traceable to internal organization and behavior. The interconnected issues concerned are the dispersion and size of producers, modernization of equipment and production techniques, pricing, and efforts to develop new market openings.

Trade association and government discussions both suggest that relatively high costs may be largely explained in terms of insufficient scale: (1) the smaller firms tend to diversify production unduly in order to minimize the risks of dependence on a limited product range; (2) they do not have ready access to capital markets for external financing; (3) the large number of producers and their preoccupation with immediate survival prevent them from holding prices above variable costs sufficiently to obtain funds for investment from internal sources;

(4) the slow pace of investment resulting from limits on financing, combined with the equipment and labor cost problems cited, makes it most difficult to keep up with improvements in other countries.

The strong demand focusing on the industry at the end of the war brought back into production many of the marginal firms eliminated during the long prewar stagnation. Between 1946 and 1950 the number of firms increased and the average scale of plant fell. In the latter year, the proportion of employees in textile plants with over 1000 workers was one-third lower than in either Germany or Italy [62, p. 410]. Judging from similar data available for the cotton textile industry in 1954, its situation closely paralleled that for all textiles [14]. About 14 percent of all workers in the cotton textile industry were then employed by firms with more than 500 employees, compared to 70 percent in the United States [149, p. 131].

Even during the influx of firms and the decrease in average plant size up to 1950, the largest firms were tending toward greater concentration of their production. The five largest companies in the spinning branch owned 38 plants in 1946 and 31 by 1950, with 10 percent more spindles per plant in the latter year. The integrated firms stood out sharply from the rest of the industry in the speed of their shift toward automatic looms and modern types of spindles [162, pp. 222–39]. The slow drift toward concentration of production, with a minority of firms making considerable efforts to modernize techniques, exactly paralleled the evolution of the industry in the United States. The only difference was the rate of change. By 1953, nonautomatic looms had practically disappeared from the American industry, but they still totalled three-fourths of all the looms in use by nonintegrated firms in France, and 42 percent of those in use by the integrated companies.

In the American industry, the pressure of competition was allowed to work out freely enough, if far from painlessly, until protectionist measures began to come to the fore in the late

1950's. In the French industry, the firms did have the pressure of their own excess capacity and poor markets, but were well insulated from foreign rivals and were less inclined to tactics of mutual destruction. The results were recognized to be poor. Both sets of producers found it difficult to sell in competition with less industrialized countries, but French costs were also far above those of the more thoroughly modernized producers in countries paying higher wages than their own. The solution chosen was not one of encouraging greater competition, but of organizing a coordinated program of improvement through the trade association.

The trade association of the cotton textile producers is, along with that of the steel industry, one of the most active in France. Prior to the war, it was little more than an instrument of negotiation on tariff questions. During the war it began to play an important role in coordinating allocation of materials. Subsequently it has developed an impressive system of organizing information, promoting research and market development, and providing advice to member firms. The association itself, in cooperation with the Ministry of Industry and the Planning Commission, but with perhaps most of the initiative coming from its own side, drew up a special five-year program for the industry in 1953. The program envisaged accomplishing in an orderly way exactly what forceful competition might have promoted had it been obtained. It focused on elimination of small plants, modernization of equipment without increasing capacity, and greater specialization [169]. The government made available to the association part of the receipts from a tax on textile sales, to aid in the purchase and destruction of old equipment. The association attempted systematically to promote mergers among capable firms, and to induce marginal producers to seek help from the government for reconversion to alternative industries. It took charge of establishing a new industry-wide research organization focused particularly on market trends and on the development of new products combining cottons with artificial and synthetic fibers. The trade association also established a productivity center to study methods of improving plant efficiency. Among other devices, this office developed the useful technique of issuing periodic reports to all member firms showing levels of efficiency (by multiple criteria) for each separate plant, thus enabling each firm to locate its own areas of weakness relative to the best practice being achieved in the industry.

At the completion of the association's five-year program in 1958, 240 plants had been withdrawn from production, the number of looms reduced one-fifth and the proportion of automatic looms raised from 45 to 60 percent. This still left a goodly crowd: nearly 2000 plants, including only 255 with more than 200 employees [15, table II, pp. 30–47]. Output per man-hour increased nearly 50 percent. One-fourth of the plants withdrawn from production were converted to other uses, some completely on their own initiative but most with marketing advice and financial help from the association and the government [3, pp. 221–22]. The Planning Commission cooperated on all aspects of the program, but did apparently raise some objections to purchasing old equipment for purposes of destroying it. The Commission advised the trade association against such action, and other government agencies against providing any help which was not accompanied by measures to ensure reinvestment in other fields of the funds obtained from sale of old textile machinery [8, pp. 128–30].

The French producers no longer have any significant competitive disadvantage within the Common Market [149, ch. 6]. As compared to the German industry, their output per man, and the ratio of automatic to total looms now in use, are both superior. The general picture of competitive strength in terms of costs was validated by the pattern of change in French retail prices for consumer goods, once trade barriers were lowered. For a wide variety of consumer goods French retail prices had to be greatly reduced to meet newly available foreign alternatives, but for most cotton goods the trend went the other way as the French producers reached new markets in other countries [175, January 14–15, 1962].

The industry's improvement in the period of its five-year plan was genuine, but the achievement might be deflated somewhat if compared to the unplanned results in the American industry during the same period. An investigation of the American industry by the French productivity center indicated that both sides had improved labor productivity at similar rates. In cotton spinning, the 30 best French plants observed for comparison required in 1958 slightly more man-hours per unit output than the American industry had required in 1950. In the interval, American firms sampled had reduced labor requirements per unit output by nearly half. In weaving, the 4 American firms observed required from 12 to 30 hours per 100 kilograms of a standardized product, with a mean requirement of 21. The 21 best French firms compared required from 39 to 81 hours, with a mean of 56 [165, pp. 6–11].

As the report emphasizes, the pressure for labor saving is much greater in the American than in the French industry, because wages are much higher relative to costs of power, equipment, and raw materials. But the close comparability of the rates of improvement of the two industries is also indicated by measures other than efficiency in the use of labor, such as the rate of reduction of spindles in use, or simply the trend of product prices relative to other domestic prices. The American industry kept pace with the French, without any of the latter's apparatus of intervention. This may perhaps be regarded as no astounding feat, but it is a good deal more than the metals and automobile industries managed to do.

The conclusion is not that the French industry's cooperative plan was irrelevant. It replaced an earlier drift, which had moved costs and prices adversely relative to those of other industrial countries, with a rationally oriented program which made the industry's progress closely comparable to that of the competitive American producers. Since the British cotton textile producers seem actually to have lost ground compared to the American industry in the postwar period [163], the French producers apparently gained when compared to those in England as well as to Common Market countries. In the light of the industry's own history, the performance of the 1950's was a major improvement.

3. The Differences Between Positive Competitive Pressure and Absence of Monopolistic Control

The cotton textile industry presents a case which does not quite fit the usual market categories applied in discussing competition. It has an exceedingly low level of concentration, low entry barriers, and probably minimal economies of scale. Almost all the conditions for the existence of competition have been present. And there definitely has been price competition, in the sense that price levels went down rapidly in adverse cyclical conditions, even during the 1953–58 period of joint industry guidance under the trade association's plan. Some firms were driven out in the 1930's and again in postwar recessions, and some companies did make relatively good progress in reducing costs. But up to the mid-1950's there was no general pressure sufficient to ensure that the weak firms became a marginal problem rather than the dominant form of the industry. The more progressive companies seem to have moved slowly, improving their relative position by the wider margins their lower costs permitted, rather than trying to capture larger markets in a hurry. The gap between high- and low-cost producers remained extraordinarily wide, and the former set the tone for the industry [162, pp. 397–400], [164, pp. 175–78].

The differences in behavior between the French and the American cotton textile industries have been matters of degree rather than kind, but they have nonetheless been important enough to hold down living standards and to slow economic progress on the French side. Structural conditions were favorable to competition, and attempts at collusion usually broke down, but it requires more than this to secure a positive thrust forcing an industry to move rapidly forward.

The relative absence of such positive pressure in the French industry probably owed something to social traditions and the prevalence of family-owned enterprise [42] [162, pp. 21–26, 173–79]. François Capronnier's excellent discussion of the issue warns against generalization, contrasting the observed dynamism of the Alsatian producers with the reluctance of tradition-bound Northern families, and emphasizing the growing diversity of more recent behavior. His conclusion is nevertheless that prolonged ownership stability had been accompanied by a weakness in competitive drive, particularly with respect to efforts to maintain exports and investment, from at least 1910 onward. The evidence supports the thesis, but it leaves open the question of the contrast with foreign performance. The American textile firms were long established too, and few students of the industry have remarked on any blinding speed in their instinctive reactions to change, but until very recently these firms collectively did much better than the French in taking advantage of possibilities of improving efficiency.

Two other factors, more nearly within the scope of social choice, seem to have been at least as important as attitudes of national producers in maintaining the French industry in a relatively weak state. One of them was its tradition of thorough protection against foreign competition [162, pp. 37–41, 63–67, 304–08]. This would not have been fatal if the industry had experienced strongly independent behavior within its own ranks, as did the automobile industry in the postwar period. In the absence of the basic tendency at home, the reliance on protection ensured that it would not be replaced with pressure from the outside. The policy of protection neatly succeeded in restricting real income in France and keeping unnecessarily high the costs of clothing for people in colonial territories, while retaining resources in unproductive employment through the inflationary postwar years.

The second special factor is that the producers have been relatively free of the push toward efficiency exerted on the American industry by large buyers. Americans who find themselves in the position of buying cotton products on French retail markets are prone to develop a new affection for Sears Roebuck. The independent importance of the action of large buyers oriented toward low-margin retailing in the United States, and of the relatively passive role of such organizations in France, is not possible to evaluate quantitatively. But it may be that this is one of the key explanations of the long-term record of weaker drive in the French cotton textile industry.

The large retail organizations are undoubtedly good buyers. When the department stores were establishing themselves in the nineteenth century they apparently did exercise pressure on unit margins and aid the development of volume sales by passing on the effects of such savings in order to undercut retail rivals [162, p. 38]. But the big stores grew older, legislation inhibited the emergence of chain-store techniques in the period when they were developing in the United States, and healthy pressure from large buyers failed to continue. This situation in turn has been evolving in a favorable direction. Legislative changes encouraging new techniques of distribution have permitted a steady expansion of retail chains. Price fixing of the American "fair-trade" variety has been prohibited since 1953, favoring the expansion of volume distributors.

Several chains have in fact been pulling away from the rest of the retail distributors in the soft-goods fields during recent years, providing lower-cost textiles through pressure on producers supplemented by retail handling efficiency. The fact that the presence of large numbers on the selling side does not preclude cooperation was evidenced in 1960 when the newest and most aggressive mass distributor, Leclerc, was temporarily blocked by a collective refusal of the producers of all leading textile brands to supply these stores. Such refusal has been used to break other discount operations in the past, and was finally made illegal in 1953. Illegal or not, this particular impasse was not quickly corrected.

If positive competitive pressure had been provided by either domestic or foreign forces, the program of the trade association would have been both unnecessary and undesirable. In the actual situation, it did accomplish at least some of the objectives that active competition would have secured. The association itself was one of the few which took on the explicit task of eliminating weak producers and lowering costs of production. It undoubtedly would have lowered the country's welfare by charging high prices if the multitude of producers had not prevented stable agreements, and it would gladly have restricted consumer choices in both France and colonial territories to the goods produced in France had its political influence been sufficient. In the absence of power to control the market, the association focused on improvements in efficiency. To a degree decidedly rare in French trade association activities, it did obtain positive results through group effort to lower costs. If resources moved swiftly to optimum employment in all cases, the program would have had no point—but the cotton textile industry would have been more thoroughly modernized in the first place.

The industry's record makes clear that dispersion is not enough. In fact, the conditions which make a high degree of ownership dispersion inevitable make it simultaneously difficult for a progressive minority to have the impact that it may provide in a concentrated industry such as automobiles. The progressive few can move ahead for a long time without seriously disturbing the rest, because the lesser significance of economies of scale makes it difficult for them to raise their relative weight in the industry at all rapidly, even if they try. The best way to keep such an industry alive is to encourage competitive pressure by keeping open recourse to imports, and to allow the exercise of strong buying power by large distributors. The second-best alternative in the absence of these choices was probably that adopted in France in 1953: a planned group program aiming at methodical reduction of costs, supervised by government agencies to minimize abuse. Fortunately for the French, the recourse to such a program was followed, in 1960, by the elimination of quantitative import restrictions and the reduction of tariff barriers against other producers in the European Common Market. Just when the American industry is turning toward the protective devices that undermined the vitality of the French industry in the past, the French more and more seem to be establishing the conditions that contributed so much to the formerly superior performance of the American producers.

9 | Cross-Section Comparisons of Performance

The five preceding studies cover industries with widely divergent structures of production and varying fortunes, but they constitute a very small sample for generalization about French manufacturing. The opposite approach would be to carry out detailed statistical comparisons, attempting to locate significant explanatory factors by correlation and isolation of unusual values. The important gaps in published data make such an analysis difficult at best for French industry, but several recent improvements make it possible to put the present discussion in a clearer general context. This chapter ventures on fairly thin ice, statistically speaking, to provide brief cross-section summaries of performance with respect to output, labor productivity, relative prices, and exports.

1. Changes in Output and Productivity

In an interesting article covering the period 1950–60, François Hetman demonstrated a fairly close correspondence between rates of expansion and rates of gain in output per worker, along with a tendency toward decreasing relative prices for the products of the more rapidly expanding industries [35]. The data used apply to broadly defined groups and include mining and utilities as well as manufacturing. An alternative source of data, available only for the years from 1954 on, makes it possible to apply similar tests to more narrowly defined categories of manufacturing. Table 5 combines this information with Hetman's results, summarizing changes in production and in output per man-hour for the period 1954–59.

TABLE 5. Increases in Production and in Output per Man-Hour in French Manufacturing Industries, 1954–59

	Production index in 1959 (1954 = 100) [a]	Index of output per man-hour in 1959 (1954 = 100) [b]
Durable goods		
Primary metals	147	134
Steel	147	n.a.
Aluminum	148	n.a.
Fabricated metal products, other than machinery and vehicles	130	127
Nonelectrical machinery	143	115
Machine tools	128	118
Agricultural machinery	195	128
Electrical equipment	173	146
Railroad equipment	89	116
Automobiles, cycles and their equipment	171	154
Furniture and wood products [c]	139	139
Nondurable goods		
Textile mill products	109	122
Cotton textiles	100	145
Apparel [c]	102	107
Leather and products	98	103
Paper and products	147	137
Printing and publishing	150	137
Chemicals	193	181
Rubber products	140	130
Food processing [c]	115	94
"All industry," including power and mining but excluding industries designated by note [c]	142	132

Sources: for all industries other than mechanical-electrical products and cotton textiles, production indexes from *Etudes Statistiques*, April–June 1960, pp. 89–104, and indexes of man-hours worked from Hetman, "Crois-

With the exception of the mechanical and electrical industries, the information on hours worked which underlies the calculations of output per man-hour is plagued by serious statistical nightmares. In particular, the sampling process used covers only those plants which employ more than 10 workers, providing an acceptable measure in many industries but leaving a high proportion of production out of account in others. In a period in which average plant size was increasing, this may lead to unequal overstatements of the upward trend in hours worked. This factor may be one of the reasons for the especially doubtful productivity figure for the food processing industries. Observation and widespread comment in France suggest that it may indeed be true that in this field output per worker has fallen with increasing production—a possibility in no way inconsistent with classical economic theory—but the activity figures do not provide strong independent confirmation. In general, the only productivity data which merit a high degree of confidence are those for the electrical and mechanical product industries. Since 1954, these have been covered by consistently defined comprehensive reporting organized by the Ministry of Industry.

None of the specific deficiencies of the production or activity data falsifies the basic picture of extreme divergence in growth rates and productivity improvement, a natural consequence of rapid economic expansion. Granting that labor mobility is not exceptionally high in France, this has not pre-

---

sance Comparée des industries françaises," *Bulletin SEDEIS*, May 1, 1961, supplément; for mechanical and electrical equipment industries, Direction des Industries Mécaniques et Electriques, "Principales Statistiques Annuelles, Année 1959," Paris (mimeo), 1960; for cotton textile productivity data, information supplied by the trade association.

Notes: [a]) The weight base of the production index used here is 1949.

[b]) Man-hours here refer to wage-earners, corresponding more nearly to American data for production workers than to "all employees."

[c]) Industries so designated are not included in the regular French index of industrial production because data on their output are particularly doubtful. Production indexes are calculated for them by the INSEE on an annual basis only.

vented marked shifts in the structure of production. Output of chemicals and of agricultural machinery practically doubled in the five-year period, while that of clothing, leather, and textile mill products changed hardly at all.

The improvements in output per man-hour were also highly uneven. The general pattern of change corresponded closely to that for production, as is surely to be expected. There were interesting departures in two of the industries discussed in preceding chapters. For nonelectrical machinery, the gain in labor productivity was only one-third that of output, compared to a ratio of three-fourths for "all industry." For textiles, the relationship was off in the opposite direction, with gains in productivity more than double those in production. The contrast centers in cotton textiles, where output did not rise at all but the reduction in hours worked was so swift that output per man-hour rose faster than in "all industry." It should be noted that the activity data here were supplied by the trade association, since published government measures do not go into detail within the textile group. This does not mean that the figures are less reliable. On the contrary, they are probably more precise, though not fully comparable to other industries. The experience of the textile producers was paralleled by that in railroad equipment, in which a good increase in productivity was achieved despite falling production. The climate of expansion with rising job opportunities, supplemented in the case of railroad equipment by government help for reconversion of facilities, apparently did permit rapid labor transfer out of industries lacking strong markets.

Comparisons between the patterns of productivity gain in American and in French industries involve a juxtaposition of data that are not established by the same techniques in the two countries, but they may still be useful to clarify the main contrasts in rates of improvement. Table 6 lists indexes of output and labor productivity changes in the 1954–59 period for American industrial groups which have elements of comparability with the French, and also lists the ratios of French to American indexes for approximately corresponding industries.

Table 6. Comparative Changes in Output and Labor Productivity between Approximately Corresponding American and French Manufacturing Industries, 1954–59

	American Industry (1954 = 100)		Ratio of French to American Index	
	Production index in 1959	Index of output per man-hour [a]	Production	Output per man-hour [a]
Durable goods				
Primary metals	110	114	134	118
Fabricated metal products	117	117	111	109
Nonelectrical machinery	115	115	124	100
Electrical equipment	132	123	131	119
Motor vehicles and equipment	122	132	140	117
Furniture, wood products [b]	120	118	116	118
Nondurables				
Textile mill products	122	129	89	95
Apparel	138	130	74	82
Leather and products	116	113	84	91
Paper and products	130	126	113	109
Printing and publishing	120	111	125	123
Chemicals	149	148	130	122
Rubber (and plastics in U.S. industry only)	144	135	97	96
Food and Beverages	114	123	101	76
All manufacturing (U.S. only)	123	124	—	—
All industry, including power and mining (France only)	(142)	(132)	—	—

Sources: American production data from Board of Governors of the Federal Reserve System, *Industrial Production, 1959 Revision*, Washington, 1960; index of weekly hours of production workers from U.S., Department of Labor, *Monthly Labor Review*; French data from Table 5.

Notes: [a]) Man-hours refer to production workers only in the United States, and to hourly paid wage workers in France.

[b]) The separate American categories of lumber and wood products, and furniture and wood, were combined on the basis of 1957 weights in the Federal Reserve index, p. 35 in source cited.

Table 6 stretches doubtful data to the limits of endurance, but it does give a consistent picture. The two production structures moved along quite different paths, with French output and productivity gains centered in durable goods, chemicals and paper, while American gains were relatively greater in textiles, clothing, leather, food processing, and rubber products. Every American industry for which production increased more rapidly than the counterpart French industry also raised its output per man-hour more rapidly than the French industry. Nearly every American industry which grew more slowly in output than the French also fell behind in productivity gains.

The two exceptions in which American industries with lower increases in production obtained equal or greater increases in productivity were food products and nonelectrical machinery. The former case involves particularly doubtful output and man-hour data on the French side, which does not necessarily mean that the weak performance indicated in Table 6 is wrong. The other case, that of nonelectrical machinery, is of particular interest here. The relative expansion of the French industry was among the highest for all these groups, yet the productivity gain was no greater than that in the United States. It is the only durable goods industry in which the productivity improvement in France was not definitely better than that in the United States. It was a consistent supply bottleneck, as discussed in Chapter 6. The productivity comparisons, admittedly subject to extra precaution for groups with such great internal product diversity, underline the earlier conclusion that the industry's performance was inferior to that of French manufacturing generally.

2. Wage Increases and Unit Labor Costs

Gains in labor productivity on the French side ran ahead of the American for most industries, but wage rates ran ahead even faster. The cost of production labor per unit of output rose faster in French manufacturing, but the effect on international competition was offset by the successive devaluations of 1957 and 1958. The two devaluations reduced the dollar cost of francs by 28 percent, converting the increase in relative labor costs into an effective relative decrease for most industries. Table 7 risks yet one more extension of the data on productiv-

TABLE 7. Comparative Changes in Hourly Wages of Production Workers and Implied Unit Wage Costs for Approximately Corresponding American and French Manufacturing Industries, 1954–59 [a]

	Index of hourly wages of production workers in 1959 (1954 = 100)		Implied index of wage costs per unit of output [a] (1959 = 100)	
	U.S.	France	U.S.	France
Durable goods				
Primary metals	133	154	117	115
Fabricated metals	125	157	107	124
Nonelectrical machinery	124	144	108	125
Electrical equipment	122	150	99	103
Motor vehicles	122	153	92	99
Furniture, wood products	119	151	101	109
Nondurables				
Textiles	115	144	89	118
Apparel	113	146	86	136
Leather & products	117	149	103	145
Paper & products	126	151	100	110
Printing and Publishing	119	159	107	116
Chemicals & rubber [b]	126	152	87	89
Food and Beverages	126	150	102	160
All manufacturing (U.S.)	123	—	100	—
Mechanical and electrical equipment industries (France)	—	155	—	114

Sources: gross hourly wages of production workers for the U.S. from U.S. Department of Labor, *Monthly Labor Review*; French wage indexes from INSEE, *Bulletin Mensuel de Statistique* for all except mechanical and electrical product industries; for latter industries, wages per hour from Direction des Industries Mécaniques et Electriques, "Principales Statistiques Annuelles, Année 1959"; productivity indexes from Tables 5, 6.

Notes: [a]) Wage costs for both countries are for wage payments only, not including social security charges and other elements of labor cost. [b]) Chemical and rubber products industries combined on the basis of their relative weights in the production indexes of the two countries.

ity, listing changes in wage rates as measured in domestic currency, and the implied changes in wage costs of production labor for approximately corresponding industries.

In view of the more rapid economic change in France, and the much greater rise in hourly earnings, it is striking that the wage increases were more nearly parallel among industries there than in the United States. The range from high to low among the American industries listed in Table 7 is 20 index points (16 percent of the median), and on the French side 15 points (10 percent of the median). The relative homogeneity of percentage increases on the French side was due to the persistence of good employment conditions, which helped to raise wages in those industries not expanding their labor forces, and to government intervention in the wage setting process, which worked in general to hold back increases in any industries tending to raise wages at above-average rates. One of the forms of government intervention was the use of price control as a pressure device, threatening firms or industries with the prospect of being denied compensating price increases if they raised wages at unusually rapid rates.

The effect of comparatively equal rates of wage increase among French industries was to translate changes in relative labor productivity directly into changes in relative labor costs. For the 13 industrial groups cited in Table 7, the coefficient of rank correlation between increases in labor productivity and decreases in implied unit wage cost is .98. In the United States, the greater dispersion of wage increases yields a rank correlation of .88.

In both countries, the increases for the textile, apparel, and leather industries were at the bottom of the scale. The only difference was that these American groups fell further below the rest of domestic industry than the French groups did, although they were among the minority of industries in which output grew faster than in France. The result was that their implied unit wage costs fell markedly, relative to the French industries, by 25 percent for textiles and fully 37 for apparel.

At the other end of the scale, the wage increase in American primary metals production was 38 percent greater than the median increase, a difference greater than that between the highest and the lowest increase in French industry. This aberrant rise came in the group with one of the lowest productivity increases on the American side, and in the face of a decline in hours worked. The combined effect of an unusually large wage increase and an unusually small productivity increase was to raise the implied unit wage cost relative to that of the corresponding French industry. This was the only group for which this happened.

The deterioration of markets for the American motor vehicle industry in this period can hardly be attributed to wage increases: the rise in output per man-hour was sufficient to offset the increase in hourly wage costs. In the French motor vehicle industry, hourly wage rates rose twice as fast as in the American industry, but output per man-hour kept pace and left unit costs almost unchanged. On both sides, the comparison leaves important supplementary wage costs out of account, and on both sides the productivity data are particularly suspect because of changes in output composition. They do serve to suggest a much more rapid productivity increase on the French side, roughly parallel movements of unit wage cost when expressed in domestic currency, and, therefore, a marked decrease in French wage costs expressed in dollars, following devaluation of the franc.

In an earlier discussion of such comparisons, using data for the periods 1950–58 and 1954–58, the author drew the conclusion that the relative advantage in terms of productivity and unit wage costs shifted favorably toward the United States for the more dispersed industries, and toward France for the more concentrated industries [47]. The different time periods did not have a great effect on the results. They were closely similar to those above for 1954–59. But the conclusion now appears too simple. If one were confined to a single explanatory factor, it would be more defensible to point out that American efficiency and labor costs gains were associated with industries where production increased relative to that of the corresponding French industries. This would fit otherwise inconsistent data for printing and publishing and for furniture and wood products, neither of which are highly concentrated industries, but both of which show relatively large productivity gains on the French side. Still, there was a high degree of consistency between relative growth and more dispersed structures of production, particularly among the nondurable goods industries. Further, the two least concentrated metal products industries, fabricated metals and nonelectrical machinery, were, of all the durable goods industries, the two for which the American industries achieved the highest relative increases in output per man-hour and the greatest relative decreases in unit costs.

The more important point is that differences in growth rates, while statistically associated with relative productivity and cost changes, do not "explain" the pattern of gains in efficiency because the growth rates were themselves partly consequences of production and marketing choices determining costs and prices. In France, government policies were often more helpful to the concentrated than to the dispersed fields. In the United States, management choices in some concentrated industries were adverse for their own output growth, while the dispersed industries were denied the luxury of noncompetitive choices inimical to expansion.

It is also true that many of the French gains can be explained in terms of economies of scale, technologically always possible but not previously realized. But the interesting question is why some industries got into motion to realize such gains much more rapidly than others. Desirable scales in such fields as textiles and machinery are well below those in automobiles and primary metals, but they are still well above those achieved so far in France. The basic explanation must include the choices of government and of business. The gains on the French side were always possible, and there are more ahead, in all fields. They could have come earlier than they did in the more concentrated industries, and would have been more generally obtained by the dispersed industries in the 1950's, if the main lines of policy had not been inappropriate to their structural problems.

3. Relative Prices

The pattern of change in wages acted to re-enforce the effects of the changes in productivity, swinging the American relative advantage away from metals and other durables toward consumer nondurables. The changes can be further compared by bringing together a sample of relative data on the evolution of wholesale prices for some of these industries, as in Table 8 following.

As in the preceding tables, the French data on prices are from two different sources. The figures for the mechanical and electrical equipment industries, not reported in the official price indexes, are deflators calculated from the ratio of changes in sales value to changes in production volume. The other French figures are direct price indexes, as reported by the INSEE. The difference introduces a further element of possible bias. In general, the deflators might be expected to show lower increases than direct price indexes, because of the tendency of buyers to shift toward substitute products for which prices rise least within each group. This does not seem to have had an important effect on the wholesale deflator for the motor vehicle industry: it rose by the same percentage as the retail index of automobile prices.

Taking the figures in Table 8 at face value, the motor vehicle and electrical equipment industries stand out as the two instances of relatively increasing prices on the American side. Both rose less than prices of steel and nonelectrical machinery in the U.S., but the latter two were also cases of rapid increase in France.

The index of American motor vehicle and equipment prices

TABLE 8. Comparative Changes in Wholesale Prices for Approximately Corresponding American and French Manufacturing Industries, 1954–59

	Index of prices (1959 on base 1954 = 100)		Ratio, French index to U.S.
	United States	France	
Durable goods			
Primary metals [a]	123	138	112
Iron and steel	129	141	109
Aluminum	123	129	105
Nonelectrical machinery [a]	126	140	107
Metal-working machinery	131	—	
Machine tools	—	152	
Agricultural machinery	117	118	101
Motor vehicles & equipment	120	112	93
Electrical equipment	123	114	93
Nondurables			
Textiles and apparel	100	103	103
Leather and products	121	170	140
Paper and allied products	114	122	107
Chemicals	103	114	111
Rubber products	114	145	127
Transformed industrial products (France)	—	124	(111)
All commodities except food (U.S.)	112	—	

Sources: data for American industries from U.S., Department of Labor, *Monthly Labor Review*, and *Wholesale Prices*, 1954–56; price indexes for all French industries other than mechanical and electrical equipment from INSEE, *Bulletin Mensuel de Statistique*; for latter group, calculated from ratio of sales to production indexes in Direction des Industries Mécaniques et Electriques, "Principales Statistiques Annuelles, Année 1959."

Note: [a]) American indexes for primary metals and for nonelectrical machinery calculated from indexes for included subgroups, weighted by December 1954 weights from *Wholesale Prices*, 1954–56, Table 4a, pp. 34–53.

rose 20 percent, while the French index increased only 12 percent, despite greater wage increases and a pair of devaluations on the latter side. The explanation offered in Chapter 7 is twofold. With respect to market practices, the French industry was more competitive, was under mild surveillance by price control authorities, made more effective choices with respect to model innovation, was favored by better domestic demand conditions, and made an effective drive in export markets. On the production side, the increase in sales was accomplished with a generally efficient expansion program, raising labor productivity so rapidly that the markedly greater wage increases were offset in their effects on unit costs.

The causes of the relative rise in prices of American electrical equipment would be interesting to seek, but no detailed study of this industry has been carried out to permit any explanation here. The indexes of relative changes in implied wage costs, from Table 7, do not provide any useful clue: they apparently fell on the American side, though the difference was slight. It might be noted that: (1) the American industry, probably even more than the French, shifted output composition toward more complex equipment, notably in meeting military orders; (2) leading firms in the industry were convicted in 1961 of collusion in price setting during the period concerned.

The third highest American-to-French price ratio is that for textiles. American prices did hold steady while the French increased three percent, but the difference is much less than the contrast in implied unit wage costs shown in Table 7. The narrower difference in pricing might be explicable in terms of demand conditions. The American industry's output rose 2.4 times as rapidly as the French in this period. On the cost side, this was a period in which American subsidies for cotton exports helped bring down relative input costs for foreign producers. It is impossible to be sure without specific study of all the various textile industries, but the discrepancy between price and labor cost movements would not seem to be attributable to any lack of competition or effective effort within the American textile industry. It was one of the minority in which labor productivity did rise faster than in France, and its average prices were the only ones on the American side which did not rise at all, although production increased at practically the same rate as the index for all manufacturing.

The relative decrease in American prices of nonelectrical machinery was also less than the relative decline in its implied labor costs. The price increase for agricultural machinery was on a par with that in France, so the decrease for other types was a good deal more pronounced than that for the group as a whole. Prices of American metalworking machinery rose only 60 percent as much as those of machine tools in France, consistent with the group data on relative wage costs and with the general picture of relative weakness for the French nonelectrical machinery industries discussed in Chapter 6.

The one important reversal of pattern was in primary metals. Unit wage costs seem to have risen more than in France (Table 7), but prices rose much less. The increase for the iron and steel industry was double the average rise on the American side, but that on the French side was 60 percent above average too. The discussion in Chapter 5 helps clarify the reasons, without providing any completely satisfactory solution. French steel prices rose much less than American when the former were under tight price control, from 1952 to 1957 (Table 10 below). With controls relaxed in 1958 and 1959, and with two devaluations providing the basis for increases up to the level of steel prices in competing countries, French steel prices jumped. The rise from 1957 to 1959 was 17 percent. This may be understood as the delayed but inevitable consequence of previously exaggerated price controls, which is the way the French steel industry considers it. It may alternatively be considered as a joint government-industry group decision on the leeway for increase opened up by the devaluations: a bonus to the industry to encourage more rapid investment, rather than a necessary part of supply cost. Either way, profits of the French steel producers were allowed to widen precisely when the effects of previously rapid price increases on the United States side were generating international competitive difficulties so great as to check profits. As described by M. A. Adelman, the American steel industry may even have overshot temporarily the profit-maximizing monopoly price [127]. The net result was that the American prices were checked with a lower increase than that of the French producers, with little credit to domestic competition on either side.

The relative changes in prices shown in Table 8 do not link up closely with relative changes in output, wage rates, or implied unit wage costs. There is a weak inverse correlation between relative changes in output and price, with several important contradictions. The only consistently extreme groups are leather products, for which United States output and productivity growth were relatively high while wage and price increases were low, and primary metals, for which the reverse was true on all counts except for prices.

4. Export Performances

It would be defensible to interpret the preceding information in terms of differences in demand structures between France and the United States. French industry has been catching up in capital equipment and production techniques, and consumption has been shifting toward the durable goods which went through rapid growth stages earlier in the United States. The industries favored by demand trends (chiefly durable goods plus chemicals and paper), have been able in most cases to raise production rapidly in France and in the process have been able to adopt improved techniques raising labor productivity and holding down relative costs. This thesis would go far to explain the comparisons with American performances, but not far enough. It fails to account for the consequence of differences in domestic managerial effectiveness and competition in affecting the growth of the domestic markets, fails to explain the deviant case of the French equipment industry performing weakly despite vigorous demand, and neglects the quantitatively significant role of exports in determining differences in growth of output.

Exports by French manufacturing industries to countries outside the franc zone were equal to slightly less than one-tenth of total production in 1954. Increases in such exports accounted for 16.7 percent of the rise of production between 1954 and 1959, pulling the ratio of exports to production up to 12.3 percent by the latter year. Table 9 presents the data assembled on a homogeneous basis for seven broad industrial groups by the Ministry of Finance, supplemented by somewhat less dependable adjusted data for the main branches of the mechanical and electrical products industries.

Table 9 overstates the growth of exports relative to production slightly, because the comparisons are in terms of current prices. The increase in franc receipts for a dollar's worth of export sales was (happily for the French), greater than the increase in domestic prices. But the difference was not great, because the devaluations were accompanied by a reduction of subsidies and because export prices expressed in foreign currencies were reduced. For all exports taken together, prices in francs rose by only 33 percent, compared to 32 percent for domestic prices [23, pp. 333, 343]. There was a marked upward bias in two groups only: nonferrous metals and mechanical and electrical equipment. For both of these, domestic prices remained well below the average rise.

Export growth accounted for almost exactly one sixth of the rise in output of French manufacturing in this period. The degree of success in escaping from the constraints of domestic demand varied widely among industries. With two-fifths of

Table 9. Exports Relative to Production for French Manufacturing Groups, 1954 and 1959; Increases in Exports Relative to Increases in Production, 1954–59

	Exports outside the franc zone (current prices)		
	Relative to production in 1954 (percentage)	Relative to production in 1959 (percentage)	Increase in exports relative to increase in production, 1954–59 (percentage)
Construction materials and glass	4.1	5.2	6.9
Iron and steel, ore and metals	20.7	28.9	37.4
Nonferrous metals	15.0	19.6	23.8
Mechanical and electrical products	8.8	13.4	19.2
Fabricated metals [a]	n.a.	9.3	n.a.
Nonelectrical machinery [a]	11.5	12.7	13.9
Electrical equipment [a]	6.0	8.0	10.1
Motor vehicles [a]	6.9	22.0	37.4
Chemicals	9.8	10.7	11.7
Textiles, clothing, leather	9.5	11.3	15.8
Wood, paper, misc.	5.3	6.1	7.2
Total of seven major groups	9.1	12.3	16.7

Sources: major groups from Ministère des Finances et des Affaires Economiques, *Les Comptes de la Nation*, Paris, 1960, vol. 1, pp. 310–17; four subsidiary groups within mechanical and electrical products from Direction des Industries Mécaniques et Electriques, "Principales Statistiques Annuelles, Année 1959." The Saar is counted in the franc zone.

Note: [a]) The official data for the four groups within the mechanical and electrical equipment industries give domestic sales at market, including taxes, but export sales net of taxes on sales or value added. Comparisons in the table between exports and production for these groups were made by adjusting export figures upward to the same basis as domestic sales, adding in estimated sales and value added taxes. The correction factors were based on an average tax of 17.1 percent for 1954 and 20 percent for 1959 [27, p. 3]. These rates applied to the value of sales with taxes included, so published export figures were multiplied by 1.206 for 1954 and 1.25 for 1959.

their increases in production exported, the performances of the French steel and automobile industries relative to their American counterparts can hardly be explained in terms of domestic demand differences—especially not in a period when exports of both of these American industries declined in absolute value [181].

Growth rates for the French machinery industries, chemicals, wood, and paper can be explained more nearly in terms of domestic demand. This does not necessarily mean that these industries were weak competitors in export markets. The structure of world demand itself favored exports by some industries and discouraged them for others. One way to attack this problem would be to compare French to world exports for particular groups. But a useful study by the INSEE points out that even this approach may have an important element of bias. "Each economy is placed by its internal structure and geographic position in different conditions with respect to world demand" [16g, p. 455]. The solution adopted in that study was to compare the evolution of imports from France to the total imports of manufactured products by fourteen of the country's major trading partners outside the franc zone.

In the period 1954–58, the share of imports of manufactured goods from France in the total import market of the fourteen countries varied between a low of 5.7 and a high of 6.1 percent, with the higher percentage achieved in both 1955 and 1958 [16g, p. 463]. For three product groups, the imports from France in 1958 ran at or above 10 percent of the total import market: iron and steel (15 percent), leather (11 percent), and automobiles (10 percent). Textiles ran surprisingly high (8 percent) and non-electrical machinery expectably low (3 percent). For all mechanical and electrical products except transportation equipment, the ratio was 3.5 percent [16g, graph 6, p. 470].

The changes over time in the relative roles of imports from France for the different industrial groups were marked by wide cyclical swings, making it difficult to summarize the evolution other than by the ingenious graphical techniques in the study cited. For the period 1954–58, only one group detached itself from the rest in an upward direction, namely, inevitably, automobiles. Their share in total automobile imports of the countries examined was below 5 percent from 1952 through 1956, then rose to 10 percent of the expanding total market by 1958. On the downward side, textiles fell from 10 percent in 1954 to 8 in 1958, and steel from 17 to 15 percent. The collection of all mechanical and electrical equipment industries, excluding transport equipment, moved sideways between 3 and 4 percent of the import market [16g, graphs 7–8, pp. 472–73].

The study of French exports relative to foreign demand brings out clearly the fact that the high ratios of exports to production for automobiles and steel shown in Table 9 do rest on successful export competition, raising the French market share in the first case and holding an unusually high one in the second. It also makes clear that the low ratios of exports to production for machinery are not due to weak foreign demand. French exports of these products were unable to reach a market share as high as that of all manufacturing combined.

The INSEE study cuts off at 1958, and thereby presents a weaker picture than that in Table 9. The latter includes 1959, a year in which all French exports increased significantly. Apart from the then continuing rise in automobile exports, the dollar value of sales by the persistently weaker groups of textiles and nonelectrical machinery turned up sharply. The machinery group continued to move ahead rapidly in 1960, while automobiles ran head on into the obstacle of the long-delayed competitive reaction by American producers.

The performance of the equipment producers since 1958 does not as yet demonstrate any more than a possibility, but it is a possibility supported by the logic of the change in the country's economic policy at the end of that year. Correction of the exchange rate, combined with a reduction of import barriers, has provided a new pull toward exports and a new force requiring previously protected industries to improve their techniques. The increase in exports of industrial equipment in 1959 and 1960 may be much more than a temporary reaction to a specific stimulus. It may well signal the beginning of a period of healthier growth for these industries and for French manufacturing, in a context of international competition from which they were previously overprotected.

5. Technological and Market Factors Bearing on Performance

The excellent study of technical change in the United Kingdom and the United States by W. E. G. Salter [66], covering the period 1924–50 for the United States, provides a particularly suggestive contrast to the results summarized in the present chapter. The most striking difference in approach and interpretation is that his analysis focuses on technological determinants of performance, while the present discussion emphasizes the role of market structure. The ways in which the two approaches conflict, and the ways in which they unite, cast considerable light on the nature of structural change in both France and the United States in recent years.

The central point of conflict is that Salter explained the pattern of structural change primarily by the scientific character of the pace-setting industries. "Under the impetus of rapidly improving technology and allied economies of scale their costs are continually falling relative to other industries, making possible falling relative prices, rapidly expanding output and, in the majority of cases, increasing employment" [66, p. 148]. In this analysis, Salter provides both empirical content and analytical amplification for Perroux's appealing but tantalizingly elusive concept of "poles of development" [77]. The whole approach comes close to a suggestion that choices of market structure are of minor importance, although both Perroux and Salter indicate clearly that they do not intend an extreme negative conclusion on this point. The French and American data considered here may help clarify reasons that any such conclusion should be rejected, even though technological possibilities may in some circumstances be greatly more important than questions of market organization.

Salter provides a particularly helpful clue to the intimate relationship of technical progress and market structure. One of the key aspects of such progress is the time lag between improvements in the "best practice" plants within an industry, and the adoption of the new techniques by the rest of the industry. He points out that monopolistic industries may choose to emphasize high unit margins, with the direct consequence of slower long-run market growth and the indirect result of a lower rate of new investment. Since it is primarily through new investment that major technical changes are implemented, the lack of competitive pressure which permits higher margins serves to retard the spread of new techniques [66, pp. 90–93]. The contrast between the performances of the French automobile industry in the interwar period and in the 1950's may provide a useful demonstration of the point. More generally, there is abundant evidence that rapid growth in production helps an industry to raise efficiency, and it is equally clear that such factors as price competition, efforts to export or to undersell possible imports, and willingness of firms to upset market positions by independent offers of different products, help to obtain the rapid growth that facilitates technical change.

At one extreme, it is probably true that market organization is of little relevance to the rate of technical advance in a new industry. If a new product is to be developed successfully, the firms introducing it must emphasize active selling techniques. They have an overwhelming interest in achieving high volume and secure reputations before possible rivals can enter the field. At the other extreme, the performance of an established industry is less likely to be dominated by radical technical change, and the continuous progress that does occur may be either accelerated or retarded by alternative forms of market organization.

For both France and the United States, the industries which provide the greater share of the value added in manufacturing are older fields in which the pace of technical change is strongly conditioned by the presence or absence of competitive pressure. Salter's data for the period 1924–50 may be taken to indicate that differences among industries in technical possibilities remain dominant even in this situation: the industries with a more strongly scientific character were able in that period to raise the productivity of all factors of production at above-average rates, and thereby to reduce their relative costs and prices. "Less fortunate industries where the pace of progress is much slower—coal, textiles, leather goods, shipbuilding, etc.—have few opportunities for reducing best-practice costs and thus their relative prices tend to rise" [66, p. 80].

It may be noted that Table 8, summarizing data on relative price changes for 1954–59, contradicts Salter's observation. The textile industries were the most successful of all fields in both France and the United States in their relative reduction of prices during this period. The fact that they outperformed even the chemical and electrical equipment industries in this respect can hardly be ascribed to any inherently superior technical possibilities. The textile industries were aided by significant improvements in productivity, but these in turn were promoted by the competitive pressure bearing on performance in the American industry and by direct reorganizational efforts in the French industry. The steel industries of the two countries were singularly unsuccessful in reducing factor requirements or costs. This may be ascribed to the age and lack of rapid scientific advance of the industries, but it is not clear that they were more seriously hampered in these respects than the textile industries. The differences among market organization factors bearing on the steel and textile industries of the two countries in the 1950's were notable, and were consistent with differences in the performances observed. These differences would fade to secondary importance if fundamental technical revolutions occurred in either field, but life goes on, sometimes happily and sometimes not, even betwen revolutions.

For most of the manufacturing industries in France and the United States in the 1950's, uneven technical progress along lines partially explicable by differences in market organization was the general rule. But the question is not one of choosing between mutually exclusive explanations in any case: it is rather one of illuminating policy choices by searching for understanding of the ways in which multiple causes interact on each other.

PART III | Policies

10 | "Indicative Planning"

Economic planning as practiced in France has a splendid goal: the improvement of productive efficiency and social welfare without recourse to authoritarian control. Its use since 1946 has been accompanied by one of the most impressive advances ever recorded in French economic history. In 1961, it received the surprising accolade of attention by the Conservative Government of the United Kingdom, followed by discussions on the possibility of adapting the approach to English problems. It has become an export product competing with American sermons on the value of free enterprise and Russian advice on central control. As such, it is a most welcome addition to the world of relevant ideas, and a fit subject for dissection by potential consumers.

The domestic model of planning that France offers for consideration should be regarded as a package with variable components. Some of the components have been altered by the French themselves in the process of making successive adaptations to a changing situation. But they have kept two principal elements which should be most carefully distinguished by possible buyers. One of them is the element of promotional stimulus provided by raising incentives to invest or to adapt production in new directions. The second is that of group agreement on objectives, established through consultation among firms and government agencies. To most of the people concerned with planning in France, these aspects of the system seem to be inseparable. But they may be doubly wrong. The two aspects may be both separable and, if not separated, partially offsetting rather than complementary. The first stimulates action, the second may either support or inhibit it.

As practiced, the promotional side of planning has been the stronger. But the government keeps flirting with an idea that could easily, with the best intentions in the world, tip the balance the other way. The troublesome idea is that group decisions on planning goals should be applied in such a way as to keep the blind optimism of misguided individual firms from carrying them to the creation of capacity or products not intended by the group. In short, the danger of planning as practiced in France is that it sets up the possibility of a system of rewards and penalties ensuring adherence to a plan. The great blessing, in practice, is that group goals have not been made binding on individual firms, that disorderly and consequently vigorous movement has been favored instead of the deadening goal of rational coherence.

1. The Monnet Plan (1947–52)

The French often refer to their technique of planning as "indicative," in the sense of spelling out goals and providing help in reaching them, as opposed to those forms of planning which prescribe required action [103]. This was the ideal established by Monnet in the first plan, when the Commission actually had extensive powers of direct control. The ideal remains the same, but the ambiguity at the core of the notion lends itself to a considerable range of emphasis in application. If the Planning Commission is to encourage specific action in any sense at all, it must operate on incentives in some manner. If it operates strongly enough, if the rewards of cooperation and the penalties of noncooperation become potent enough, altered incentives come to resemble orders to march. Under the same formal system, "indication" can mean either complete direction or mild persuasion. The first plan came very close to the sense of overt direction.

The Monnet Plan was a somewhat ill-coordinated but vigorous attempt to change the economic structure at the same time as promoting recovery by focusing effort on a few basic industries: power, transportation, steel, cement and farm equipment at first, then basic chemicals, fertilizers, artificial fibers and other groups considered to be lagging [1] [2] [30] [104]. The emphasis was less on general expansion than on reorganization of these particular industries to establish efficient production conditions [5, pp. 4–8]. The Commission tried to promote high levels of investment combined with elimination of older productive facilities, aiming at larger scale and more specialized production units. Its theme was "modernization or decadence," amplified by Monnet as "in reality nothing but a way of expressing the ceaseless adaptation required for survival of the life of each man, each enterprise, each nation" [2, p. vii].

The production targets specified for particular industries were derived from direct estimates of probable markets. They did not rest on any refined interindustry analysis. According to Baum, "No systematic studies were attempted of the comparative costs and benefits of alternative investment projects. Some rough pragmatic judgments along these lines must have been made, but the over-all criteria were never made explicit. . . . Similarly, no comprehensive study was made of how the use of resources by the investment program would affect consumption standards, or how the necessary resources could be diverted to the program without adding to inflationary pressures" [30, p. 23].

The targets set through the course of the first plan were based on the idea of a fairly prompt return to prewar production peaks, expected to be followed by continuing expansion. At the time the Planning Commission was ahead of most economists in rejecting the idea of a probable depression. It was also ahead of many of the industries concerned, partly in the expansion of markets foreseen and very much so in the degree of reorganization and investment required. From 1946 on through the period of the first plan, most of its effort was spent trying to lead and push industries forward faster than they wished to go.

In its efforts to alter behavior, the Commission did not attempt to force compliance by direct orders. It had access to licensing and allocation powers up to 1949, but then and since has relied instead on persuasion backed by its ability to exert influence within all spheres of government policy. The initial concept of the Commission was in fact that it would serve as the coordinator for all economic agencies of the government [100, pp. 49–56]. Given the enormous range of administrative discretion possessed by government agencies, this would have provided great leverage for ensuring cooperation by specific industries, as well as authority to shape the nation's aggregative policies. Not suprisingly, it did not prove possible to establish such a position. In the words of an economist associated with the Commission: "The extreme distrust of various ministries, jealous of their prerogatives, the privileges of the nationalized firms, did more to prevent the Planning Commission from playing a decisive role, did more to menace its existence, than all the the political forces hostile to the idea of planning" [100, pp. 56–57].

The Commission quickly learned to live with a situation in which it became primarily a bargaining agency dealing between private industries and government agencies, without authority to compel decisions on either side. It had mixed success on both sides. Within the government, its influence was and is fairly strong in budgetary affairs and in the allocation of credit from public funds, and minimal in the sensitive areas of agriculture, public works, and overseas policies [100, pp. 80–83]. In dealing with private industry, it had considerable success precisely because it became an important agent at court, particularly with respect to the critical problem of access to financing.

The aggregative choices of French economic policy in the immediate postwar period made it practically impossible for any industry to carry out a major investment program without government help. The high level of liquidity deriving from wartime monetary distortions, the overwhelming desire of consumers to restore earlier living standards and of business to acquire resources quickly, and the disrupted conditions of supply, provided all the necessary ingredients of a ferocious inflation. In principle, drastic deflation combined with monetary reform might have checked the inflation. This could have reduced the misdirection of resources to speculative inventory accumulation and to redundant investment in small-scale commerce [104]. The Planning Commission was among the advocates of fiscal and monetary discipline, but did not succeed in controlling the decision. The government accepted the inflation and resorted to direct controls on credit and prices as possible palliatives [89]. The attempt to regulate prices in this situation was utterly futile. The restrictions on bank lending and security flotations made it very difficult to carry out any programs of industrial investment without state authorization. The one way to obtain important investment financing was through direct access to public funds or loans from the major state-owned credit institutions.

The industries for which investment was favored by the Planning Commission were able to obtain investment financing when most others were not, and were further aided in obtaining imported materials and equipment in a period when quantitative import controls were very tightly applied. Much of this help came accompanied by quite specific advice on regional reorganization, consolidation of production, and creation of larger new firms to replace long-established smaller enterprises. The Planning Commission offered a great deal and at the same time asserted a right to share in critical management decisions. The industries concerned accepted much help and were most careful in accepting the advice.

Since the plans came close to the goals of the more progressive people in each industry, and offered concrete advantages for implementation, it is not surprising that they were fairly well implemented. The main resistance to reorganization came from smaller enterprises whose independent existence was at stake. Since the nationalizations had eliminated this problem in some of the industries concerned, and the other fields involved in the first plan were relatively concentrated, this resistance was not an overwhelming handicap. It did delay reorganization in the steel industry, but in this instance was successfully attacked by the ingenious device of exposing the industry to international competition through establishment of the Coal-Steel Community: competition was brought in as an ally of planning.

Revisions of goals and changes in the period of the first plan make any attempt to compare investment or production targets with realizations a most subtle exercise [30, pp. 21–42]. The frequency of revisions itself suggests that any such comparison misses the objective of the Commission. The Commission was not trying to compile an accurate record of prediction demonstrating analytical ability, but to get industries which had been highly cautious or downright sluggish to wake up. In this it and its semi-independent allies in control of the nationalized industries succeeded very well.

The first plan did achieve a high level of investment in the basic industries and some if not all of the helpful measures of reorganization sought within them [2] [104] [108] (Ch. 5 above). The cost was a tightening of the squeeze on resources for the sectors not included in the plan. The housing program was held back to some extent under pressure from the Planning Commission [104, p. 69]. The whole range of consumer goods and the more dispersed producer goods industries were left to shift for themselves in an environment made more difficult for them by the diversion of resources to the fields favored in the plan. Given the fact that the excluded opportunities were never evaluated, it is practically certain that the consequences were suboptimal. Given the observable duplication of wasteful small-scale investment in overexpanded fields such as commerce and textiles, it is probable that the consequences were better than they would have been in the absence of the plan.

Within the areas covered by the plan, the coal and railroad industries probably drew in more resources than needed [104], basic chemicals and artificial fibers lagged far behind objectives [2, pp. 7–8, 91–103], the steel industry dragged on reorganization until pushed by establishment of greater international competition through the Coal-Steel Community, and probably every effort of the Planning Commission met resistances that held gains below conceivable possibilities. Still, all the basic industries did carry out major modernization programs, the steel industry became a more potent exporter than ever, the experimental plant established under the plan in the field of artificial fabrics helped break a long-standing block in that industry, and the problem of sustained growth shifted almost entirely toward the sectors left out of the first plan. The rationale of the fundamental choice was clear enough, and eminently sensible in an economy which had become adapted to slow growth. The drive aimed at reduction of supply restraints in the basic industries whose reorientation was a prerequisite for a higher rate of aggregate expansion.

2. Planning Since 1952

The success of the Planning Commission in overcoming resistance from industry and in guiding government policy to establish the Coal-Steel Community in 1952 marked the high point of its leadership in the 1950's. From that time, the Commission ceased trying to run industries, and turned instead to fostering group cooperation in the context of more comprehensive plans for the whole economy. It retained the use of credit controls and other promotional devices to alter incentives, but ignored any further possibilities of changing pressures by promoting international or domestic competition. Planning achieved increasing formal coherence and a more comprehensive contact with all sectors of the economy, but lost in the process much of its original independent thrust.

The transformation of emphasis and technique beginning in 1952 was due to changes in both directing personalities and in the economic environment. In that year, Monnet left the Commission to head the Coal-Steel Community, and the newly established conservative government of Antoine Pinay began to cut back on credits for the investment program. In the background, reconstruction had been accomplished, the fear of further nationalization had died, leaders of private industry were regaining confidence in the possibilities of either using government for their own purposes or resisting intrusion, and business was becoming less reliant on government aid in financing investment. The remaining problems of inefficient industry organization were the more complex headaches of the dispersed industries rather than the broad obstacles tackled in the first plan. Further, a clear-cut recession developed in 1952 and carried on into 1953, shaking confidence within the Commission on the outlook for continuing expansion. Differences in preferences of the people concerned, and differences in the situation of the economy, led to a new spirit of caution in pushing for specific investment decisions and to a new emphasis on development of a comprehensive, logically integrated program.

The second plan, covering the years 1954–57, was prepared a good deal more carefully than the first [30, pp. 28–32] [110, pp. 268–73]. The technical skills available for the purpose were greatly improved, especially through the cooperation of the newly formed group of national accounting and interindustry analysts in the "Service of Economic and Financial Studies" within the Ministry of Finance. This group has then and since provided the Planning Commission with both the initial aggregative forecasting required for discussion of specific programs and with the necessary checks on consistency of developing goals.

In addition to its greater coverage and consistency, the second plan differed from the first in "the modest character of its goals. . . . No increase in the share of the GNP devoted to investment over the comparatively low levels of 1952–53 was projected" [30, p. 31]. The steel industry, after years of being told that its modernization program was too cautious, was advised in the second plan that its expectations of market growth were too optimistic. As noted in Chapter 5, the advice preceded by two years the emergence of a drastic shortage.

During the period of the second plan, the economy moved ahead so much faster than anticipated that the four-year production goals set in the program were exceeded by most industries in the first two years [102, p. 11]. Further, the unexpectedly rapid expansion in 1954–55 was accompanied by improvement of the balances of trade and payments. The plan was clearly not aimed at maximum possible growth in the first place. But the continuance of expansion in 1956–57, accompanied by the development of the bitter war in Algeria, did promote all-out inflation and a severe balance of payments deficit. The expansion had to be halted in 1957 because of the inflation and drain on reserves. The third plan was drawn up in this context, emphasizing reorientation of production to achieve a combination of external balance with domestic expansion.

The third plan set as its objective the establishment of conditions permitting external balance by 1965, through growth with emphasis on exports rather than through limitation of demand. The basic policy decisions of 1958, which radically altered the economic structure through devaluation, reduction of trade barriers, and establishment of convertibility, were not among the objectives, or consistent with the outlook, of the plan established in 1957. The changes which reshaped the economy were chosen and established outside of the planning process. One of their consequences was that the goal of external balance envisaged for 1965 was achieved in 1959.

Although the Planning Commission was explicitly working

toward a goal of external equilibrium, its documents covering explicit choices in particular industries suggest that it took continuing import protection as a working rule. The program drawn up by the subcommission concerned with the transformation industries turned down the idea of allowing duty-free imports of machinery *not* produced in France, because this might discourage eventual production by domestic firms. The group found it "shocking in effect to note that equipment credits drawn on the metropolitan budget and put at the disposition of overseas territories have been and are still largely utilized to purchase foreign equipment for which the equivalent could be found in France" [8, p. 110].

The same specialized commission did stress the necessity of achieving lower costs through investment, research, and improving labor productivity. It did not achieve any distinction between the laudable goal of reducing costs and the criterion of success as a condition in which French prices would be "competitive in all sectors" [8, p. 104]. The specific organizational recommendations to achieve more efficient production concerned mainly the need for larger-scale units, through mergers or working agreements permitting division of markets. Unhappily, two major obstacles were seen to check progress in these directions. "The essential psychological obstacle is the individualism and the concern with independence that characterize many of the French in general, and heads of enterprises in particular . . . many industrialists see in their colleagues only competitors, and not eventual associates" [8. pp. 125–26]. The other important obstacle to effective reorganization was seen to be the nation's antitrust legislation. The commission took due note of "the embarrassment of public authorities before that legislation which declares a general prohibition of agreements among firms, at the same time as they recommend the modification of industrial structures" [8, p. 127].

Statements of this type from particular documents cannot be taken as considered presentations of the views of the Planning

Commission. They could be matched by others in favor of competition and international trade, and they do not prove anything about the position of the Commission in taking specific decisions. Still, it is hard to find evidence in the actions of the Commission after 1952 which suggests that it did consider it possible to achieve structural changes other than by supervised agreements among firms. As Stanislaw Wellisz observed, the Commission's personnel have not been oriented toward competitive market solutions [110, p. 272]. This is not surprising, in view of an intellectual history in which competitive ideals have never been held in high esteem. But it is more meaningfully explained by the mechanics of the methods of planning itself. The process of group negotiation promoted cooperative arrangements as the central vehicle of policy. The Commission became a participant in cartel decisions, leaving its personnel little scope at best for enthusiasm over possibilities of competition.

It might well be considered surprising that a method of planning built on joint discussion by officials of industry, labor, agriculture and diverse government agencies—and all Frenchmen at that—could end up with a neat set of agreements on complex economic issues. In fact, the exterior appearance of calm does mislead. The published documents represent skillful presentation of views that do not embody complete accord. More importantly, the original concept of consultation including representatives of all groups within the planning process, checked by parliamentary review, postulated more democracy than proved feasible. On the one hand, the erosion of parliamentary authority in France permitted development of a system in which all important decisions are made within executive agencies. The legislature does little more than register approval. On the other hand, the role of both agriculture and labor groups within the planning process became greatly circumscribed. The largest labor union, the *Confédération Générale du Travail,* withdrew from participation in the second and third plans, though it returned at the start of preparations for the fourth plan in 1960 [100, pp. 46–48, 96–98]. According to officials of the Commission, the trouble was that these groups conceived of participation in the unacceptable terms of the corporate state, in which they represented their particular group interests and fought to dominate the plan for their purposes. According to labor union officials, they were not the only ones trying to influence planning in their interests, they were simply the losers. In either case, the return of the CGT in 1960 may help obtain more balanced consideration of competing group interests.

The second and third plans apparently were strongly influenced by leaders of the financial community and of some of the basic industries which had been initially antagonistic to the first plan [34, ch. 6]. The point is not that the government officials involved were forced against their wills to accept a business-oriented approach, but that the top officials of both business and government, coming from similar backgrounds and sharing concern for prosperity and growth, found themselves in basic agreement as soon as the men on the business side disarmed enough to realize that they had much to gain from cooperation. The Commission engaged less and less in its earlier efforts to force structural reforms within industries as the latter swung toward fuller acceptance of the possibility of new growth through higher investment and greater efficiency.

Published policy positions of the Planning Commission during the second half of the 1950's include consistent support for higher business profits and reduction of the rate of wage increases, frequently argue for lower taxes, and generally oppose price controls. They always encourage mergers, without giving any evidence of discrimination among them on grounds of differences in forseeable gains, or even of any detailed study of the question. They give singularly little attention to questions of income distribution. On the other hand, they stress the necessity of public investment, especially of greater expenditures on housing, education and social services. And at all times, except during the 1956–57 inflation, the Commission has been a more forceful advocate of full employment and expansion than might be deemed desirable by a conservative business community interested in ready availability of labor and low wage rates.

3. The Role of Nonauthoritarian Planning

When one visits the quiet offices of the Commission's pleasant old house in the rue de Martignac, it is difficult to take seriously the thought that this is the nerve center of anything so much admired by some, and feared by others, as national economic planning. In fact it is not, if planning be given the sense usually intended. This is the home of a group of well intentioned and intelligent people trying to help clarify alternatives for government and for business. That is a useful function, but not one that satisfies proponents of active direction of the economy through planning. The main issue is the degree to which enterprise decisions should be made to conform to the plans.

Throughout the 1950's, the French technique of planning used a mild system of differential favors to secure cooperation, but attached no direct penalties to the refusal to cooperate. Recalcitrant firms simply lost the opportunity to obtain possible assistance, and incurred the diffused handicap of more difficult access to investment financing because of the direction of credit to cooperating companies. The difference between participating and excluded firms was important in the immediate postwar years of severe capital shortage; but the rapid increase of business incomes and restoration of private capital markets thereafter made credit allocation a much less powerful device. Promotion remains possible, but handicaps imposed for ignoring the plans have become less important. With existing government powers of persuasion weakened, the process of group consultation is in danger of drifting toward simple acceptance of collective industry proposals. The system has succeeded so well up to this point that it runs grave risk of being turned by its own dynamics into a source of impediments to progress.

Proponents of active planning in France have recognized the possible loss of control through established methods, and have uniformly drawn the conclusion that the remedy is to strengthen the government's position by adoption of more effective devices for ensuring enterprise adherence to the plans. During the 1950's, the problem they usually had in mind was that of the industries which simply failed to carry out investment programs shown to be desirable, sometimes even after the firms concerned had secured government help for such programs. Individual companies did not always translate the collectively accepted industry targets into actions on their part which would add up to the group objective. One device suggested to meet this problem is that of "quasi contracts," under which firms would sign specific individual agreements rather than simply assent to a collective program. This implies a fairly active form of market allocation, but that would not be a major departure from the present system. It would have all the defects of market sharing among established firms, but it would not close the loophole which has acted to lessen their negative consequences in many French industries: it would not in itself crack down on any firms which aimed beyond their traditional market shares and overshot planning targets by greater investment, product innovation, or pricing competition.

Positive actions not envisaged in the plans have never been blocked, except in the indirect sense that they have been handicapped by lack of help in dealing with general restraints on financing and import allocations. Since these indirect restraints have been greatly lessened in recent years, it is true that for most practical purposes nothing in the planning system prevents independent action by those firms which wish to carry it out and can find their own financing. The automobile industry provided an outstanding example in the last half of the 1950's. The firms were so vigorously competitive at home and so successful in developing exports that they shot way past all planning targets. Such actions may be interpreted as unexpected contributions to the country's economic advance, or they may be interpreted as just another form of refusal to cooperate, diverting resources away from planning objectives and making results differ from collective goals. To some exponents of planning, the exuberant independence of the automobile firms seemed inferior to the orderly, if somewhat slow, cooperation of the steel producers [100, pp. 34–36]. Leading officials of the Planning Commission and the Ministry of Industry have recently taken the argument one step further. They began to propose explicit restraint on investment throughout the Common Market, in those fields in which such investment threatened to create capacity exceeding markets [175, May 3 and June 22, 1961].

Pierre Massé, the present head of the Planning Commission, proposes a "concerted development program" for the Common Market countries, ". . . in order to avoid the overequipment that is tending to appear in certain branches. I realize that each country may think that it will win the race. But it may also think that other countries have the same idea. I readily concede the tonic value of competition, but it is essential to be able to recognize the dividing line between incentive and waste, especially where costly investments and risks of underemployment are involved" [106, p. 18].

M. Massé's point applies equally to the crucial internal option of imposing limits on the separate investment programs of firms. It is completely logical if one accepts as a premise that the plans embody an optimal allocation of resources. Expansion in any one line beyond specified objectives would then lessen the rate of growth by diverting resources from superior alternatives. Even if one takes the more modest view that planning cannot foresee newly evolving opportunities, and hence that independent action outside the plans in order to take advantage of them may make positive contributions, it still follows that diversion of scarce capital to the creation of productive capacity that will not be used is a serious loss. But it may nevertheless be true that attempts to impose administrative restraints on investment which seems likely to create excess capacity would constitute one of the worst mistakes that could conceivably be made.

Planning is based on the known, the foreseeable, that which can be assessed. It leaves out the unknown, the unpredictable, that which may have value beyond the measured limits of the expected. One of the strongest aspects of the method used so far in France is that it has accepted the possibility of free change of enterprise decision outside defined objectives, and has thereby encouraged the rebirth of experiment and vitality in French business. General restraints on investment outside the plans would ruin this. Specific restraints on a few major industries investing in fields of existing excess capacity would not be quite so bad, but this does not make them wise. They would serve a useful purpose only under two assumptions: that planning authorities were able to predict the upper limits of future markets, and that creation of excess capacity had no effect on the search by firms for methods of promoting its use. Both of these assumptions are untenable.

The first French plan underestimated demand growth in one of the few instances in which central guidance was attempted, the classically dependable field of electric power; the second French plan grossly underestimated the whole economy's expansionary potential and advised restraint in the steel industry at exactly the wrong time; the third plan failed to propose or even envisage a feasible set of policy revisions which, when adopted on the basis of the recommendations of the Rueff Commission, accomplished almost immediately some of the main objectives expected to require nearly a decade. The automobile industry is repeatedly singled out as the most likely candidate for government restraints to minimize excess capacity, but if the industry had been held anywhere near planning targets in the 1950's the country would have been the poorer. It is easy enough to retreat to the comfortable notion that better forecasting methods would have given better results, and undeniable that the methods used in France have greatly improved. But the best econometric analysis in the world will never reveal the opportunities that have not yet been created by technical innovation, new commercial opportunities, or new achievements of the human imagination.

Individual firms can easily take too optimistic views and overinvest accordingly, as the government monopolies in coal and rail transport have demonstrated in France. The traditional restraint of lower profits for those firms which do overestimate and cannot take corrective action retains a definite validity. But the addition of administrative restraints is doubly dubious. They may easily create too low a capacity limit in the first place, especially if based on the preferences of producers trying to calculate maximum profits for the group as a whole. Secondly, they may destroy a powerful incentive to seek new methods of using productive capacity.

Harold Lubell made the last point very effectively when the same issue came up during the period of the Monnet Plan. In the brief recession of 1949, the Economic Commission for Europe issued a report emphasizing the existence of idle capacity in the steel industry. It suggested that the French plan should reduce investment in this industry, in cooperation with a general European effort to avoid excessive expansion of steel capacity [104, pp. 130–31]. Monnet ignored the advice and kept up the pressure for investment, thereby facilitating recovery from the recession and helping meet the subsequently intense demand of the Korean War period. The decision happened to be validated by events, but Lubell correctly argues that the choice was the right one apart from the particular verification. Productive potential is a direct stimulus to the effort to develop markets for it. "The 12.5 million tons of steel potential may be sufficient incentive for the unenterprising businessmen to be good Schumpeterian entrepreneurs. The risk of course is that overcapacity may breed restrictionism; the capacity, however, is a necessary condition for improving the material welfare of the French nation" [104, p. 131].

Avoidance of restraints on investment outside the plans does not preclude use of the government budget to shape the society's goals on what to produce, nor the use of the planning system to improve information and ease supply restraints. It does lessen the accuracy of stated programs, by leaving the door open for unforeseeable gain. It trades limited certainty for high possibility.

The group consultation process builds into the planning system a method of discouraging individual expansionary measures not approved by the industry as a whole. For the reasons advanced above with respect to direct administrative restraints, plus the problem of group interest in the level of private profit, this process probably works against enterprise initiative and economic advance for the society. The defects have been offset by the government's use of the consultation system to encourage greater action by the group. This is a method of introducing representatives of the public interest within the decision process of a cartel. When private industry was less oriented toward expansion, and when government advice was potent because its help in investment financing was critical, the gains may well have outweighed the losses. It is most uncertain that they do so any longer in France, or would do so in any other country in which management is strongly oriented toward growth.

In the absence of the system of group consultation, the intimacy of joint government-industry determination of national goals would be lessened. One way to state this is that the representatives of the public would be less influenced by the preferences of the business community. It is perhaps not astonishing that the present system has a certain attraction for conservative governments. In any event, potential users of such planning techniques should not confuse the establishment of worthwhile goals, or the use of direct aids to efficiency in meeting them, with the conceptually independent and possibly unhelpful system of group cooperation in establishing decisions on the supply side.

The foregoing may possibly be interpreted to mean that the useful component of planning in France is its aspect of clarifying national objectives, a normal function of government in all societies, and not the system of intervention in supply decisions. But this is not the intent. The argument is not that interventions are unhelpful, but that the useful forms should be distinguished from those that are not. French planning has contained positive elements going beyond the type of direction embodied in national budgets of the United Kingdom and the United States.

On one level, planning interventions on the supply side may help considerably to improve efficiency in so far as they aid in offsetting defects in the price system. This is the defense of French planning advanced by Wellisz, who found many problems in its application but concluded that it did help overcome distortions caused by the use of administrative controls on prices and by aggregate monetary disequilibrium [110, esp. pp. 282–83]. This position would leave the French Planning Commission with little excuse for being since 1958, with price controls greatly reduced and monetary equilibrium reasonably well re-established. The discussion of the problem needs to be taken a step further. Aggregate disequilibrium and controls were not the only causes of distortion in the market system in France, and pricing imperfections do not provide the only basis of an expectation of gain from planning.

The second level of possible improvement over the results of purely independent market choices is that planning may help to locate discrepancies between private and social gains and to counteract their continuously changing causes. Even given completely competitive markets, with a legal framework precluding all business practices directly inconsistent with social goals, and with forceful entrepreneurs seeking to maximize profits in a well-conceived, long-run sense, interdependence beyond the horizon of the firm and discontinuities associated with major investment decisions make it likely that unguided separate decisions will be collectively suboptimal [105, chs. 9, 10]. If all these conditions are fulfilled, the scope for further gain may be small. If they are met only to the unsatisfactory degree observable in France immediately before and for some time after the war, the scope for gain may be large. But in either case, action by a planning authority—or by a lively Council of Economic Advisers—to locate and measure inconsistencies between profits for the enterprise and gain for the economy, to devise taxes and subsidies taking them into account where they cannot be directly corrected, and to provide soundly based estimates of the consequences of current decisions, can surely guide individual firms toward more helpful choices. Any society stands to gain from such efforts when intelligently conducted, whether they are called planning or not. To quote Massé once more, the plan "replaces fragmentary and poorly linked anticipations with *coherent global anticipation* . . . if it disappeared as an official institution, its detractors would probably decide to restore it unofficially as a center of information" [105, p. 477].

A conclusion that planning has a highly useful role as a system of information and promotion falls well short of the view that it should provide active direction of the economy. Hamlet is still missing. Information and promotion do not require that individual economic units conform to any coordinated plan. Precisely so. If a nonauthoritarian system is desired, this objective is not feasible. If conformity is pursued, it is practically certain to do more harm than good.

In fact the planning operation has been and remains a potentially deadly instrument. Sufficient concern with avoidance of possible excess capacity, coupled with power to restrain investment to this end, could easily bring the country's growth rate drastically downward. The French version of planning has not been deadly, for two reasons. On the one hand, its directive personnel have usually been oriented toward investment and expansion, less rather than more inclined than private industry to worry about excessive capacity. On the other hand, the Commission has not had the power to block individual firms which did wish to move ahead more rapidly than collective planning seemed to indicate as desirable. Planning helped raise the industries' original targets, and then ceased to constitute a plan in the sense of controlling the result. It left the field open to enterprise choice. This often meant that the producers fell below the stated targets, but also meant that very often they ran way above them because they found openings never envisaged in the plans. The system has not been one of government control, but decentralized enterprise decision plus a promotional push.

11 | Government Enterprise

The extensions of government ownership at the end of the war might be better described as examples of spontaneous political combustion than as an economic program. But they were expected to yield significant advantages for the economy, in particular for the implementation of planning, and they did have some important consequences. Attempts to evaluate these consequences have given rise to a debate that has taken an interesting and new twist. That debate is not primarily concerned with questions of the compatibility of government and private enterprise, or their relative efficiencies, but rather with definition of the objectives and means of control of the state firms themselves.

The consensus of the best studies of the question is that the government firms have largely escaped direction by other agencies of the government and have acted very much as private enterprise might have done in the same markets. Their general conclusion that this is unfortunate is well expressed by the outcry of Bernard Chenot: "What good does it do to nationalize a firm if it is to be directed in exactly the same way as a private enterprise?" [99, p. 163].

1. Social Efficiency and Enterprise Profit

The question posed by Chenot, and most of the investigations underlying it, have a built-in confusion. They imply that behavioral characteristics of all firms seeking profit are interchangeable. If this were so, government enterprise oriented toward the welfare of the firm itself would indeed do little good. But if it be recognized that in most markets there are many alternative ways of trying to earn profits, with varying implications for economic efficiency and social welfare, it becomes clear that there may be important scope for gain by introduction of new decision groups with different methods of promoting the welfare of their firms.

Three main groups of reasons suggest that private markets may fall significantly short of possible levels of efficiency. The first is that managements may fail to search aggressively for improvements, for such reasons as reluctance to accept dilution of ownership to the degree necessary to reach optimal scale, high valuations on leisure or on present location leading to rejection of profitable changes, or simply the potent capacity of humans for repetition through habit and inertia [40] [56] [69]. The second, often related to the first, is the possibility of agreements on pricing or other aspects of performance that lower community welfare even though they aid profits. The third is that lack of information beyond the horizon of separate firms may lead to inferior choices even by well-managed, competitive firms. All three of these factors may be affected by the introduction of government enterprise, even if the state firm does aim primarily at its own growth.

In those cases in which concern for retention of control by separate managements impedes the realization of possible gains from concentration, the economy may gain from nationalization of the group even if the new state firm does single-mindedly pursue its own welfare. This possibility is clearly not relevant to the cases of coexisting government and private enterprise, as in artificial fertilizers, automobiles and oil. It was not realized in practice by any evident organizational gains in banking or insurance [91, p. 177]. It pales into insignificance beside the loss of diversified producer initiative and buyer alternatives that would be implied in the overwhelming majority of the nation's industries if complete concentration were attempted.* But in three basic industries—coal, electric power and railroads—the case for gain through concentration was probably valid.

In coal and in rail transport, particular companies had proven highly efficient but some had been extremely slow in readjusting ancient decisions of location and technology to changing alternatives. They had left capital and workers in areas where exhaustion of more easily worked coal deposits, or the emergence of transport facilities alternative to rails, yielded high costs and subnormal factor incomes. France's longer history of accumulating mistakes, and lower factor mobility, made the problems of these industries considerably worse than in the United States. They would ultimately have been corrected anyway, but nationalization did permit quicker movement toward regrouping and concentration of effort within the industries [90] [92] [93] [96].

Improvements inaugurated in these two cases were by no means free of offsetting defects. The coal industry exhibited both great concern with the adequacy of employment in the mines during the reconstruction period of general labor shortage, and a weakness for installation of the newest types of equipment even in mines where the structure of operations made it of little use [92, pp. 154–62] [96, pp. 117–18]. Both the coal and rail industries greatly overestimated postwar markets and embarked on partially wasteful investment programs [104, pp. 102–27]. Both of them showed an extreme interest in measuring improvement by engineering criteria, sometimes to a

* The most painful example of excluded opportunities and social loss through concentration of ownership has without question been that of the radio and television news services of the government-owned system. The natural instincts of the monopoly enterprise at its worst have been demonstrated by the purchase of control over a particularly influential station operation just outside the French border (Europe I), by blacklisting of performers critical of government policies, and by systematic suppression of information crucially important for intelligent political decision by the population.

point suggesting neglect of the effects on average costs [96, pp. 131–33]. Nationalization permitted organizational improvement in these fields, but did not ensure that optimal actions would follow.

Although the electric power industry was not subject to general criticism for inefficiency prior to the war, its nationalization did not replace competition, and did permit gains in efficiency [90] [95] [96]. Coordination of investment plans and a national system of power exchange were both feasible means of reducing costs. Such gains can be closely approximated through organized cooperation of privately owned utilities, but even the efforts of unusually alert private power companies in the United States have at times been deflected away from optimal choices by inconsistencies between market and social benefits [94].

2. Behavioral Characteristics of Government Firms

The direct effects of the initial reorganizations have in any case been overshadowed by the cumulative consequences of the new behavioral characteristics shown by the managements of the state firms in the course of the 1950's. The two more important such characteristics have been a high degree of expansionary drive, involving continuous pressure for investment and introduction of new techniques, and a surprisingly intense concern with the development of economically rational methods of determining prices and budgets. "The nationalized firms have known how to develop their productivity, enlarge their fields of action, and watch their costs . . . In an economy where the spirit of conservation has too often taken the place of the spirit of enterprise in the psychology of the private entrepreneur, the nationalized sector sometimes appears to be the last refuge of those traditionally 'capitalist' virtues: audacity, the taste for large scale operations, dynamism" [99, pp. 401–02].

Both those state firms with monopolies in basic industries and the government automobile firm competing with private enterprise have consistently acted as if they placed extraordinarily high value on expansion of their operations, and paid decidedly little attention to the risks of overdoing it. This has given them a striking resemblance to the more aggressive leaders of private industries. The resemblance does have a possibly misleading aspect. Private firms which are strongly expansionary, but overshoot possible markets too far, or pay insufficient attention to efficiency, simply get reclassified as failures. The expansionary ones that are left are those which did the job well. In the government sector, all the expansionary ones are left, whether they did the job well or not. On the whole, most of them did it well. The government firm subject to market tests in the automobile industry did it brilliantly. But all of them at all times exhibit the happy faith so neatly described by André Delion as "The belief that demand will adapt itself to the internal planning of the enterprise" [91, p. 189].

The eager approach to expansion by the government firms was amply demonstrated during the reconstruction period. Their newly installed managements quickly drew up individual plans for reorganization and modernization, antedating the adoption of the Monnet Plan. They used their preferential position in access to financing granted to them under the Monnet Plan to implement these programs with a wholehearted vigor going well beyond that of the similarly privileged private steel industry. The state firms operating in commercial fields accounted in the aggregate for slightly under 8 percent of total value added in 1951 [96, pp. 14–15]. They carried out approximately two-fifths of all investment in Metropolitan France in the years 1947 through 1952 [92, p. 140].

The disproportionate share of investment by government-owned firms in the reconstruction period was to a considerable degree explicable by their capital-intensive technology and by the fundamental fact that they provided the country's basic communications, power and transport facilities. The capacity of these industries had been geared to a slow rate of industrial expansion, and had to be raised as a necessary condition of more rapid growth for the economy. Investment in most of them had been negligible from 1930 to 1945. This was less true of the electric power industry than of coal and transportation, but its facilities were far from adequate for the new rate of industrial growth that the postwar economy proved able to obtain. The nationalized industry's management started an expansion program, was apparently amazed at the much higher target subsequently recommended by the Planning Commission, and then discovered that the latter's projections were below the actual requirements of the revitalized economy [104, p. 110] [109, p. 214]. Adaptation of this capital-intensive industry to a sharply higher rate of demand growth required a high rate of investment, and was itself a precondition of continuing expansion for the economy as a whole.

The fact that useful objectives were served by the vigorous investment programs of the nationalized industries certainly does not imply that the allocation of resources to them was ideal. In particular, programs of the coal and railroad industries proved radically overoptimistic on the growth of their markets. The program for the electric power industry proved too modest in its demand estimates but at the same time it may have drawn too heavily on investment resources because its initial expansion emphasized the ultimate in capital-intensive methods: hydroelectric power derived from high dam, large reservoir systems.

The main alternative to the program of hydroelectric power would have been the development of thermal plants based on domestic coal. The choice between these methods is a classic problem of investment criteria, whose solution depends on specific parameters that must be calculated for the particular alternatives open. If any such calculations were made for the first plan either by the *Electricité de France* or the Planning Commission, they were not brought out in the debate which subsequently exploded. In the reconstruction period, with widespread bottlenecks throughout the economy and an acute shortage of capital to resolve them, it seems most unlikely that any calculation of alternatives using reasonable interest rates would have yielded a solution favoring initial emphasis on hydro plants. The recurrent emergence of marketing difficulties in the coal industry—partially alleviated by the willingness of the electric power industry to undertake the extra costs of buying and storing surplus coal [96, pp. 197–202]—made the choice of avoiding new power facilities based on coal seem particularly unfortunate.

In the early 1950's the Planning Commission did attempt to redirect electric power investment toward thermal plants. Opposition became particularly strong to the biggest project of the E.D.F., a hydroelectric system utilizing a large reservoir to be constructed at Roselend, in the Savoie. The objection was that the capital cost per kilowatt hour was about triple that for a hydroelectric plant without a reservoir [107, p. 149]. Several econometricians associated with the E.D.F., notably including the same Pierre Massé who subsequently became head of the Planning Commission, replied to these objections with a set of linear programming solutions indicating the desirability of a high component of hydroelectric power using large reservoirs in the long-term program [105, pp. 154–90] [107]. Their analysis showed that a budgetary limit on total investment would, if sufficiently low, exclude recourse to hydroelectric power but would thereby increase the capitalized total cost of the whole program. The higher the initial budgetary limit, the more completely an optimal program would shift away from thermal power in the interest of lowest total cost.

The programming analysis was explicitly based on 1954 factor prices and an assumed interest rate of 8 percent. It was not intended to be a justification of the stress on hydroelectric power during the reconstruction period, when the opportunity cost of capital was surely higher than 8 percent. It remains a welcome addition to the literature of economics, providing the type of clarification that planning ought continuously to elicit. It did not prove the past correct, but helped guide the future.

The analytical capacities of the E.D.F. have been accompanied by a goodly degree of political tenacity. Its proposals submitted in 1951 for the second plan included three alternative programs. The Roselend Dam was in the third set, emphasizing hydroelectric power. The Planning Commission put this alternative third, advocating thermal power first. The subcommission concerned with energy ignored this decision to the extent of moving Roselend up into the preferred program. The Minister of Finance agreed with the Planning Commission and refused the necessary credits. The E.D.F. then went back to work and the credits needed for Roselend appeared in a ministerial decree in 1955 [95, pp. 298–99].

The state firms undoubtedly overdid their bid for investment resources in the reconstruction period, but this does not mean that their expansionary vigor was harmful to the economy in the 1950's. It probably was one of the country's more important assets. The government firm in the automobile industry was one of the first major enterprises in the country to plunge wholeheartedly into the fruitful pattern followed later by the best private firms in many fields: the deliberate development of production facilities in excess of domestic market requirements, coupled with investment in the creation of important new export markets. The private firms which did this served the country's interest at the same time as they ensured more rapid expansion for themselves. It is uncertain whether the public or the individual enterprise objective was the more important in Renault's case, but the motivation matters a good deal less than the result. This company, and the government firms occupying monopoly positions less subject to market tests, contributed by their bias toward expansion to both the strength of demand and the improvement in capacity to meet it. They moved quickly to exploit the openings available to them, and beyond that worked constantly to develop new opportunities themselves.

It is certainly possible that a consistent expansionary bias may work out to the disadvantage of the economy by causing a waste of resources, and downright probable that some such wastes were incurred in the reconstruction period. But in the 1950's, as the supply flexibility of the economy improved, the state firms helped push the economy toward the full utilization of resources which encouraged bolder choices by all industry. Since bolder choices which involve the creation of new capital facilities themselves add to the productive resources of the future, the pressures generated by the state firms may well have added to rather than subtracted from the creation of capacity in private industry in this decade. Both a general reluctance to invest and a generally optimistic approach to investment tend to be self-justifying. If firms err, it is better that they err on the side of trying to do too much than that they sit still.

The conceivably negative consequences of persistent expansionary bias in the state firms have been minimized by external restraints on their access to financing for investment, and by their own concern with the creation of principles to improve the efficiency of their decisions. The firms in the monopoly fields have rarely been allowed much freedom in setting the level of their prices, and have frequently been forced to accept losses rather than allowed to accumulate funds for expansion. They must seek financing either directly through the budget process, or by sales of bonds on the public capital market. They had perhaps too much freedom in securing finance during the first postwar plan, but since then have had to make a good case for major new operations, in the face of often unsympathetic administrations.

The problem of setting prices and obtaining funds in fields such as power and transport is so complicated as to facilitate defense of politically based opinion, because of the peculiar importance of economies external to the firm and the absence of competitive market standards. Perhaps this is one of the reasons that the French nationalized firms in these fields have made extraordinary efforts to adapt general principles of economic rationality to their problems [97] [99, pp. 243–333].

The state railroad system, *the Société Nationale des Chemins de Fer*, has been one of the leaders in the application of modern econometric techniques to its decisions on pricing, traffic handling, and investment. The French system was well ahead of the American railroad network in the realization of the economies to be gained from piggy-back types of combined transport, and in the effort to build profitable volume through greater utilization of capacity by promotional rates. One of the more critical of the observers of the state firms, Monique Maillet-Chassagne, concludes that introduction of promotional pricing by the railroad company has added at least 10 percent to its traffic volume [96, pp. 42–44].

The nationalized electric power industry has been at least as assiduous as the S.N.C.F. in seeking means to ensure efficiency in its methods. The application of linear programming to investment decisions in the dispute over hydroelectric and thermal power was cited above. Perhaps its most interesting work has been on the side of price analysis, where, as Thomas Marschak has pointed out, the econometricians of the E.D.F. developed independently and applied in practice some of the more interesting principles of modern welfare economics [97].

The contributions of the state firms to efficiency and expansion did to some extent include an improvement of competitive pressures, but not to the degree that might have been predicted from any assumption of natural conflicts of interest between government and private enterprise. Improvements could have come from the creation of more powerful and better informed buying services in the monopolized industries, and from a change of competitive pressure in fields with coexisting public and private firms. In both respects the courses of action taken have been mixed.

In their buying habits, the nationalized firms have exerted helpful pressure for improvement of supply practices through technical advice and enforcement of standards fostering more effective markets. The E.D.F. in particular has been given much credit for establishing and enforcing standardization in equipment supply, permitting lower production costs and clarifying alternatives for all buyers. Renault led a whole new industry by its successful experiments in the development of automatic transfer equipment, both innovating and changing alternatives for buyers and sellers in associated markets.

The S.N.C.F. has been able to exploit possibilities of market shading in the steel industry [19], and most industrial spokesmen are ready to complain that government buying agencies drive hard bargains [149, p. 46]. But it has apparently not been a common practice for state firms to use their buying leverage in the aggressive style of the Great Atlantic and Pacific Tea Company. Rather, they have come under the influence of the most actively interested selling groups, even to the point of siding with their private suppliers against outside alternatives [96, pp. 196–97]. In one interesting case, the major electrical equipment suppliers collectively refused to handle an important order of the E.D.F., unless the latter agreed to pay a price well above that established under existing price controls. The E.D.F. joined its suppliers in arguing that the control agency should accept the ultimatum of the producers [95, pp. 306–07]. This position might well be judged to be in the interests of efficiency in the particular instance, since controls were being enforced in conditions of excess demand. But the argument as reported points directly at a real weakness of the French state firms as efficient buyers: it apparently never occurred to the E.D.F., and practically never to any of their colleagues, that recourse to imports might be the best way around a problem of unusually expensive domestic supply. The government firms "buy French," with decidedly few exceptions.

Horizontal competition between government and private enterprise has been genuine and vitally helpful in the case of the automobile industry discussed above. Similar pressure and leadership in technology operated in the machine-tool industry, though to a much weaker degree because of the great range of products and dispersed producers remaining outside the area of impact of Renault's innovations. The state firm which was introduced in the field of artificial fertilizers in 1924 also seems to have followed the pattern by becoming the group's leader in research and innovation [172, February 2, 1956].

The oil industry offers a very different picture. Government enterprise was created in the first instance to accelerate exploration and did succeed in this. But the establishment of government-owned distribution outlets was neatly integrated into a completely collusive system without any observable change in market practices. Conflicts of interest were restricted to questions concerning the proportions of government oil that had to be purchased by private distributors. The government eventually bought out the Caltex distribution system in France to aid in this disposal objective. It did not rush to the wild extreme of lowering prices. Rather, the prices are set by negotiations between the oil companies and tax officials, in a process and by criteria which would merit greater public illumination than they have so far received.

The contact points between government firms and possible private competitors would make interesting areas for further empirical investigation. Baum suggests that the state-owned coal industry has been a contributor to forces acting to keep oil prices high, and that the railroad industry has not been above semicollusive arrangements with the private truck industry [30, p. 213]. These fields are so involved with questions of decreasing cost and of external economies that the effects of apparently unhelpful practices can hardly be assessed without full-scale study of each individual case. Still, it does seem that the government firms here too have a tendency to follow the same course of action that one might expect from private management, and that the society must rely on outside supervision exactly as if private monopolistic behavior were involved.

In the cartelized fields, government firms join in customary practices. In fields where private firms behaved independently beforehand, and government enterprise is added without eliminating the private firms, the state firms have behaved independently but better. The number of cases and information available about them are too limited to preclude either optimism or pessimism about the probability of gain from introduction of new government enterprise. They certainly do not offer great hope for improvement of markets in cases where previous collusive practices are officially accepted; they do suggest the real possibility of increased competitive pressure in industries where it is favored by other aspects of government policy but is not in fact overly active.

3. Government Firms and the Implementation of Plans

Investigations of the behavior of the state firms amply document, and usually deplore, the fact that they have been almost as free of control in the interests of national economic policy as has private industry [91] [95] [99]. "From the moment that economic policy lost its significance in providing direction of the economy by the state, the nationalized enterprise ceased to be a means of action to be no more than a practically ordinary enterprise. . . . If nationalization has ceased to be a myth inspiring the reformers of tomorrow, it is doubtless because the state has not given to the nationalized enterprises the task for which it created them" [95, pp. 320–21].

The location of responsibility for control of the state firms has remained an open question despite repeated attempts to answer it through legislation. New laws and decrees have alternated between efforts to direct their behavior through a wide variety of specific controls and advisory boards, and the contrary technique of allowing their managements freedom to make the choices that seem to them most efficient [92, ch. 10] [95, pp. 151–90] [99, pp. 31–71]. Georges Lescuyer observes that the E.D.F. is subject to external control through twenty-seven channels defined in existing law, but the sheer number of the forms of attempted control only serves to underline the fact that none of them really works [95, p. 319].

The basic problem is much the same as that with external supervision everywhere. The managements of the firms know much more both about what they are doing and what else they may usefully do than any outside agency possibly can. Moreover, they can legitimately argue that for efficiency they need the right to move quickly, without continuous administrative restraint. Local politicians anxious to keep the state railroad from closing down an inefficient repair facility or branch line do not hesitate to demand legislative controls, but the Planning Commission and other economic agencies of government are understandably reluctant to get in the way of actions by the state firms. When they try, they meet potent resistance.

One of the more forceful and successfully independent among the managers of the government firm was Pierre Lefaucheux, head of Renault until his death in 1955. He pleaded the case for operating independence with all the fervor deriving from years of effort to maintain it. "The worst fault that one can commit against the nationalizations consists precisely of effacing the notion of a responsible head and developing the notion of the state as boss . . ." [95, p. 204, n. 18]. "Impardonable error would be committed if one organized the functioning of the nationalized enterprises on a single model . . . with the sole goal of facilitating the work of the controllers by the always harmful method of uniformity, impeding the free play of the spirit of initiative of the responsible people and the efficacy of their action" [95, p. 207].

Operating independence for the state firms may still leave room for helpful intervention in the crucial areas of pricing and investment. Even in the fields in which the state firms are not monopolies, it is conceivable that they might align prices with nominal competitors at excessive levels. And where they are monopolies it is perhaps not entirely safe to assume that the individual firm will judge the general interest so accurately as to obviate the need for outside supervision of its pricing.

In the automobile industry, Renault has been subject only to the same type of weak price control applied to all its competitors. In the coal, rail and power monopolies, changes in price levels or important aspects of the pricing structure are subject to decision by the Minister of Finance. The Planning Commission may influence such decisions, but they have rarely been made on the basis of any objectives of national resource planning. They are dominated rather by a political tug and haul among the state firms trying to get financial resources, finance ministers using them as pawns to sacrifice on the altar of price stability, and private interests demanding low-cost state services. As André Delion observed, private business interests exert pressure for reductions of the prices of public services, and then cite the fact of losses by the government firms as evidence of the inefficiency of state enterprise [91, p. 136].

Since the state firms are not in principle concerned with making profits, it might perhaps be thought that it would be preferable to exempt them from external interference in their pricing. They have shown great interest in calculating efficient systems of marginal cost pricing, and are surely capable of adapting such systems to their usual objective of avoiding either profit or loss [93, pp. 484–85]. But all the concern with difficulties of public control of the state firms, and the more spectacular experiences in Italy [92], provide a useful warning. It is perfectly possible for a managerial group interested in the public welfare, totally exempt from the private firm's concern with recorded profits, to arrange its costs and prices in such a manner as to facilitate the finance of an endless list of worthwhile new projects. Even with controls on their pricing, and with erratically harmful political intervention, some of the French public corporations have shown great capacity for expansion both directly and through proliferation of new subsidiaries [91, pp. 168–69, 177]. Empire building is built into the race. It is a highly valuable instinct, to be encouraged rather than blocked by arbitrary obstruction of particular projects, or by preventing access to finance so that none can be carried out. But at the same time it requires some form of constraint, to lessen the likelihood that more valuable alternative claims on resources are not blindly sacrificed. Further, it is an invitation to the creation of power beyond the reach of the political process to turn over to any dynamic group with a monopoly position the right to decide the extent of its own control over resources.

The objective most nearly consistent with economic efficiency for those state firms with monopoly positions would be to allow them to apply their carefully devised pricing systems in such a way as to yield positive returns comparable to those in competitive private industry, while trying to ensure the same set of outside checks on cost manipulation or excessive returns that is the intent of American public utility regulation. There is no economic reason why the state firms should aim at lower profit rates than those obtainable in private industry under competitive conditions, or why they should be subject to political interference in their pricing. But there is also no basis for expecting that optimal results would follow from allowing them any greater freedom than would be allowed private firms in similar monopolistic positions.

The nationalized firms would seem to be particularly apt subjects for the application of over-all planning to improve efficiency through control of their investment programs. They must submit their capital budgets to the Planning Commission, the Fund for Modernization and Development, and the Minister of Finance. In the first plan, the coal and rail industries simply submitted their own programs and went ahead with them [104]. But in the course of the 1950's the Planning Commission did apparently request sets of alternative proposals, and debated their relative merits. In the Roselend case discussed above, the conflict of views served to sharpen the criteria of decision. Such review should in principle be helpful for any independently formulated investment program not subject to check by competitive markets, whether the programs are those of private or government-owned firms.

Whether the firms are state-owned or not, the initiation of basic proposals must in the usual case come from the industry itself. The Planning Commission must take the subsidiary role of the critic who can force debate on the basis of outside knowledge, but can be only one voice among many in the final decision. Whether the voice makes any difference or not depends ultimately on the intelligence and political skill brought to bear on the matter. In a particularly acute exploration of the actual results in France, Jean Rivero concludes that the firms themselves dominate the decisions. Their recipe for success is to prepare a good position in the first place, and then allow outside government agencies to "affirm authority in lengthy discussions over points of detail, once the essentials are accepted" [99, p. 403].

It is conceivable that the Planning Commission may, through its greater knowledge of the over-all situation, be able to make a good case for either upward or downward revaluation of particular projects. Where conflicting judgments involve demand or cost forecasts, presumably objective solutions can be reached on the basis of correspondence between welfare for the firm and for the economy. Where the question involves external social costs or benefits not marketable for the firm, it calls for selective taxes or subsidies to alter the firm's preferences, exactly as with private business. The only difference made by public ownership is that the E.D.F. would never have to be coaxed very hard to do more than it originally intended. The readiness of the firms to cooperate with outside advice may be higher for public than for private enterprise, at least for changes involving increased investment, but the logic of the possible gain from reorientation of decisions to take account of external economies is independent of the nature of ownership.

The conclusion here rejoins the discussion of planning itself. Decentralized separate decisions aimed primarily at the welfare of the enterprise are more fruitful for welfare than restraints imposed through a preconceived pattern, provided that the framework within which all firms operate is well organized in the first place. Good organization itself requires important positive steps of government, to promote full employment and monetary stability, to provide for the accomplishment of specific social objectives through the budget, to prevent undesirable choices such as child labor through social legislation, to establish a workable exchange rate, and to eliminate arbitrary restraints on supply. But the background framework and the definite rules should guide enterprise choices without reference to the nature of their ownership. Where the Planning Commission can identify conflicts between enterprise profit and social goals, it can increase welfare by altering incentives to induce firms to seek the latter, whether the firms be public or private. Where the search for enterprise welfare leads firms to take socially useful actions, the country gains by allowing them maximum freedom, again without reference to ownership.

Specific intervention in the decisions of state firms, apart from the aids and regulations applied to all firms, is likely to be useful only when it offsets initial distortions deriving from their institutional role. In an important example, the nationalized firms have been required to use interest rates designated by the Planning Commission in their investment calculations. They have recently been required to use a nominal rate of 7 percent [109, p. 227]. Such a rule has a definite justification, because state firms are often able to borrow at lower rates than private companies, and may therefore carry out projects which have a lower expected yield than some of those which private firms are prevented from implementing. The rule itself may be partially misguided in this case, because the accounting rate specified is actually above that at which major private firms can obtain funds. But it does have a logical foundation and the great merit of influencing enterprise decisions without recourse to detailed control of managerial choices. It does not constitute a genuine exception to the basic argument that private and public firms should be treated alike, because it is essentially an offset to institutional factors tending to distort decisions.

The preceding suggests a twofold answer to Chenot's sharp-edged question. First, it may do, and probably has done, some good to nationalize the coal, electric power, and railroad industries, as well as Renault, even if the government firms do act very much as private enterprise might in the same positions. It probably did help because some of the nationalizations solved a number of organizational problems that had persisted in conditions of private ownership; because the government firms turned out to be more strongly oriented toward expansion and experiment than the majority of private firms; and because they exerted some helpful pressure on private firms in the same and related markets. They did act much like private enterprise, but the more enterprising examples of it.

Secondly, the question aimed wrong in the first place. There is no logical content to the idea that economic welfare can be promoted by specifying separate behavioral rules for public enterprise, or by second-guessing their managements in normal operations. They need incentives and restraints, but exactly the same set as that applied to private firms. With a favorable aggregative environment, and with specific alteration of incentives through the planning process where enterprise preferences clearly run counter to public welfare, efficiency is best promoted by allowing decentralized decisions by private and public firms alike.

12 | Effects of Price Control

Price controls have a bad name among economists primarily because they have most often been used, and have most often failed to work well, in efforts to hold down the level of prices during periods of general excess demand. As a substitute for aggregative deflation in such conditions, they deserve the bad press they have abundantly received. But the French experience in their application has not been confined to this situation. It provides some instructive information on their effects under conditions of recession, recovery and expansion with low unemployment, and outright excess demand as well.

As described briefly in Chapter 3, the control process sounds rather arbitrary. In fact it is more so than American regulation of the public utility type. On word from the Minister of Finance, the Director of Prices may immediately order a freeze or even a reduction of prices in any industry. The companies involved may protest in any way they choose, but they cannot go to the judiciary and get an order enjoining the directive. This does not mean that they are helpless. They are protected from erratic rulings by the inevitable network of custom, common interest of all concerned in successful business expansion, interacting objectives of the government agencies participating in the decision process, political pressure, and public debate on important cases. The control agency must be able to defend its orders against highly organized trade associations devoting much effort to influencing decisions in this critical area.

But the agency is less subject to the checks of judicial review and effective parliamentary inquiry than, for example, the Interstate Commerce Commission. As is generally true of business-government relations in France, executive discretion is greater than in the United States [34].

1. The Trend of Industrial Prices

The use of controls did not prevent markedly greater postwar price increases in France than those experienced in most other countries. The results may be divided into four periods: (1) a raging inflation from the beginning of 1945 to 1949, during which wholesale prices rose nine times; (2) a temporary lull in 1949, followed by a new inflationary outburst in 1950–51; (3) a complex period from 1952 into 1956, including a remarkable stretch of combined price stability and aggregative expansion; (4) renewed inflationary pressures developing in 1956 and culminating in 1957, followed by greater emphasis on aggregative measures to combat rising prices and lessening use of controls [18, pp. 106–76, 258–90].

The inflation that carried through 1948 was a straightforward case of enormous excess demand in conditions of full employment. Against a background of exceedingly liquid monetary conditions and budgetary deficits running from 30 to 60 percent of total government expenditure, the proportion of national product available for domestic consumption was considerably reduced by increases in the relative volume of both investment and exports [18, pp. 86, 125] [30, pp. 46–51] [37, pp. 217–38]. Attempts to check the resulting pressures by controls were not aided by any extraordinarily high level of public cooperation, but the failure should not be ascribed to a peculiarly French impatience with authority: evasion of regulation in markets experiencing excess demand is in the interest of both buyers and sellers. Rapidly rising prices in these markets pulled up material costs and helped build up wage pressure in the sectors more amenable to control, making restraints there scarcely more effective. It is a moot question as to whether temporary local successes by the control agency reduced the rate at which price and wage increases interacted on each other or made the inflation worse by creating an added handicap to supply adjustments.

The renewal of inflation that began in 1949 and carried into 1952 was a different experience, with an interesting end result. Controls were relaxed at the start of this period, in the belief that the worst supply shortages were over. Prices began to rise with the first signs of recovery from the brief 1949 recession, caught fire in the general Korean War inflation of 1950, and then kept on going up after world demand and raw material costs eased in early 1951. Signs of lessened pressure on productive capacity began to appear in the second half of 1951, and unemployment began to rise from November. Wholesale prices of industrial goods leveled off but did not fall, while wages and retail prices kept moving up rapidly until they were attacked directly in March 1952.

The government's approach to the situation in March 1952 was not sophisticated. Although signs of recession were developing, retail prices were still rising, wholesale prices had stopped shooting up only in January, and unemployment was not over 2 percent of the labor force.* In the belief that the main objective of policy was to fight inflation, and that the way

* The French Government does not publish a continuing measure of unemployment as a percentage of the civilian labor force. Estimates in the text are based on INSEE sample surveys taken in October of 1952 and 1954. These references are extrapolated to other dates by use of the regular monthly series of unsatisfied requests for work, which greatly understates unemployment as defined in the United States but may serve as a defensible index of change in the degree of unemployment. The 1952 sample survey indicated an unemployment ratio of 1.6 percent in October. The monthly series shows that the level of unemployment in the first half of 1952, when prices were reduced, was less than in October. The sample surveys, which should be free of the main factors causing understatement in the monthly series, have unfortunately not been continued in more recent years [11, p. 72] [18, pp. 34–58] [173].

to do it was to reduce prices, the government attempted to do exactly that. Some industries were ordered to reduce their prices, negotiated decreases were worked out with major trade associations and retail chains, and everyone else was asked to make voluntary reductions. On its side, the government undertook to hold down taxes, while its expenditures continued to rise. The budget deficit rose from 2.7 percent of GNP in 1951 to 4.5 percent in 1952 [18, pp. 198, 291]. The government fed increased money income into the economy through the deficit, while raising the real purchasing power of its addition to money income and of existing cash balances.

If the behavior of prices had been an accurate indicator of a basic situation of excess demand, the policies adopted would have been explosive. In fact, demand moved slightly downward, both because it was headed that way in the first place and because the check to retail prices discouraged speculation in inventories. The cost of living fell 3.4 percent between March and June. It stayed below the March 1952 level until the end of 1956.

The available interpretations of this 1952 operation stress that the government was lucky: the demand situation was about to bring prices down anyway [30, pp. 68–79] [116]. The fact that demand pressure and raw material costs had been easing for some time without bringing down prices of industrial products does not invalidate this suggestion. Prices may simply have been making lagging adjustments to the cost increases of 1951, notably to the general increase in wage rates implemented in September.

It is not possible to be sure whether the actions taken in 1952 just happened to coincide with a price reversal that was about to occur, or that they brought about a correction that might have taken a good deal longer to work out without the direct intervention. But perhaps the point of chief interest is that a situation of rising prices and low unemployment was not treated as one requiring aggregative deflation. The direct attack on prices worked because their increases were not in fact accurate indicators of genuine scarcity. The lack of any real pressure on prices after they were reduced by authority suggests both that: (1) arbitrarily raised prices provided scope for arbitrary reductions, and (2) unemployment below 2 percent of the labor force can be consistent with price stability, if there are no specific shortages and if price increases in the absence of shortages are prevented.

It is not surprising that retail prices stayed down in 1952 and during the first half of 1953, while the recession continued. It is of greater interest that they did not rise promptly with the recovery beginning from mid-1953, and in fact stayed down through two subsequent years of rapid expansion with very low unemployment. It might be suggested that this is what could be expected to happen in any competitive economy: prices fell in conditions of excess capacity, and did not move back up again until pressure on capacity became strong again. This is probably what would happen in a thoroughly competitive economy but this is not what prices have usually done in France. Apart from the experience under discussion, industrial product prices rose along with each increase in production, and stabilized or continued rising in recessions. In this one instance, controls helped move prices more in the manner they would have moved had they been set under competitive conditions.

From December 1953 to December 1955 industrial production increased 18 percent. The index of retail prices of industrial goods rose 1 percent and that for wholesale prices of industrial goods fell .5 percent. As measured by the census of May 1954, unemployment near the start of this period was only 1.8 percent of the civilian labor force. As measured by the employment survey of October 1954 it was 2.3 percent. Judging from the higher bench mark, the unemployment ratio was down to 1.9 percent by September 1955, 1.2 by September 1956, and 1.0 by September 1957. The situation in the latter part of 1956 and 1957 was unambiguously one of excess demand. The 1954–55 unemployment ratios, though low by U.S. standards, proved consistent with both a high degree of price stability and rapid expansion of production.

The maintenance of stable prices for industrial products well after the economy had moved to extremely low levels of unemployment was considerably aided by the behavior of raw materials prices, which fell 4 percent in 1954 and recovered only half that amount the following year. This helpful factor was related both to unusually rapid increases in agricultural production at home and to a decline of one percent in the average price of imported materials. On the other hand, hourly wage rates in manufacturing increased 15 percent from 1953 to 1955. Further, the stability of prices was not purchased by a rising import surplus. The economy was able to deliver an increase of one-third in export volume, an increment more than double the increase in the volume of imports [178]. This raised the value of exports relative to imports from 79 percent in 1953 to 93 percent in 1955, despite a slight deterioration in the terms of trade [18, p. 239].

The ability to provide rapidly rising output under conditions approximating full employment came partly from increases in hours worked, and from a movement of labor out of agriculture into industry, but chiefly from a striking improvement in output per hour worked. Average hours worked per week, which had reached a peak of 44.8 during the 1951 inflation and then fallen to 44.0 in 1952, went back up to the earlier peak without inflation during 1955, and then on up to 45.7 by 1957 [178]. Simultaneously, the labor force responded to demand pressure by resuming its movement toward nonagricultural employment. With a stable population of working age, employment in nonagricultural occupations increased 3 percent between 1953 and 1955, and another 3 percent in the following two years. But both the rise in hours worked and the helpful movement of labor toward higher-income occupations were overshadowed by the fact that output per hour worked in the industrial sector increased approximately 7 percent per year from 1953 to 1957 [35, table IV]. The increase in productivity provided the goods that balanced the concurrent rise in demand, and almost exactly offset the increase in average hourly wages. Absent these gains in efficiency, price controls would not have prevented increasing prices. Absent the controls, the pressures in labor and product markets would surely have brought about an early demise of the stability of industrial prices.

In the course of 1956, with the full weight of the Algerian War added to the previous close balance, aggravated on the supply side by a costly drop in the volume of agricultural production, the situation again turned toward outright excess demand. This was signaled by a deterioration of the external balance and by spreading bottlenecks, rather than by rapidly rising prices. A survey of production conditions in November 1956 indicated that practically all firms were operating at the maximum rates possible.* The retail price index did not clearly express the demand situation because it was systematically falsified. Selective subsidies and detaxation of items in the index were used to hold the index down, feeding basic inflationary pressures in order to maintain the pretense that they were under control.** Controls were converted from a check

* *Etudes et Conjonctures* carries periodic reports concerning unused capacity, obtained from INSEE sample inquiries on the outlook and intentions of business management. This series provides a measure of "the proportion of firms declaring that they could increase production if they had more orders." The lowest point recorded was that for November 1956, when only 3 percent of the firms sampled said that they could increase production [16d].

** The French Government is surely not the only one in the world which likes to choose its statistical techniques with a view to keeping the consumer price index down, and the particular government in 1956–57 had domestic precedent in this respect, but this seems to have been an unusually determined operation [18, p. 265] [175, January 10, 1957]. *Le Monde* estimated that the index was falsified by 4.8 points (3 percent) in the course of a year. The Fifth Republic has not entirely resisted the temptation to indulge in this form of deceit, though it has so far avoided the extremes of its predecessor [175, October 31, 1961].

against arbitrary price increases into an instrument for forcing industry to absorb rising costs through lower margins. The preceding improvement of the trade balance was radically reversed. As in the early postwar years, intense efforts to enforce regulation in a situation calling for aggregative deflation only added to the fundamental difficulties and soon broke down.

In the latter part of 1957 emphasis shifted toward aggregative deflationary measures. Subsidies aimed at the price index and reliance on direct controls were both reduced. The process of moving away from price regulations in the industrial sector continued in 1958–60, although they have been maintained for steel and brandished threateningly at several other industries believed to be getting too aggressive. With relaxed controls, industrial prices have neither risen wildly nor shown quite the same stability as in 1954–55. They increased 7 percent in 1959, following the increase in franc prices of imported raw materials caused by the devaluation of December 1958. In 1960, with raw material prices stable, they rose a further 3 percent. The latter increase is not readily explicable in terms of labor costs: hourly wage rates in manufacturing increased 7.6 percent, but output per man-hour in the industrial sector simultaneously increased 7.2 percent [35, table IV] [178]. It might have been due to excess demand in particular markets, but the INSEE surveys have reported that most firms believed they could increase production if they had more orders. All these considerations refer to a small price change in any case. The experience has at least demonstrated that the French economy is no more liable to explosive inflation in conditions of full employment than most other industrialized economies. But the result in 1960 may be an indication that the maximum rate of expansion consistent with stable industrial prices has shifted downward with the reduction of controls.

2. Effects on Competition and Efficiency

In one of the best books on current problems of monopoly and competition in France, Jacques Houssiaux makes a forceful case for elimination of price control on the ground that it favors oligopolistic collusion [59, pp. 200–201]. His evidence on the structure and performance of French industries indicates that concentration is in most cases lower than in the United States, but widespread agreements serve to moderate competitive pressure and maintain market shares. He suggests that controls favor collusion because they lead to a negotiation process in which trade associations can easily serve as instruments for moderating competition, and because the establishment of official ceilings provides a focus for individual quotations which might otherwise have differed. He also argues that these negative effects are not counterbalanced by any genuine success in blocking increases that firms believe to be in their interest: that the trade associations dominate the control process.

Without denying the significance of Houssiaux's suggestions, two countering qualifications seem to be necessary: (1) most of the clearly competitive industries have been free of controls, and (2) some of those under strict regulation have well-established records of effective collusion, long antedating price control. France does not have a tradition of attempts to enforce competition. The agency created in 1953 to survey business practices and to attack harmful restraints on trade may be the forerunner of a significant change in this respect, but its cautious approach has not yet revolutionized traditional practices. Important industries are permitted such techniques as joint selling agencies, market sharing agreements, and group decisions on pricing, as long as the Commission does not decide that a particular industry is acting in a manner clearly harmful to the public interest. The general point that industries in which firms exhibit independence in their pricing decisions should be left free of controls remains valid, but this category does not include all manufacturing industries in France.

The suggestion that prices evolved much as they would have done in the absence of controls is most difficult either to support or to refute. For the periods of open inflation up to 1952, the changes were so violent and so general that regulation can hardly be considered to have had more than temporary delaying effects. The period of greater interest is again that of 1952–57, in which controls were actively enforced through successive conditions of recession, recovery, and continuing expansion in conditions of full employment. Two nonconclusive tests indicate that controls did affect pricing significantly in these years: the trend of profits relative to sales was not consistent with normal expectations for uncontrolled markets, and the pattern of price change was systematically different from that for American industry during the same period.

The movement from conditions of recession in 1952 to a situation of excess demand in 1957 should in principle have acted to raise ratios of profits to sales in most industries. In the aggregate, for all firms subject to regular profits taxation, the ratio of net profit after taxes to sales fell from 3.9 percent in 1952 to 3.6 in 1957.* The nature of the data is such as to cast doubt on the accuracy of small changes, but the results fairly well rule out the possibility that margins increased as would be expected in the absence of controls. In some industries (notably machinery and heavy electrical equipment), margins were greatly reduced despite the change from excess capacity to excess demand. In others, including nonferrous metals, automobiles, chemicals and textiles, margins did go up in the same period, either because productivity gains were especially rapid, or, in the case of textiles, because price controls were not well

* Data here refer to firms subject to the "régime du bénéfice réel," which includes all medium and larger enterprises, accounting for 91 percent of sales by all reporting firms in 1957 [25].

enforced for them. Controlled industries for which productivity gains were relatively slow were apparently subject to a genuine squeeze. This is not to argue that the effect was desirable. It is only to refute the suggestion that controls were irrelevant for the behavior of prices.

Comparison of the pattern of price changes in 1952–57 to that in the United States is handicapped by differences in classification of data, and by the scarcity of official indexes for narrowly defined groups of industrial products in France, but the small sample included in Table 10 serves to bring out some suggestive contrasts.

TABLE 10. Changes in Wholesale Prices for Selected Manufacturing Industries, France and the United States, 1952–57

	Percent Increase in Price Index	
	United States	France
Primary metals	30	9
Electrical machinery	19	−6
Motor vehicles	13	3[a]
All manufacturing	9	0.4
Chemicals	5	−8
Leather products	4	7
Textiles	−7	−3

Sources: *Bulletin Mensuel de Statistique* for all French prices except electrical machinery; Syndicat National de la Construction Electrique, "Rapport Statistique, 1959" for electrical machinery; Levinson, "Postwar Movement of Prices and Wages in Manufacturing Industries," Study paper no. 21, prepared for the Joint Economic Committee, Study of Employment, Growth and Price Levels, January 1960, p. 14, for American prices.

Note: [a]) The French index for motor vehicles is based on retail rather than wholesale prices, but retail margins were fixed and dealer concessions rare in this period, maintaining a close correspondence between changes in wholesale and in retail prices.

To anticipate two relevant questions concerning the above comparison, output of French manufacturing increased more than twice as rapidly as that of American industry in the period considered, and hourly wages in manufacturing rose 36 percent as against 24 in the United States [178].

During this period of active control, the dispersion of price changes was considerably less in French than in American manufacturing. The range from greatest increase to greatest decrease was only 17 percentage points, compared to 37 in the United States. Taking "primary metals" as a central objective of control, and an area in which it was most easily exercised, it is noteworthy that this stood out on the high side in France as well as in the United States. The only difference was that it did not stand out so far. Leather products and textiles present the opposite situation of relatively dispersed production structures, not in fact subject to close control. In both these cases, and in no others, French prices rose relative to American.

The data cited do not prove that price regulation changed the course of events. In the first place, independent choices of firms, guided by competitive objectives, may have been more important than controls in holding down prices in some industries. This was definitely the case in the automobile industry. In the second place, differences in factor cost changes were such as to favor the pattern of pricing indicated. The restraint on prices of primary metals itself acted to hold down costs for all the metals-using industries. The pattern of wage changes had the same effect, and is worth considering in more detail.

The recent study of costs and prices in American industry by Charles Schultze and Joseph Tryon concluded that the evolution of unit labor costs was better explained by differences in productivity gains than by differences in wage rates, except for five important cases [67, pp. 42–45]. Their exceptional cases included the two extremes in the table above: primary metals (where wages stood out on the high side), and textiles (where the wage increase was below average and the productivity increase above). One of the key differences in France is that there are no marked exceptions in this sense. As indicated by Table

7, hourly wage increases have differed moderately among industries, but the degree of dispersion has been smaller than in the United States. Differences in unit labor costs are more fully explained by differences in productivity, because the dispersion of wage increases is more limited.

The fact that the structure of wage change in France favored the pattern of price change observed does not mean that the former determined the latter. Regulation was explicitly used as a warning device against firms or industries tending to raise wages markedly faster than the general pace, and may have been responsible in part for the relatively low spread among wage increases. This factor was surely of secondary importance in determining the wage pattern, but it probably did help shape the evolution of wages as well as prices.

The faster pace of wage increases in France in the period discussed was offset by more rapidly rising output per man-hour, in turn made possible by the greater rate of increase in production. Comparison of changes in labor productivity indicate that the improvement in France relative to that in the United States was particularly high for primary metals, motor vehicles, electrical machinery and chemicals, and considerably lower for textiles and leather products [Table 6]. These structural differences are consistent with the possibility that selective application of control to highly concentrated industries little inclined to price competition may, by making it more difficult to pass on wage increases, help shift the effort of firms somewhat more toward cost reduction as a means of raising profits.

For competitive industries, arbitrarily set prices surely do distort resource allocation and lessen efficiency. Where an economy is split into competitive and noncompetitive producing groups, both prices and wages in the latter move too high relative to their levels in the competitive industries. Price control limited to the minority of noncompetitive industries, checking their profit margins and holding their wage increases in line with opportunities elsewhere, may in principle improve allocative efficiency. As practiced in France, controls did not make any such neat distinction. But, by the accident of the fact that highly concentrated industries are easier to control, they may well have held prices and wages in a pattern more nearly consistent with efficient resource allocation than would have resulted in the absence of controls.

3. Relationships to Aggregative Expansion

Regulation of prices was definitely not fatal for the growth of manufacturing output. From 1950 to 1960 the index of industrial production rose 89 percent, slightly above the expansion rate for all OEEC members, and markedly above that in the United States. This performance cannot in any sense be explained by changes in the efficiency of the pricing system, but it is of some interest to consider the treacherous question of the effects of regulation on the rate of expansion.

In the periods of strong excess demand through 1951, controls did no more than provide a temporary impediment to increases in the sectors more readily supervised. Their incidence was thus focused on the more organized industries. They may well have hampered investment selectively in such sectors, impeded the transfer of resources to the more productive areas of the economy, and favored the survival of inefficient operations beyond the reach of regulation. In so far as effective at all, they deflected the flow of income and control of resources from firms toward consumers, restraining investment and the possible rate of economic growth.

In the recession of 1952 and the subsequent period of balanced expansion, controls cannot be considered to have been uniformly negative. In 1952, the temporary decline in sales created excess capacity and reduced investment demand. Price increases in this situation would have altered the flow of funds from recipients with a high propensity to spend toward business firms eager to improve liquidity and uncertain about the desirability of further investment. In so far as controls checked the ability of noncompetitive firms to implement price increases in such conditions, they may well have sustained aggregate demand and facilitated recovery.

From the latter part of 1953 to the beginning of 1956, expansion proceeded in conditions of full employment and generally restrained industrial prices. As noted above, the restraints brought down profit margins (though not absolute profits), in the aggregate and particularly in capital equipment industries. Since this was a period of general pressure on capacity, it may be assumed that an increase in the flow of income to firms would have raised investment [86]. Blocking price increases for industries operating at capacity and endeavoring to raise investment favored current consumption at the expense of growth. Moreover, the squeeze on profits was particularly pronounced in the machinery and electrical equipment industries, focusing the negative effects in a manner restraining the increase in capital equipment. Recourse to imports to the extent permitted did act to ease this bottleneck, but they in turn contributed to the heavy balance of payments deficits of 1956–57.

The combination of strong demand conditions with restraint on profits did prove more favorable for investment than the initial 1952 combination of weaker demand and higher profit margins. Fixed capital formation rose slightly faster than GNP while profit margins were being held down. As measured in constant prices, the ratio of fixed investment to GNP rose from 16.0 percent in the 1952 recession to 18.7 in the 1957 boom [22, pp. 13, 339]. This does not exclude the probability that the economy's supply ceiling would have risen faster if higher prices had cut into consumption and allowed greater investment.

In a sense, price control under conditions of excess demand provides an alternative to monetary policy as a means of checking investment. It does reduce the funds available for investment financing, perhaps more effectively than ordinary credit rationing or high interest rates. But the net result is not the same. This technique allows purchasing power of households to gain to the extent that firms are restricted. It is not a deflationary instrument, but a means of favoring consumption at the expense of investment.

While controls were outrightly unhelpful in conditions of genuine excess demand, they need not have been harmful for growth during the years when aggregate demand and supply rose in close balance. Their worst aspect was that they restrained profits and held down investment in the capital goods industries, where demand did exceed supply. If they had been administered under a rule allowing freedom for those industries subject to excess demand, while maintaining a check for those noncompetitive industries for which supply remained adequate, the price level might have risen earlier but resource allocation would have been improved. The restraint was overly general. Its negative side became more important as more industries passed into the category of bottlenecks with the surge of demand in 1956–57. Up to that point, the positive side of price supervision was quite real. It made clear that a situation of rapid growth with unemployment on the order of 2 percent of the labor force was not in fact one of excess demand requiring deflation.

Regulation of industrial prices in France has had such varied and contradictory effects that any judgment as to whether the balance has been harmful or not must be highly arbitrary. One basic distinction does help clarify the results. When used in conditions of general excess demand to hold down the price level, direct controls hampered efficiency, restricted investment, and did not achieve any positive objective. When used to check arbitrary price increases in the one period when demand and supply were in close balance at low levels of unemployment, they helped preserve a condition of rapid expansion without inflation. In this favorable period their application to concentrated industries created a pattern of price change markedly different from that in the United States. This pattern might well be judged to have come closer to a competitive structure than that in the United States, in the sense that regulations in general bore down on the less competitive industries, keeping their price and wage changes more in line with those in the competitive sectors. Controls caused nothing but trouble when applied to industries for which demand exceeded capacity to supply, but they did help avoid false signals of inflation deriving from market power of sellers rather than genuine scarcity.

13 | Selective Promotion and Protection

The use of price controls constituted an aberration from the basic purpose of intervention in French business, which is to promote and to protect industry. The Planning Commission, the Ministry of Industry, and the various agencies interested in export aids have been trying to ensure vigorous industrial expansion, not to hamper it. In conflicts with labor or consumer interests, these agencies have been fairly consistent in their support of the business side. Within the business sector, they have particularly tried to facilitate the growth of the larger firms, opposing policies which tend to freeze the economic structure in the interest of preserving smaller companies.

Much unnecessary confusion has been generated by a tendency to lump all government promotional operations under the general head of "planning." This is wrong as to fact, since a great deal of the selective intervention actively practiced is decided on and implemented outside the planning process. It is misleading to thought, because it mixes up the positive function of planning as a system of coordinated guidance with an ambiguous and possibly harmful practice of altering private decisions by selective subsidies and protection. The fact that some of these techniques promote the ends of planning does not mean that they are integral to the process. Apart from planning as guidance, there are some unduly neglected questions about the wisdom of so much selective promotion.

Promotion refers here to a wide variety of aids to particular companies or groups, such as subsidized loans, special tax privileges, guided orders from state agencies, differential access to imports of equipment ordinarily restricted, and the like. The ingenuity of the officials concerned in thinking up new promotional techniques has been amazing. And they change frequently, as a given method either fails to work or works so well that it bothers somebody. E.g., a special depreciation allowance for new equipment applicable only when the equipment involved was itself produced in France, was tried out in 1959 and abandoned, following protests by the Italian Government, before the year was out. Rather than try to follow through such individual techniques in any detail, the assumption is that they may be treated as falling into two types: (1) selective subsidies, or (2) import protection.

1. The Implications of Selective Promotion

All the forms of selective subsidies used may be assumed to be helpful to the recipient, usually by facilitating investment, sometimes by reducing current input costs, and more rarely by improving the market. In the eyes of the giver and the receiver, they stimulate economic activity in useful directions. Granted that they stimulate differentially, they are generally regarded as raising aggregate investment and aiding the expansion of the economy as a whole. But this is a most uncertain conclusion. The question of whether the economy gains or not depends on the alternatives open. In the course of the postwar expansion, the alternatives have changed markedly, from a situation in which selective promotion probably did help considerably to one in which more general techniques might often be preferable.

It is undeniable that subsidies which act to raise rates of return on capital will encourage decisions to invest by their recipients. Subsidies to all potential investors, up to the point of full employment of resources, will raise investment as a share of national income and increase the rate of growth. But subsidies to particular groups, in a context of generally restricted credit and high business taxes made necessary by pressure of demand on productive capacity, may not raise total investment at all and may very easily reduce the marginal efficiency of the capital formation which is undertaken.

If government policy succeeds in ensuring full employment of resources, available to all on the basis of prices reflecting relative costs, then there is a sound basis for the expectation that investment will be undertaken in the directions in which it adds most to national income. The basis for the expectation is that firms will gain if they choose the alternatives which secure the maximum difference between the market value of the product realized and the increase in the firm's own costs. The major weaknesses in the assumption that the results will be optimal is the real possibility that individual firms will make mistakes because of their limited knowledge of actions by others, and the fact that they will neglect possible advantages to the economy that cannot be converted into gains for the company.

The positive aspect of planning as practiced in France is that it does attempt to provide guidance as to the future, filling in gaps in knowledge without taking decision powers away from the enterprise. Further, the Commission makes some attempt to identify discrepancies between market prices and opportunity costs, at least on such basic questions as interest and exchange rates, and has helped establish generalized procedures for correcting incentives accordingly. Given these well-conceived efforts, there is a fair presumption that further selective measures, such as the tax and credit favors accorded to the steel industry, will actually reduce the economy's possible rate of growth. Subsidized investment by any one group, pushing it ahead faster than it would have gone in the absence of subsidy available on differential terms, implies the sacrifice of investment with higher real rates of return in other directions. If the ghost of Say will permit, what one sees is the gain in investment by the subsidized industry; what one does not see is the greater loss by the community as a whole.

The prevalence of direct subsidies and differential fiscal treatment among industries in France reflects a somewhat superficial belief on the part of government agencies and favored companies that each selective aid contributes a net gain for the economy as a whole. The many ways in which this system might or did lead to distortions inimical to progress have been thoroughly cataloged by Baum [30]. But it is rather unsettling to observe that such a compelling list of errors has been accompanied by such a potent economic performance. The difficulty is that selective promotional techniques are neither automatically helpful nor inherently harmful. They can only be judged individually in terms of the alternatives open. Some techniques which might have been harmful if used in the United States, and might equally be harmful in France now, may have been much better than general methods of guidance under the conditions prevailing in the French economy in the early postwar years. The main reasons that considerable reliance on selective techniques was appropriate in the early postwar period were that the price system was thoroughly disorganized, and that entrepreneurial reactions were dismally negative.

Given the basic mistake of failing to reduce excess demand, selective aid to the better organized private and state industries quite possibly made the allocation of resources a little less inefficient than it would otherwise have been. Such aid was usually linked to reasonable programs of investment, export promotion and import substitution. The sectors from which resources were diverted by these programs undoubtedly included many able businessmen interested in at least equally vital programs. But careful long-range programs in these sectors were in any case seriously impeded by the incoherent speculative process encouraged by the over-all inflation. Those businessmen who aimed at cost reduction or systematic plant expansion were less likely to earn profits and remain in the bidding for resources than those who focused on hoarding inventories, or on high-margin operations in the grossly overexpanded retail trades. At least in the late 1940's, it is easy to condemn aggregative monetary policy, but not the selective help practiced by the Planning Commission and the Ministry of Industry.

From early 1952, with reconstruction accomplished and inflationary pressures under control, selective investment subsidies lost a good deal of their earlier utility. They retained it only in so far as they twisted sales effort toward export markets. This remained desirable because the currency continued to be overvalued until the end of 1958. Again, a general policy choice in the background was in error—everyone was understandably overcautious about another devaluation—but selective subsidies acted to raise the yield on export sales toward what they would have been if the currency value had been corrected. Since the successful devaluation at the end of 1958, this defense of the subsidy apparatus is no longer valid.

Apart from the problem of distorted prices, that of poorly oriented producer choices did provide a basis for helpful direct promotion. The fact that the steel industry resisted to the extent it did the principle of regional specialization and joint investment in modern facilities when proposed by the Planning Commission in 1946, even though offered extraordinarily favorable conditions for doing so, underlines the attitude dominating industry generally. The pent-up demand at the end of the war did encourage investment, but when left alone it took the form of multiplication of small firms and repetition of outmoded techniques, even in those industries where significant gains from scale could be stipulated from experience in other countries.

Given the preferences of the French business community at the start of the postwar period, preferences completely understandable in terms of long experience, it does seem legitimate to conclude that government pressure directed toward concentration of facilities, specialization, and larger-scale investment decisions did secure greater efficiency in the industries concerned than would have been achieved in the absence of the intervention. At the same time, the selective process pushed resources toward these industries, diminishing their availability to fields which were not at the time using them to lay the groundwork for sustained expansion with competitive costs. It is perfectly true that nobody proved that the gains in the favored directions exceeded possible losses elsewhere. Under the particular conditions of the society at the time, it seems a reasonable presumption that they did.

Some of the economic historians concerned with characteristics of French management, and some government officials today, are inclined to the belief that reluctance to carry out major expansionary efforts is an ingrained characteristic of the country's businessmen. The reasons for such belief have been found in a wide variety of aspects of French society [36] [40] [46]. Kindleberger rightly suggests that many of the factors used to explain poor performance in the past look surprisingly unimportant in the light of the postwar achievements [39]. The traditional impediments were real, but those on the government side have been altered by a more progressive policy emphasis, and those on the private side have become less and less serious as expansionary choices prove to be more often the correct ones. As with respect to price distortions, reluctance of private industry to expand appears less and less a valid reason for selective promotion of cooperating groups.

Assistance to particular industries on special terms does seem increasingly likely to inflict a net loss on the society by holding back alternatives not considered by the government agencies administering subsidies. But this does not mean that subsidies in themselves reduce growth. If they were available on equal terms to all, they would play a role similar to that of accelerated depreciation, or to a general shift in taxation from business to households. They would act to raise investment relative to consumption, and thereby permit more rapid growth, without holding back producers outside the favored circle. It is true that this argument makes no reference to the relative valuation of sacrificed present consumption and future gain. There is no reason that it should, when investment decisions are made by firms and by government, as is the case in every industrialized society, rather than by households deciding to abstain from consumption. The relative distribution of resources among private consumption, public consumption, and investment is essentially a community decision, not one that is or could be made by the private consumer. It could be made adverse to consumer welfare, but that has not been the general practice in France. When an economy can combine a high share of investment in total resource use with a higher rate of growth in consumption than it has achieved in many preceding generations, it is not unduly neglecting the welfare of consumers.

Finally, there are many particular circumstances under which subsidies of a type different from the low-interest loans to the steel industry may have a positive function in raising the efficiency of resource use. This is probably true of subsidies for industry research organizations, educational programs, and location in areas of surplus labor. It may also be true of efforts to help companies, trapped in fields with long-term excess capacity, to transfer their plant and retrain their labor forces to enter new activities of greater promise. The transfers would work out eventually, as they have so slowly in American textiles and agriculture, but efforts to facilitate them may both alleviate special hardships and keep resources more effectively in useful production. Such programs have been particularly relevant to the process of adaptation to the new environment of greater international competition.

2. Protection

Practically every OEEC meeting on trade liberalization up to the end of the 1950's featured a good deal of special criticism of French import restrictions. It was not merely that tariffs on imports of manufactured goods averaged unusually high, or that the percentage of trade allowed to enter without quantitative controls was unusually low, but that the small areas of competition permitted were restricted to those few industries in which French firms were able to hold their own anyway. As is commonly the case in protection of manufacturing, but perhaps to a greater degree than in most industrialized economies, the protective system in France was designed to build barriers in proportion to the weakness of the producing group concerned. Imports of fuel and raw materials were usually regarded as inescapable, but the policy applied to manufacturing was a massive exercise in the art of balanced growth.

It would be wrong to think of French trade policy as an immovable blank wall against which the other OEEC delegates thundered in vain. Slightly wrong. A careful step-by-step description of changes by Gérard Marcy makes it clear that there was an erratic trend toward greater liberalization underneath the ballet of timid advance and quick retreat [74]. General moves toward greater liberalization were taken in periods when the balance of payments improved, perhaps more than otherwise would have been taken because of the pressure from other countries through international organizations. Imports of manufactured goods did increase through the 1950's, drastically so during 1956–57 when deliberate acceptance of a major trade deficit was used as a means of fighting inflation.

Alongside this general trend, at least one sector of the French Government was extremely active in promoting regional trade improvement. The bitterly fought battle over the Schuman Plan provided the opening wedge in the early 1950's, putting the coal and steel industries under graduated but nevertheless increased competitive pressure. Once the pending change became certain, the French steel industry mitigated its antagonism to the Planning Commission's remaining proposals for regrouping and greater specialization. Most of the change, and the accompanying spurt in the industry's investment, came before trading restrictions were seriously altered [138, pp. 357–69]. It was the process of intensive preparation for new conditions which were conceived as threatening the life of the industry, more than the reality, softened by this preparation, that made the difference.

The reorganization of the steel industry was a joint product of two pressures: direct intervention carried on during the most active period of the Planning Commission, and the exposure to import competition through the Coal-Steel Community. The other industrial sectors picked out as being in need of modernization, notably industrial equipment and textiles, were not brought into reorganization programs until the quieter period of the second plan. Industrial equipment became the center of consistent administrative efforts. It was widely considered, with some reason, that French economic progress required a dynamic group of equipment industries able to meet changing technological opportunities rapidly and at competitive costs. The equipment producers were given plentiful advice on the fast growing requirements of French industry, on opportunities for achieving lower costs through specialization and scale, and on means of securing financial help in carrying out necessary investment. They were also given a phenomenal degree of import protection, even at the visible cost of slowing expansion for the rest of French industry. A few firms responded with definite progress, including the development of specialty exports outside the franc zone. The great majority did little. Import barriers were kept selectively high in those areas of the equipment market where the producers made least progress. Those exposed to trade because they could do well, did so; those protected from it because they were inadequately efficient, remained so.

By 1958, the theme that something had to be done about the equipment industries had gained in vehemence what it had lost in novelty. The administrative proposals of that year included the idea of competition, in this instance to be fostered by a projected new government firm built around the machine-tool branch of Renault [28]. This was not tried, partly because Renault was not eager to part with its machine-tool division. It might have worked.

If the French economy had remained on its 1946–58 path of persistent expansion combined with direct stimulation, it is more than likely that the equipment industries would have improved their organization and efficiency. Some firms were doing so, and they would surely have placed gradually rising pressure on the rest, whatever the level of external competition. There is no evident reason in terms of resources why an economy capable of meeting international competition in basic metals and in automobiles should remain indefinitely weak in industrial machinery. As of 1958 this was seen as a matter requiring time and infinite effort. As of 1960 it was still possible to be dissatisfied, but the major miracle had been accomplished. The equipment industries were suddenly in the limelight as a newly progressive field whose exports were rising remarkably. The key to the change was a radical change in policy, namely correction of the currency value and exposure to international trade.

The sheltered industries did indeed have a legitimate complaint on the necessity of protection until the end of 1958, in that they were handicapped by a serious overvaluation of the franc. It would have involved an irrational slaughter to open trade freely in this situation. It was in this respect a perfect combination of policies to correct the value of the currency and at the same time announce an early deadline for the elimination of quantitative restrictions. The government wasted no time in starting on a joint course of tariff reduction within the context of the Common Market, supplemented with step-by-step elimination of quotas. By mid-1961, practically all the machinery industries had been exposed to the beginning of trade without quantitative limits. Tariff reductions were more than offset in most cases by the increased cost of foreign currency resulting from devaluation, but the net effect was to concentrate competitive alternatives for the first time on the weaker sections of manufacturing.

France has not plunged wholeheartedly into free trade in manufacturing, but the climate has been radically altered. Producers still have notable elements of protection, especially toward countries outside the Common Market, but this is no longer crucial for French structural change. They also still have the whole arsenal of administrative support available to help them modernize within old industries or shift to new ones. These measures of direct assistance have actually grown in practical importance, because the willingness of those businesses previously reluctant to use them has perceptibly increased now that the alternative has been changed from one of limp progress to possible annihilation. Measures of direct assistance have undoubtedly helped achieve a transition with minimal waste of resources, rather than one strewn with local disaster.

To pose the issue as one of opposition between selective help and international competition probably misses the main point of the French results. As long as the less progressive industries were guaranteed survival without change, they were not greatly interested in administrative measures aiding them to achieve it. Exposure to trade made them seek it more actively. Direct aids then minimized the disorganization that might have resulted if they had been left to shift for themselves in the new context. A coercive system might have worked without trade, with different costs of its own. It is most doubtful that it would ever have worked as well as have the recent steps toward a working coalition between administrative assistance in shifting resources and international competitive pressure pushing change in the right directions.

14 | Concentration and Competition

When an American economist publishes an analysis of the size distribution of firms, the underlying concern is usually the possibility that concentration may be so high as to make it difficult to secure competition. When a French economist tackles the same subject, the concern is more often with the possibility that concentration may be too low to be consistent with efficiency.

The two approaches, to which exceptions may be found on both sides, reflect a fairly general acceptance of competition as a method of control of manufacturing industries in the United States, and an equally general contrary attitude in France. As noted in Chapter 3, neither country has found any completely consistent set of policies on which agreement could be indefinitely maintained. The political balance between those who would prefer to limit the specific disruptions caused by competitive pressures and those who focus more on the possibilities of general gain moves continually in both countries.

French policies before the war leaned heavily in the direction of protecting present interests at the expense of possible progress. The leaders of economic policy after the war reacted strongly in a different direction. They did not try to create any movement toward more active competition. If they had tried, they would have found precious little support. Instead, they used direct methods of promotion and control to force through selective changes. They attempted to increase cooperation among firms and to raise industrial concentration through mergers. Competition was not regarded as a significant possibility. This original emphasis has slowly moved toward a more complex approach including efforts to reduce collusion. Aided by a new fluidity deriving from expansion and reduced trade barriers, the effort to move toward competition has generated increasing conflict with the ideal of coordinated group progress.

1. Concentration and Efficiency

The idea of measuring concentration in American industry grew out of preoccupation with two possible dangers. One is that competition in individual industries can be undermined by tacit agreements when a small number of producers supply almost all of a given commodity. With many producers, agreements are hard to maintain without a formal apparatus that may be attacked under antitrust legislation; when three or four firms account for nearly all production, they can more easily reach informal understandings difficult to attack from the outside. In such conditions, independent behavior by any of the smaller firms in the industry is not too likely in the first place and incapable of constituting great pressure if it does occur. The second concern of American economists is that a concentration of the bulk of economic decisions in the hands of a small number of firms, regardless of their shares in particular markets, might enable them to dominate social choices. In the light of these two concerns, then, concentration has been a negative word, meaning that a possibly harmful share of economic activity may be in the hands of a small number of firms.

The thought that concentration or average size might in some cases be too low for efficiency has not been common in American studies. After all, if gains from greater scale are available, the profit motive should lead to their realization by all capable entrepreneurs. The further gains possible from reduction of competition through mergers, or agreements facilitated when there are not too many firms involved to agree, are generally considered as added reasons for expecting business to adopt or to go beyond the sizes necessary for efficiency.

On the basis of one of the few careful empirical studies of both sides of the question, Joe S. Bain concluded that concentration is often higher than is necessary for efficiency, but that there is also a significant component of stagnant, persistently undersized companies in American manufacturing. "The findings from this small sample of [twenty] industries could hardly be hoped to be exactly representative of tendencies present in manufacturing industries in general. But they do lend support to the thesis that in at least half or more of all such industries the leading firms are in a significant degree larger than necessary from the standpoint of efficiency in production and distribution, and that seller concentration is, in a corresponding sense, unnecessarily high" [52, p. 356]. But the industries studied also had typically an "inefficient fringe" of unduly small plants, supplying from 10 to 30 percent of output. They "show a strong tendency to persist over time, not only in the collective but in the individual sense, so that inefficiently small plants in general are *not* young, expanding plants which later grow to efficient scale. The condition is chronic, and not apparently an incident of the process of healthy growth" [52, p. 353].

French economists interested in the same questions start from the assumption that most firms are too small. They do not have any great confidence in the potency of the profit motive as a force leading business to seek efficient scales of production. They know that government policy prior to the war had the effect of operating against any such trend, and they believe on the basis of direct comparisons that the "inefficient fringe" has been extremely important in most French industries. The literature on causes and factual evidence is suggestive, if often confused. One clear point is that the emphasis of policy choice since the war has been much more in the direction of pushing for greater concentration and scale than in that of encouraging competition.

The concern of the Planning Commission with promotion of mergers and concentration has been noted above. Practically every annual report of the Commission notes the more important mergers of the preceding year along with the other welcome signs of reform. If any of the government agencies interested in promoting concentration make distinctions between consolidations in the particularly dispersed industries which have lagged in postwar progress, and the 1959 agreement under which those infinitesimal firms, Pechiney and St. Gobain, combined their chemical operations, they have not spoken out [175, November 22, 1959]. The process of attacking outdated structures proceeded in the field of synthetic fibers to the point in 1961 at which the all-embracing arms of the Celtex group have combined the interests of all the firms in the industry [175, June 24, 1961].

Perhaps the most influential of the economic studies which helped crystallize opinion in the direction indicated was that published in 1956 by J. M. Jeanneney, who was then outside the government, but became in 1958 the highly active Minister of Industry. "The small firms have too often lagged behind possible technical progress. The reasons are intellectual and financial. New techniques are hard to find out about, to choose, and to put into operation. The head of a small firm, who has to keep track of everything, often lacks the time and qualifications necessary. . . . The direction of family firms being hereditary, they risk falling into incapable hands. When they need to carry out investment, they cannot tap public savings through bonds or stocks. Their owners, fearing the loss of full control of their business, often hesitate to use the financial help that they could obtain from banks or individuals" [37, pp. 258–59].

Jeanneney recognized that the backward characteristics of

small business would normally have led toward an increase in the average size of firms, as the minority which did choose to expand found their profits higher and opportunities for further growth improved. According to his evidence, such a trend was in progress up to 1931 but was then reversed. He interpreted the reversal as a result of government policy fostering small business in the 1930's, leading to distortions which require positive action to redress the balance by promoting concentration. "Up to 1931, the number of large plants constantly increased. In 1906 there were 205 industrial plants employing more than 1000 workers and 421 in 1931. . . . Since then the movement of concentration seems to have been stopped. . . . In 1952, although industrial production was 26 percent above that of 1931, one finds only 332 industrial plants employing more than 1000 workers (instead of 421 in 1931). . . . Now, in the United States, between 1929 and 1951, the number of manufacturers employing more than 2500 workers nearly tripled. . . . If the turnabout taken by the French industrial and commercial structure towards 1930 were explained by the fact that the medium and small firms had found the secret of a new efficiency, one could only rejoice. . . . (But) the true reason for the halt in concentration was the protection afforded by the state" [37, pp. 259–60].

Jeanneney's discussion helped strengthen the gradual change in sentiment away from protection of small business and excessive distrust of large firms. Such a transformation away from crippling bias is devoutly to be wished, but the wholehearted stress in the opposite direction by government officials with extensive powers for direct intervention is perhaps less warmly to be welcomed. His comments raise questions concerning both factual accuracy and economic objectives.

The trend toward an increase in the number of plants employing more than 500 workers was indeed checked in 1931. By 1936, the number of such plants had fallen 20 percent [37, p. 259]. This decline appears in perspective only when it is noted that aggregate industrial employment fell 18 percent between the same two years [18, p. 38]. The apparent reversal of structural trend was mainly a manifestation of the drastic nature of the depression.

Major changes in census definitions and methods make the figure for the number of plants with over 1000 employees in 1931 most dubiously comparable to postwar data [16a, pp. 842–43]. If Jeanneney's figure for 1931 were considered comparable to postwar figures, his conclusion would have to be changed. In 1954, the industrial labor force was smaller than in 1931, but the number of plants with more than 1000 employees was 479, as against the 421 cited for 1931. By 1958, the figure had risen to 506. The 1954–58 data show the trend unambiguously. While industrial production increased one-third and the industrial labor force rose about 3 percent, the total number of plants decreased 4 percent and the number with more than 1000 employees increased 6 percent [15, tables I and II, pp. 4–47].

It will be noted that all this discussion concerns the number of plants above a given size, not concentration in the sense of market shares. The emphasis has been a characteristic of French economic studies, both because of data limitations and because they have been concerned more with the adequacy of scale than with relative shares. One exceptionally interesting article has recently drawn on a newly developed fiscal series to study concentration in terms of firms and relative sales for the period 1951–56 [17b]. Considering the distribution of sales among all industrial enterprises for which sales were over one million NF in 1951, the author demonstrates that "the industrial structure was not sensibly modified from 1951 to 1956." The degree of concentration fell slightly from the boom year 1951 to the recession of 1953, then rose slowly back up again during the expansion through 1956 [17b, p. 36].*

* The one measure of concentration used in this study was the slope of a straight-line approximation to a Pareto curve, obtained by plotting

The study of concentration pointed out that the ratio of labor costs to sales falls, and that of profits to sales rises, with size of firm. Profits were taken in this case as the sum of reported net income plus depreciation charges and reserve provisions. Without any reference to profit in the sense of rates of return on invested capital, the author concluded that this information validates Jeanneney's position on the advantages of size. "The larger firms seem to lead in productivity; they thereby realize larger profits than medium-sized firms, while paying higher wages. . . ." Industrial expansion favors concentration and affirms the preponderant role of the large firms ". . . concentration and general improvement of the standard of living—it is in this framework that our industrial rise is inscribed . . ." [17b, p. 53].

The study cited, using material never previously organized for this purpose, provides much useful information. It is not the first analysis of concentration for which the conclusions seem more to be drawn from policy preferences than to be imposed by the data. If the technology of a given industry requires use of relatively large scale capital-intensive methods, firms in this field will inevitably have relatively high ratios of capital charges to sales. If gross profits defined to include such charges, as in this study, did not in general rise with scale it would be a strong indication of inferior efficiency on the part of the larger firms. Similarly, if net profits relative to sales were not above average, this would imply subnormal rates of return on capital used. And if labor costs were not below average relative to sales, this would suggest failure in economizing in the use of labor despite greater use of capital. The empirical results are consistent with either greater or less than average efficiency in resource use by the larger firms.

---

for each year the log of the number of firms with sales above a given level against the log of sales [17b, pp. 36–37 and fig. 1, p. 54]. The universe consisted of the nonnationalized firms for which sales exceeded 1.0 million NF, accounting for about 60 percent of all industrial sales.

Skepticism concerning this attempted proof of a positive relation between size and efficiency does not mean rejection of the point that greater average size would be desirable in French manufacturing. The long prewar lethargy of French industry left many possible gains from scale unexploited. The "inefficient fringe" in many industries was more than the mild evidence of waste that Bain found in American manufacturing. It was the rule and the scourge of French industry. But the real possibility of gain from greater market pressure to eliminate those firms which are inefficient may easily become confused with the less helpful idea that greater size automatically means superior efficiency, and should therefore be promoted actively by any and all means.

According to Raymond Barre, the economist who became Jeanneney's assistant in the Ministry of Industry in 1958, "The large firm appears today as the most efficient unit of production; following Schumpeter, its role as a motor in growth should be underlined. Far from pushing Malthusianism and higher prices, it favors improvement of techniques and the quality of products, and excites competition by innovation, which is the source of well-being" [53, p. 914]. If this means in practice simply that discriminatory restraints limiting enterprise size should be eliminated, the objective is certainly defensible. If it is taken to be a justification for intervention favoring larger companies in the belief that they constitute the newly progressive future, it is not.

If large firms do have all the advantages suggested, and the environment does not discriminate against them, one would expect that a long-run test would reveal a pronounced increase in their relative role, measurable as an increase in concentration. This is what Jeanneney thought he saw in France prior to 1931, and what so many American economists thought they saw in the United States until Adelman and others demonstrated that the belief was not borne out by the facts [51]. During the first half of the twentieth century, with the edge in financing advantages rather on the side of the large firms, and with little serious effort by government to block mergers unrelated to market superiority, the relative position of the largest companies did not significantly change. There must have been some fairly important factors offsetting the strengths so freely attributed to them.

The offsetting factors have usually been discussed in terms of diseconomies of scale. The abundant literature on the subject has perhaps brought out no point more clearly than that the possibilities of gain from scale vary widely among industries [52] [64]. Size provides some presumption of ability, but it may be one that expressed itself in the past and is unlikely to be sustained in the future.

The policy concern is perhaps less with current operating efficiency, which clearly precludes gain from indefinitely increasing scale in a good many areas of manufacturing, than it is with the ability of the larger firms to initiate progress. This is an issue on which empirical investigation has shown such varied results that one can pick almost any conceivable position and find support for it. It is certainly true that many of the largest firms are leaders in the process of seeking improvement. They are often more willing and able than small firms to spend money on research, and they are particularly successful in securing persistent gains within well-defined technological fields. But a good deal of the factual material on this subject rather discredits the notion that the well-established giant firm is the prime source of significant change, at least in England or the United States. Even in the twentieth century, with growing organization of research and with disproportionate financial resources on the side of the larger firms, the majority of important discoveries have come from independent inventors and medium- or small-sized firms [55] [61] [68].

The fact that only a minority of important inventions can be credited to large firms is perhaps inevitable, in the simple sense that they constitute only a small fraction of the business population. The proportion of independent inventors and small firms who do make significant contributions is quite low, but it would be astounding in view of their enormous numbers if they did not generate the majority of new ideas. This hardly saves the argument on the wisdom of a policy intended to channel resources to a few large companies. It suggests rather that progress is aided by the maintenance of a large number of independent centers of initiative. The answer to this is sometimes thought to be that the industrial application of new ideas is the particular strong point of big companies. And there is much in this. So much that it might well be checked against some of the record of France's own industrial history.

In the dim reaches of the seventeenth century, there once was a royal monopoly in the important industry of mirror production. After some difficulty a new firm obtained permission to share the field, and then ran away with it through perfection of a technological break-through in the art of glass making. The invention was developed by the newcomer, now known as St. Gobain, and not by the established firm [33, pp. 135–41]. In the nineteenth century, Pechiney was the only producer of aluminum for some time. It not only did not develop the new process which laid the basis of the modern aluminum industry, it did not even wish to take the trouble to upset established routine by trying out the change [123, p. 68]. In the 1920's, it was not either of the two largest established firms in the automobile industry which pioneered mass production and industrial research techniques, but the newcomer André Citroën. In the 1950's, the newly founded Surmelec and Moulinex did more to free the French housewife from the curse of extraordinarily high-cost household electrical equipment than their larger colleagues had ever done. Similarly, the two domestic firms which emerged in the 1950's to lead the new business machine industry, Machines Bull and Meci, would not have been likely contenders for selection by a government agency looking around in the late 1940's for giant firms to be given selective support.

Much progress comes from the largest firms, and much comes from relative unknowns. It is no accident that the latter provide most of the stimulus for really important changes. Established organizations thrive on orderly progress within established channels, not on upsetting them by radical change. Schumpeter was brilliantly correct in focusing attention on the importance of innovation as a test of market performance. His error was to identify size with progress. The identification could prove to be true in a particular institutional environment, but it would have to be one in which all the weight of subsidies, government orders, and privileged contact was given to the largest firms. Under such conditions, the smaller companies might well contribute relatively little to the progress of the economy. The trouble is that the loss on this side might not be balanced by any significant gain on the other.

The preceding is meant to point to an apparent impasse in postwar policy toward concentration. On the one hand, many industries have been cluttered up with excess numbers of unprogressive firms, some small and some not so small. This does mean that real gains would be possible through a process by which the more dynamic companies took over larger shares of the market, increasing their average size and quite possibly increasing market concentration. On the other hand, direct support to the largest companies, identifying them with the dynamic component of industry, lowers the opportunities for the many newer firms which might in an unbiased system provide most of the progress of the future.

Intelligent government officials can probably score high in picking the most efficient of the largest firms of the moment. They are unlikely even to know about the smaller ones which could come up fast if given an equal chance, and decidedly unlikely to know the key sources of possible radical change in the future. A policy which focuses on the firms which grew to be the largest in the past is backward looking.

The way out of this impasse is not difficult to specify, if not easy to follow. Open domestic and international competition without selective favors to large or small, with entry encouraged and financing conditions made reasonably equivalent for firms of all sizes, with growth through the market encouraged and growth through mergers of rivals discouraged, could both reduce the inefficient fringe and keep the channels open for progress.

2. Competition

According to André Marchal, competition is "a sport much in honor in the United States . . . *une mystique plus qu'un politique.*" None of this for us adults, who must conquer "the forces of destruction dialectically contained in the principle of free competition" [58, p. vii].

M. Marchal's unequivocal position serves as a warning preface to a recent book by Houssiaux which constitutes a case in favor of legal rules to enforce competition within the Common Market. There is no "French" position on the subject. It would still be fair to say that M. Marchal's view would command the majority vote in government, industry, and the faculties of the universities. Competition is definitely not "*fort en honneur*" in France.

If one were to make the classic suggestion that the disapproval relates to a technique that has never really been tried, the answer might well be that the manufacturing sector was largely left to private competition before the war and that it did not work brilliantly. And, underneath polite ambiguities, one might detect a further point of special interest: in the postwar period, the American economy has relied on competition in manufacturing while the French have not, and much the greater progress has been on their side.

The belief that the French relied on competition in the manufacturing sector before the war, and found the results poor, is correct on two counts and wrong on one. They did not have the benefit of any positive directing force other than competition, and the results of whatever they did have were not very good. But what they had was at best a most dismal caricature of competitive behavior.

Government intervention before the war was common, but it was conceived in the spirit of protecting existing business rather than fostering change. The same spirit of preservation was the rule within private industry. This was not because public regulation blocked any fierce desire for independence on the part of firms. Roland Tavitian is surely correct in emphasizing that the consensus of the society was against the risks of change: both government and business, notwithstanding internal differences, were dominated by preconceptions inimical to progress [48].

It has been suggested that, before the war, "competition was more widespread in France than either in Germany or the United States" [54, p. 21]. The sense in which this might be defended is purely structural. Concentration apparently was unusually low. As Houssiaux notes, this means that performance could have been strongly competitive, not that it actually was so [59, pp. 184–208]. The specific impediments included widespread collusive agreements and government action promoting cooperation. The more general difficulty was an inertia born of weak aggregative progress and a desire to minimize risks of retaliation.

If active competition be taken to refer to independent efforts of firms to increase their individual markets, this may often be a factor leading to increasing concentration, as it has in the French automobile industry since the war. If collusion includes the form of cartel cooperation in which all producers are kept alive, with the more efficient accepting above-average returns but forgoing possible growth, this may be a factor keeping concentration low. A low degree of concentration has no unique meaning. In the French case, it was a sign of caution and collusion, not of independent behavior. The policy that was tried and failed before the war was quite simply private control of markets without active competition.

For inactive private markets, postwar French policy substituted a positive apparatus of planning, price control, selective promotion and protection. These techniques have embodied generous doses of internal confusion, but they have been consistent with outstanding performance. French manufacturing made greater progress relative to American in the 1950's, when the former was subject to widespread governmental interferences, than it made in any prior period. This might be taken only as a belated catching up: they were so far behind that failure to gain would have been the more surprising result. But others even further behind did not gain in this period, and the French themselves had not previously been catching up. They did so only when new techniques of government intervention were adopted to help.

The prewar failures of French industry were not attributable to competitive forces but to the lack of them, compounded by poor aggregative choices. The postwar successes have not been caused by stepping on competition, but by its revival in automobiles and probably a number of other consumer goods industries, the development of effective substitutes for its absence in some of the concentrated industries, and the stimulus of excellent demand conditions. The failures on the American side in some of these industries, notably automobiles and steel, are hardly to be attributed to excessively independent behavior of the firms involved. Where industries directly compared do seem to have been reasonably competitive on the American side in the 1950's, as in textiles and nonelectrical machinery, their performances were decidedly good compared to the French industries, despite the handicap of weaker aggregative demand.

The effectiveness of much of the intervention practiced in

France came from the fact that it was used by government agencies oriented toward expansion to provide fairly good substitutes for competitive forces which were not present and could not readily be created. Where market control exists, the next best thing to eliminating it is to bring the public interest to bear in industry decisions. In France, as in England [131] [135], government supervision of the steel industry has resulted in mistakes as well as helpful choices. The net results do not suggest that the French would have done better to stick to the American rules of sideline criticism.

The role of the 1953 legislation against collusion was not great. The competition that did occur was a result of choice by a few producers in the early postwar years, and by more and more of them as such initiative proved to pay off in a climate of expansion. Prewar aggregative stagnation encouraged cooperative caution; postwar expansion began to shift the rewards to the more courageous. Whatever the institutional framework, rapid expansion is conducive to more independent behavior [63, p. 67].

Although the domestic antitrust rules did not have much to do with the aggregative performance, they should not be dismissed as insignificant. In a few cases, particularly unhelpful collusive practices were condemned [20]. By the attack against retail price maintenance, the way was opened to the possibility of vertical pressure from large buyers on producers. It is difficult to tell as yet the practical significance of this change as far as producers are concerned, but it has been followed by a reduction in the number of retail outlets and a shift toward mass distributors using lower retail prices.

Further, the existence of a legal basis for attacking collusion provides a crucial link between the Jeanneney-Barre school of promotional government economists and those who would place greater stress on development of competition. According to Barre, "If observation reveals that the growth of modern economies results in large part from the activity of large firms and the exercise of their economic power, it shows equally that the stagnation or scelerosis of certain economies can be imputed to the exercise of monopolistic practices by groups of firms or ententes, who safeguard inefficiency and ineptitude" [53, p. 914]. If French policy were broadened to include a sustained effort to prevent collusion in those industries in which direct promotional efforts have worked poorly, instead of being confined to further elaboration of controls, the rate of progress in the 1960's could conceivably prove more consistent and in the aggregate more brilliant than during the last decade.

The conflict of the 1960's may center on the efforts to maintain government sponsored group cooperation in a situation in which it is less likely to be helpful. Both the public agencies and a majority of producers apparently prefer coordinated promotion. But if the economy retains its vigor, opening continuous new opportunities, and if trade becomes relatively free, some firms are going to want to move more independently. Rapid progress in a more open economy, a possibility just beginning to be tested, is at once easier in the sense that pressure from imports speeds change in efficient directions, and more difficult in the sense that balanced group expansion is continuously threatened with the upsetting force of superior outside achievement in particular lines. Import competition is a powerful ally in a decentralized economy capable of rapid supply adjustment. It is probably not consistent with both a high growth rate and the degree of coordinated group decision practiced in France in the 1950's.

PART IV | Empirical Results and Economic Theory

15 Market Organization and Comparative Advantage

The effectiveness of government and business choices discussed in preceding chapters has frequently been tested in terms of export performance. The test involves a trap, which French policy has not wholly avoided. If those fields unable to develop net exports are given special help to make them succeed by this criterion, the effort may reduce the availability of resources and raise costs for the more successful. Conversely, if the successful export industries are given special tax and subsidy privileges as rewards, the result may be further increases in their exports but overly compensating restrictions on other industries.

If these dangers be realized, it does not follow that the optimal solution would be ensured by simply establishing an equilibrium exchange rate and allowing market forces to operate. It is readily possible, and an important aspect of French performance, that intervention improving organization in particular markets may yield a pattern of specialization superior to that which would arise in the absence of the intervention. The superiority intended in this context is that the alternative trade pattern created by direct action may yield higher incomes to both the nation itself and to the outside world. But the position raises a familiar general question. If a country's basic factor resources, in conjunction with those of its trading partners, do determine an optimal trading pattern, then how can market intervention have any justification other than that of aiding realization of this pattern? To turn the question around, can characteristics of market organization enter significantly in determining the best trading pattern?

1. The Idea of an Optimal Trading Pattern

The idea that there is an optimal trading pattern given for each country by the proportions of its resources and the preferences of consumers owes its strength to Bertil Ohlin's brilliant but misleading extension of the idea of comparative advantage [76]. He gave the simple point of desirable specialization a new depth by providing an explanatory framework rooted in the solidly familiar terminology of land, labor, and capital. He assumed a competitive world with fully employed resources, leaving room for a great deal of action to secure these conditions but leaving no important place for choice on the supply side to shape the trading pattern that would be determined if these conditions were established.

In the most general terms, the argument provided an immediately appealing way to organize observable facts. Countries with extensive land and high population density, but with little capital, do in general focus on primary production. The Belgians, on the contrary, emphasize manufacturing, and so on. The irrationality of trying to produce wine in Scotland or coffee in Massachusetts can always be cited to demonstrate applicability of the point to specific problems. But the whole discussion breaks down when thoroughly examined either empirically or logically. When Wasily Leontief applied it to the factor proportions involved in the United States trading pattern he had to try to save Ohlin's principle by counting the American worker as equal to three foreign workers, which makes nonsense of the point that trade is determined by concrete, measurable factors [79, p. 174]. When Paul Samuelson carried the assumptions out to their ultimate implications for real factor earnings, in the unswerving Samuelson style, they were so much at variance with historical information that he rightly turned against the foundations of the analysis. The general idea can always be saved if one is wedded to form rather than significance, but only by descending to propositions of the safe but unexciting level of "the tropics grow tropical fruits because of the relative abundance of tropical conditions" [80, p. 182].

If the proposition is changed to read that a country with abundant tropical conditions should not introduce a shoe factory because of that fact, the theory backs off. If the country does not introduce the shoe factory, this can be explained in terms of the natural resource factor. If it goes ahead and introduces a wide range of industries, exporting manufactured products and eating its own bananas, this becomes explicable in terms of the availability of capital generated in the successful process of industrialization. Whether or not attempts at industrialization will work cannot be deduced from the initial availabilities of measurable factors of production. What success depends on is the ability of the people involved to organize their efforts and to channel increases of income into useful investment.

The idea of international specialization has itself come under unwarranted attack because it has been too closely identified with the subsidiary explanation of comparative costs in terms of factor proportions. If one wishes to rescue the idea of comparative advantage, the main requirement is that the dynamism of human choice be brought into the picture and given greater attention than countable land, labor and capital. "Effective knowledge ('know-how') is probably as important a variable in understanding economic history and geography as is specific factor endowment. . . . Factor proportions explain only part of the facts of international economics. We must still set up hypotheses of differences in international production and productivity, differences in effectiveness which are to be accepted as empirical facts even if not simply explainable" [80, pp. 181–83].

The potent thrust of the French automobile industry is not simply explainable, but it can to a considerable extent be understood in terms of a change in market organization leading to more independent competitive behavior and more imaginative entrepreneurial choice. Similarly, the export success of the steel industry in the 1950's would not have been possible without access to coal and iron ore, but it would have been a good deal weaker than it was if these factors had not been brought more effectively into use by government pressure toward reorganization and modernization of the industry during the first postwar plan. The complex of pressures generated by competition and direct intervention may be a vital factor in determining changes in relative efficiency and thereby in the optimal trading patterns.

Fredrick Harbison, following the line of direct empirical study of enterprise efficiency in different countries, came to much the same conclusion. "Organization may be looked upon as a resource, and in significant though not all respects it is similar to other resources such as labor, capital and natural resources. . . . Organization is the principal factor determining the productivity of labor, assuming capital and natural resources to be constant" [56, pp. 378–79]. As he uses the term, organization refers to that within the firm. But that is in turn a function of the external opportunities and pressures surrounding the firm as well as the personal abilities of the management within it. By forcing family-owned steel firms into consolidated corporations, stipulating desirable investment programs, and presenting the firms with financial help, the French Planning Commission set up new conditions favorable to more effective managerial choice within the companies. By turning around shortly thereafter and forcing them to cope with competition from foreign producers, the government then stepped up the pressures requiring more efficient choices. In a contrary display of misplaced encouragement, the government kept pressure for possible reorganization away from the industrial equipment industries until 1958, then changed the signals and quickly altered choices within the firms.

External policy variations might not have much impact if the internal organization of firms automatically moved toward maximum conceivable efficiency, but any assumption that it invariably does so would be most unreal. As Harbison further points out, with special reference to French entrepreneurs but without confining the evidence or the point to them, "Because of noneconomic factors which determine in part the behavior of human beings as managerial resources, all organizations are probably 'inefficient' in effecting the optimum combination of economic resources which is theoretically possible" [56, p. 379]. Changes in market organization altering the pressures for efficiency within the firm can shape internal decisions, and the latter in turn can greatly affect the relative efficiency of industries. Comparative advantage is a result of such measures at least as much as it is a result of objectively countable factor proportions.

The preceding point may be distorted into a proposition leading back around to the fallacies of balanced growth [81]. If comparative advantage can be altered in the short run by human choices, why should it be undesirable for the French Government to encourage domestic production of all the industrial goods that continue to be imported? The answer to this may be in small measure that of Ohlin: absence or extraordinarily high costs of production for specific raw materials, if in addition they are costly to transport from other producing areas, may make some products intolerably expensive, even with the best managerial organization in the world. It would be wrong to dismiss resource endowments as irrelevant in manufacturing industries: wrong for a society because raw material inputs do constitute a significant share of total costs in many industries, and wrong for an economist because it would bring down the rightful wrath of William Parker on his head [72, pp. 187–90]. But recognition of the importance of raw material costs in many lines of manufacturing does not take one very far either in predicting the desirability of investment in the French automobile industry *versus* investment in chemicals or machinery, or in explaining contrasting degrees of export success after the event. Something else is more important. On the surface, it is the level of managerial effectiveness in organizing production and initiating desirable changes in products. Beneath this, it is the set of inducements and pressures brought to bear on enterprise decision, a set going beyond existing input costs and product prices to include all the elements of market structure which are short-circuited by traditional trade theory.

Relative costs differ among trading countries, partly because resource availabilities differ but also because approaches to market organization by both governments and businessmen differ among societies. Recognition of the fact that changes in market organization can change the pattern of comparative advantage does not yield a conclusion that relative costs are irrelevant to the selection of industries, or that specialization can be neglected as a guide to policy. It simply opens the possibility of applying principles of explanation in an area where they now break down.

2. Market Organization and International Specialization

What is right about the principle of specialization is that concentration of resources in directions of their greatest value will raise current income and facilitate growth, and maintaining them in weaker sectors will hold back the whole society. It is probably true that any reasonably capable French producer of machine tools can make any kind of machine in the world, to any quality specified. But if the firm makes too few of them, or its management is occupied with too many lines of production at once, or if the installations required for low unit costs require more external finance than the firm wishes to cope with, or if ten thousand other common possibilities enter the picture, the cost of production relative to the costs of compact automobiles will be higher than in Germany. Every such supply impediment can be met by domestic production at a cost, but the cost is the double one of restricting the expansion of fields which have been more successful in achieving high organizational efficiency and shielding the poorly organized from the pressures that could force their improvement.

Specialization emerges naturally from inequalities of both resource endowments and organizational capacities. The traditional argument against blocking its evolution in the interests of protection for high-cost industries is not in question. But if the determinants of relative strength and weakness are less the solid facts of resource availabilities and more the nature of the pressures brought to bear on organizational efficiency, as is probably the case in manufacturing, the best choice is surely not that of allowing the weaker industries to disintegrate. Positive measures to force improvements may change the optimal allocation of resources by bringing to life some of the areas of apparent comparative disadvantage. What counts is the way changes are attempted: by protection ensuring inaction, or by promotion of competition where it may operate and direct reorganization where predictable economies are not being secured by market forces. Comparative advantage at any moment is a statement of relative successes and failures achieved, not a definition of the proper allocation of resources in the future.

Widening of analytical effort to include factors of market organization does not mean rejection of the possibility of systematic explanation of trade patterns. It simply means that a more difficult empirical task must be substituted for a falsely simple one. In the small sample of cases discussed in detail in

Part II above, the systems of domestic promotion and control provided a reasonably good basis for prediction of comparative export performance.

In the cases of aluminum and steel, relatively homogeneous end products, stability of technology, difficulties of entry, and high market concentration made the prospect of competitive pressure weak in both France and the United States. The French did something about this and American policy did not. Both price control and the reduction of import barriers in the Coal-Steel Community provided elements of social control lacking in the American steel industry. Action appropriate to deficiences in market organization on the French side would not have created improving export performance if required resources had not been available, but it helped prevent the behavior which undermined the previously strong American export position in steel. Much the same considerations applied to the aluminum industry until almost the end of the decade. But American policy allowed competition to operate when it did appear from abroad, and also helped reduce entry difficulties, leading to the creation of considerably improved market pressures at the beginning of the 1960's. Unless present choices are altered in these respects, the contrasts in market organization would lead to a prediction that, given resource and technological factors similar to the 1950's, the export performance of the American industry should improve relative to that of the French: that "comparative advantage" can again be altered by market policy.

At the opposite pole, the machinery and equipment producers of both countries operated with diversified and changing end products, relatively small-scale, and fairly good entry conditions. But the French combined extreme import protection with domestic techniques of group cooperation inimical to independent competition, while American policy intervened only to attack restraints. The structural factors in market organization were not radically different, but the policy rules differed and so did the export performances. The United States machinery producers lost ground relative to some other foreign producers, perhaps in part because they were handicapped by exorbitantly rising steel costs; but they avoided the decided comparative disadvantage exhibited by the French producers. And the latter began to turn rapidly in a more favorable direction almost immediately after the change in French policy at the end of 1958 toward lessened trade barriers, a change accompanied by substitution of the generalized stimulus of currency devaluation for that of selective export promotion.

The automobile case seems to provide a discordant note. This was a highly capital-intensive and concentrated industry, with difficult entry conditions and with much greater import barriers on the French side, but the French industry unquestionably outperformed the American in export markets during the 1950's. The most notable difference in performance was that the American producers exhibited little independence of each other and surprising ability to ignore collectively an important market opening, while the French producers created the right new products and acted quickly to take advantage of sluggish response by the American firms. The spark that made the French industry more lively was similar to new entry: a radical change in management leading to a drive toward industry leadership by Renault. Whether great or little emphasis should be given to the fact that the leadership was provided by government enterprise in the French industry, the relevant fact here is that one set of producers behaved with a high degree of cooperation and the industry lost its comparative advantage, while the other acted competitively and created one.

The strength of the French essays in intervention, in so far as they affected trade, was their ability to improve organization and efficiency in particular industries and to maintain, or create, export fields that might otherwise have been lost to foreign competition. The useful steps did not simply reveal the pattern of comparative advantage implicit in the nation's resources. They developed a different set of relative advantages, with a higher value of output per capita.

The weaknesses of the promotional measures attempted were that they included excessive protection for the more backward fields and some distortion of incentives through selective subsidies. The protective measures reduced possible pressures for improvement in the weaker fields and at the same time slowed down the more efficient. The extensive reliance on direct promotion prior to 1959 surely did help awaken producer interest in real possibilities beyond their traditional horizons, but the system lent itself to a biased concentration of advantages and actual exports. In 1959, 151 firms accounted for more than half of all French exports [171]. This situation may have been due in some measure to the ability of the larger firms to maintain good contacts with administrative agencies, even if it was basically a consequence of genuine strength in particularly concentrated fields. The result of shifting to a more accurately valued currency was to reveal possibilities of multiple-pronged export development previously untouched by the process of direct promotion. This did not mean a decrease in the degree of useful specialization: it meant a shift from export trade biased toward a few firms to a more general development of all real advantages.

A special aspect of French promotional schemes which did prove highly useful was the system of direct aids for reconversion of productive facilities. This assistance is not limited to cases of dislocation due to import competition, but may be especially helpful in this context. In the post-1958 change toward greater trade, scheduled reductions in import barriers were announced along with a program to aid firms in converting to new techniques or to entirely new fields. This has both a psychological benefit in promoting general acceptance of the program of greater trade freedom, and a direct benefit in economic efficiency in so far as it reduces the costs of change by facilitating rapid shifts of productive factors in useful directions.

It is all too true that a small number of empirical observations, every one subject to considerable debate on its explanation, does not add up to a theory. But the French experiences, and especially their contrasts with those of the United States, do suggest a case for shifting the focus of the theory of international trade. If trade theory is to be useful, it cannot dodge consideration of the complex factors which determine organizational efficiency in particular domestic markets. If factors of market organization are taken more explicitly into account, it might be possible to systematize more effectively the loose collection of clues now available. But even if the market organization side of the problem is simply given its rightful place in analysis of trade, it will be seen that the clues can be of some help. It was neither accidental nor a necessary consequence of resource availabilities that American steel and automobile exports behaved poorly in the 1950's, or that the French had a seemingly chronic disadvantage in machinery and equipment. Remedies were conceivable in all these instances, and were to be sought in the system of incentives and constraints acting on enterprise decisions. It is possible to go beyond the observation of facts to important elements of explanation, and thereby to guidance of policy concerned with both export earnings and economic efficiency. But this may be done only by recognizing that analysis of resource availabilities and the organization of markets are inseparable aspects of the same question.

16 Competition, Controls, and the Supply Ceiling on Growth

What counts in determining the possibilities of economic expansion is the ability of the productive forces of a country to respond to changing opportunities by altering the ways in which resources are used, and on the positive power to develop new capital facilities, techniques, and products.* These adaptive and initiative powers have been significantly raised in the industrial sector of the French economy during the postwar period. The question is how.

An explanation of what did happen must be a compromise with reality: millions of things happened. They do not add up to any one-dimension statement of cause and effect. An explanation relying on a single key, such as the introduction of planning, the strength of aggregate demand, a rebirth of courage, or a spurt of technological progress, is likely to be, even if it embodies an important part of the truth, too gross a distortion of reality to be a useful guide in the formulation of further decisions. What is needed is a refined distortion, recognizing multiple levels of causation but focusing on the factors relevant to future choice.

The area of choice considered here is that in which govern-

* This thesis might be said to be the organizing principle of C. P. Kindleberger's study of the process of economic development [71, ch. 7], as of Jean Monnet's explanation of the objectives of the first French plan [2, preface].

ment and business act to determine, in conjunction with relatively fixed structural factors, the organization of particular markets. This is only one aspect of the system of forces affecting economic growth. But it is a crucial part of the operational connection between the fundamental set of conditions inherent in the nature of the society and the day-to-day choices which collectively constitute the achievement of the economy. If markets are organized toward stability, toward protection rather than change, the economy may make some progress, but even the best of external conditions will still yield disappointing results. If markets are organized to promote change and growth, with acceptance of the consequence that firms unable to accomplish change will have to yield their control over the country's factors of production, supply choices are almost certain to take quick advantage of all opportunities and to create new openings in the process.

1. The Supply Ceiling

The explanatory approach used here takes the level of enterprise efficiency, and the relative valuations of expansion and risk by managements, as variables determined in large measure by the organization of markets. In a sense, it is a circle. A group of firms following accustomed techniques even after new possibilities become technologically feasible determine, by their failure to change, the existing market organization. An outside force, be it new entry, new management in one of the existing firms, import competition, or direct promotion of change by government, may in such conditions alter the pressures and cause enterprise choices to change in directions favorable for more rapid aggregate progress. The "outside forces" themselves become essential aspects of the new market organization. In the postwar French economy, the government independently created such forces in several important cases. These direct changes, accompanied by erratic steps toward more effective use of the pressure of import competition, helped improve entrepreneurial actions. The combination of stimulus and improved reaction raised both efficiency in resource use and the demand for investment to allow expansion and modernization. The process increased the rate of growth of the supply ceiling of French industry and raised the rate of growth of demand to utilize emerging capacity.

The concept of a supply ceiling on which microeconomic choices may work to facilitate growth is meant to refer to the type of production limit often described as "full employment." The departure from familiar terminology is meant to emphasize that productive capacity normally is in the process of increasing, even if there is full employment and no growth in the labor force itself, and that the rate at which it does increase is a variable affected by the quality of supply decisions. But the notion is at best ambiguous, because supply restraints may take a variety of forms.

Specific restraints almost invariably come into play before an economy is fully utilizing all its productive capacity, either in the form of particular production or resource bottlenecks, increases in the level of prices beyond those the society is willing to accept, or balance of payments deficits beyond those that can be financed. Much of the trick of improving growth must lie in the success of measures used to adapt the structure of production in ways that will minimize the waste of underutilized resources at the point of necessary restraint on demand. Some of the measures the French used did help promote such an improved adaptation, and some did not.

In the immediate postwar years, the economy was ridden with specific bottlenecks, restraining total production even when capacity was available in many areas. Progress then depended on conceptually simple, if operationally difficult, elimination of specific restraints. The change that constituted the end of the reconstruction period was itself a process of supply adaptation, in which the structure of production altered to reduce the degree of capacity remaining when bottlenecks were encountered. The economy would have accomplished such an adaptation without any government intervention at all. But the result might well have had different characteristics. Private decisions taken in the fields outside the planning process moved in the direction of restoring the prewar productive system geared to earlier patterns of mediocre progress. The changes introduced by the first stage of directive planning did alter the organization of basic industries in directions consistent with more rapid growth.

The Planning Commission never proved that the resources it pre-empted during the first plan were put to uses yielding higher rates of return than conceivable alternative investment. It would be a defensible guess that the actual alternative to their program would have been a greater diversion of resources to consumption, to more of the commercial and service facilities springing up in the wake of seemingly unlimited consumer demand, and to a massive reduplication of unduly dispersed and insufficiently specialized industrial facilities geared to protected domestic markets. The procedure of the majority of the industries outside the scope of the first plan was to multiply firms and continue diversified production techniques. That of the industries within the plan was, against much protest in the case of steel, to consolidate facilities, close out older plant, specialize within plants for lower costs, and invest in new facilities taking advantage of the most modern production techniques even when their scale implied the necessity of reliance on export markets.

Direct reorganization in the first plan secured genuine improvements in several basic fields, greatly facilitating growth in the 1950's. The reason that significant gains were possible by such methods was that the preceding organization of some industries had fallen far short of recognizable possibilities. The reasons that this situation had arisen in so many fields have been amply developed in studies of the prewar economy. The main factors were the inadequacy of demand growth, traceable to poor choices of exchange rates and domestic fiscal policies, and structural rigidity in a wide variety of fields associated with absence of competitive pressure and generalized emphasis on protection. Weak demand growth discouraged entrepreneurial initiative, promoted efforts to secure stability, congealed existing methods, and thereby ensured that periods of improving monetary demand would be handicapped by sluggish supply response. The direct attack on this system helped obtain the gains that a livelier competitive system, aided by better demand conditions, would have provided long before. This phase of planning and improvement of efficiency provided a once-for-all (or at any rate a once-for-this-time), discontinuous gain. It did not constitute the core of the growth process of the 1950's. It is not at present relevant to the problems of the United States, where entrepreneurial flexibility has probably remained higher than the level the French planners had to cope with.

The first plan left the great majority of the country's industries relatively untouched. The Planning Commission continued to provide promotional advice, with subsidies and investment financing acting to alter incentives, and did thereby provide marginal assistance with the growth process. Perhaps the more important side of its activity became that of the promotion of a high rate of capital formation. The Commission ceased to play any great role in determining industry organization, and a growing share of total investment came to be financed out of business profits for privately selected objectives. This transition to self-financing would have been slower if the Commission and allied agencies had not pushed vigorously, in a style quite contrary to that of the economic agencies of government in England and the United States during the 1950's, for government expenditure policies favorable for expansion. It could have been stopped cold if investment outside the planning objectives, or that carrying industries beyond specified goals, had been impeded in the interest of balanced plans. The government promoted expenditure, keeping capacity in use and ensuring high returns to all intelligently directed investment, while doing nothing to block independent choices. The consequence was a gradual strengthening of private investment decisions, generalizing technological improvements with lessening reliance on government help.

It is clearly conceivable that a still higher growth rate might have been obtained during the 1950's either by raising investment relative to consumption, or by better techniques of promotion. A relative increase in savings and investment might have been attempted by shifting taxes from business toward consumers, relaxing price controls, exercising greater restraint on wage increases, or any other of a wide variety of techniques for raising business profits relative to other forms of income. Many specific policy conflicts of the 1950's may be viewed as aspects of a continuing struggle between the proponents of measures to raise business incomes as a means of raising savings and investment more rapidly, and opponents more interested in favoring current consumption. The fact that government decisions were not always consistent is not surprising. They were the product of conflict between a real desire on the part of executives in both government and business to curtail consumption, in order to facilitate growth, and an opposite desire on the part of the majority of the population to raise current living standards.

Apart from cyclical swings, in which business incomes both rise and fall faster than those of the community as a whole, a democratic society tends to resist systematic attempts to shift a greater share of national income to business enterprise. The resistance is understandable. Most people want the economic system to yield them rising welfare, not simply as an ultimate promise but as a continuing fact. If the majority of the people can bring their wishes to bear on government decisions, it is exceedingly difficult to raise the savings ratio. And the effort to do so may well not be worth while, if the established ratio is itself sufficient to permit steadily rising income per capita. At any rate, it has been clear in France that the efforts to do so have helped maintain an extraordinarily high degree of social strain, and have tempted recourse to methods of blocking the political expression of majority preferences. It may be a good deal easier to retain democratic institutions under a system using direct intervention and promotional techniques to encourage improvements in efficiency than under one relying on indirect control methods coupled with persistent effort to raise the share of national income going to business.

The techniques of intervention used subsequent to the first plan included several methods, each with potentially separable positive and negative aspects. The implicit compact between the promotional agencies and business, that profitable favors would be available for the easily accepted target of continuing expansion under protected conditions, did work reasonably well in the more concentrated industries. It worked for the same reason that the industries were concentrated in the first place. The choices of a few firms determined market results because of real advantages in large-scale production of relatively standardized products. The cooperation of a few managements was sufficient to make advance probable, because they either constituted the field themselves or were able through better methods to move rapidly ahead of noncooperating firms. The role of import protection in this process is not clear. The aluminum producers did choose to expand and did it well, but always insisted that they would not have been able to do so if they had been exposed to the possible disruption of low-price external competition. The traditional argument that they would have done even better if forced to meet foreign competition does not seem overwhelming in this case, where their prices were brought down below those in external markets. On the other hand, the impetus to substantial completion of the reorganization program in the steel industry came from the decision to allow import competition in the Coal-Steel Community. The expansionary pact here did not rely on continuing protection: it took on new life when the protection was significantly reduced.

There were cooperative firms and trade associations in the dispersed industries too, willing to take part in programs of modernization, specialization, and export promotion. But it proved practically impossible to exercise direct pressure on enough firms, and selective cooperation yielded only slow progress because of the same structural factors that inhibited concentration in the first place. The variety of products needed to suit either consumer preferences or the diverse equipment needs of industry, and the necessity of continuous product change, were not consistent with efficient production on a large scale. Concentration and scale offered some gains for particular products, but these eternal objectives of the planning approach were not particularly relevant to the basic problem. What these industries needed was generalized pressure to increase specialization and intensify their search for better methods. What they got under the promotional system was selective assistance for particular firms, through methods that emphasized group consultation and protection and weakened in the process the possibilities of competitive pressure. When they got something else, after 1958, their improvement was prompt and striking.

The switch toward international competition after 1958, through devaluation and negotiation of lower import barriers, had a potent effect on market organization in exactly those fields left relatively untouched by direct promotion. It decreased the chances of survival for firms operating with unnecessarily high costs due to neglected opportunities for specialization, and increased the profitability of changes permitting entry into export competition. By altering the incentives of producers, it changed the techniques of production and redirected investment decisions in ways further reducing supply restraints on growth.

French microeconomic policy erred during the 1950's, and restrained the otherwise powerful forces acting for growth, by a stubbornly misdirected reliance on universal application of the selective techniques which worked well in concentrated industrial structures. Their mistake was an alternative version of the error committed by American policy, which relied on competition, both where it did and where it did not vigorously operate. Both countries have their proponents of an appealingly simple solution: remake the industries which do not respond properly to preferred policies into the image of those that do. In France, this took the form of frequent suggestions for the creation of a concentrated machinery industry, via such routes as nationalization or directed favors to the largest firms, as if this would set up the same conditions for efficiency as in the steel industry. The proposals have their exact counterpart in American suggestions that the steel or automobile industries be split up into smaller segments to make them more amenable to an antitrust approach. In both cases, there may very well be possibilities of gain from careful steps in the directions indicated, but it remains ultimately true that real technological possibilities preclude pushing either French diversified industries into the shape of General Motors, or of reducing concentration in all American industries to levels that would make reliance on competition completely effective.

Many of the gains that followed direct measures of promotion and control in France would have been brought about by competitive markets without such intervention, had they existed. Price regulation in particular would cause nothing but trouble in a thoroughly competitive economy. But this does not mean that all the results of direct intervention were merely "second best" approximations to the consequences of competition. The provision of incentives to plan expansion on scales aimed at export possibilities as well as in the domestic market, support for industry research programs or experimental plants, subsidy of experiment with new construction techniques, aid for reconversion of firms unable to compete with imports in older fields, and provision of information coupled with pressure for change through the planning process, acted to widen the horizon of producers and reduce the costs of change.

Absence of restraints on competition is not enough. Schumpeter did have an important half-truth. Competition makes certain that the best known techniques used by any firm will be used by all. It does not ensure that all the possibilities of improvement which may be generated by independent search will be sought or adopted by anybody. It does not ensure that resources will move rapidly in a society which has come to accept a low level of flexibility and consequent absence of rapid growth. The French Government has been attempting, awkwardly and sometimes downright badly, a little of the key process of stimulation in new directions that Schumpeter considered to be the province of great entrepreneurs.

The right side of the half-truth is that whole industries may miss opportunities, and the generation of new ones may come out of efforts which have little to do with competitive forces. The wrong side is the belief that competition is inimical to discontinuous steps forward, or that large firms with monopolistic positions provide the best hope for innovation. Competition does not guarantee innovation, but it almost certainly favors it because it undermines those who do not look for change. French experience as well as American provides good examples of the proposition that large organizations, far from being the dominant source of really new methods, have a demonstrable tendency to develop hardening of the arteries with respect to radical change. They all have to fight, some successfully and many not, a tendency to freeze in the familiar.

2. Effects of Supply Choices on Aggregate Demand

The difference in growth rates between France and the United States in the 1950's seems on the surface to be explicable without reference to such microeconomic problems, because of the crucial fact that demand usually pressed on the supply ceiling in France and did not do so in the United States. But this difference on the demand side was in part a product of decisions and actions on the supply side. If the American economy had been capable of raising production more rapidly without price and balance of payments difficulties, then aggregate demand would not have been restrained at levels so far short of the country's productive limits. If French industries had been less successful in achieving improvements in productive efficiency, the level of demand would have been weaker there. Direct promotion and controls may not only raise the supply ceiling itself, they may add something important to the ability of an economy to utilize its capacities fully.

On the American side, the primary reason for the restraint of demand in the late 1950's was the experience of rising prices and the conviction of the government that it was better to sacrifice expansion in the interest of greater price stability. A highly significant share of the problem arose from price and wage behavior in the steel industry [134], and the aluminum industry performed in much the same way. These two industries did not create the same problems on the French side, not because of any absence of union organization or greater competition among firms, but because their prices were regulated. They had to rely more completely on raising volume and productive efficiency as means of raising profits. This regulation was unhelpful in periods of excess demand, but did help avoid arbitrary increases at the root of all the metals using industries in periods of adequate productive capacity—a constant feature of the situation in the United States from 1955 to 1960.

The directed reorganization and subsequent supervision of the steel industry in France helped promote an extraordinarily rapid rate of advance in the industry's efficiency, and important gains in its export performance. Similarly, the newly nationalized firm in the automobile industry adopted the expansionary policies which led to rapid development of the whole industry's production and exports. Their modernization programs, as those of other basic industries, both improved the structure of supply and provided a good deal of the investment expenditure that kept the level of aggregate demand high. Perhaps more importantly, their exports provided both monetary demand and the foreign exchange earnings which permitted the rising imports necessary for rapid growth.

It was not demand pressure that reorganized the steel industry and brought its costs down compared to those of competing countries. It was not domestic demand, nor any growth in the American market evident to the American automobile producers, which led Renault, as it had Volkswagen, to develop dramatically rising exports to the United States in the last half of the 1950's. The initiating force came from the supply side, and the effects on demand were potent. From 1954 to 1959, the rise in exports of French manufactured goods was approximately equivalent to one sixth of the increase in domestic production. For steel and automobiles, the growth of exports equalled two fifths of the rise in their output, in a period in which exports of these American industries both fell in absolute value. Effective supply decisions provided both a high rate of technological improvement and a high level of monetary demand, but the latter was less an independent explanatory factor than a summarized consequence.

3. Relationships Between Policies and Results

Choices of promotion and protection were by no means irrelevant to the actual improvement of business efficiency, but neither were they uniformly helpful nor dominant in the result. They did not constitute the basic motor force of the expansion during the 1950's. They simply aided in shaping its evolution.

Looking back on the performance of the 1950's, it is so easy to find favorable factors operating to help the French expansion that it becomes tempting to ascribe all the results to them. Kindleberger now emphasizes, complementing his observation of 1955 that France is one of the countries "in which economic adaptability has begun to slow down," that national attitudes changed so strongly in favor of expansion during the second world war as to make the postwar growth practically inevitable [38] [39] [73, p. 253]. And apart from this change of community preferences, which does seem evident now that the economic consequences are visible, the postwar economy benefited from some highly favorable special conditions. These included American financial and technical assistance in the early years, excellent demand for possible exports throughout the 1950's as neighboring countries continued rapid expansions of their own, the existence of possible gains in some industries merely through the decision to take advantage of known but unexploited techniques, willingness of workers to put marginal earnings above any temptation to bring the length of the work week below 45 hours, and the new scope for change introduced by the wartime disruption itself.

The society was willing to accept some departure from established methods, and this created a golden opportunity for experiment. As in the United States in 1933, the situation facilitated a mutation of policies. And just as in the United States earlier, it quickly proved clear that such mutations can be either good or bad. The will to improve is hardly enough: best also that people know how to go about it. The direct promotional methods did give a good push at first, but then began to mix in mistakes to a degree that makes it most doubtful if the net result in the 1950's was to provide more than marginal assistance.

Once the reconstruction was achieved, the real driving force became something else. It was the release of the dynamic component always present in the desire of people to qualify themselves for better jobs and higher wages, of engineers and scientists to find better solutions to technical restraints, of investors to earn higher returns, and of managements to raise business profits. Pierre Uri stated it clearly in 1954. The problem then, as now, is "less one of stimulation than one of an effort to eliminate, progressively but systematically, all the artificial obstacles opposed to the natural force of economic growth" [22, p. 194].

Natural forces of growth are inherent in any economic system which makes it possible for individuals to choose freely their own occupations and business organizations their own methods of seeking income. But the pressure may not generate great results if the balance between the desire for improvement and the desire for protection against disruption by forces of change is tilted too strongly in the latter direction. The balance results from eternally opposing forces, both of them variable in strength. An economy may fail to move because there is very little initiative forthcoming, as may well be the case in one which has not known successful expansion, or in one which confines opportunities to a small fraction of the population. Or it may fail to move despite the presence of initiating forces, if the obstacles placed in the way are sufficiently serious.

In the interwar period, French governments sided with the forces of conservation against change, impeding an initially low level of private initiative, whether the particular governments were conservative in conventional political terminology or whether they were not. The basis of the transformation in postwar France was that important agencies of government, as distinct from that mythical entity, "the government," reversed alliances. They reached into the economy to side with particular business forces favorable to progress. In the first years they provided direct initiative through new managements in some of the previously weak or particularly crucial basic industries. They stimulated private initiative through plans which could, if stripped of their obsession with concentration, raise the level of performance without destroying competition in any society. They did not determine the growth rate, they merely improved it.

4. The Continuing Tension Between Protection and Stimulation

It is as much a mistake in France as in the United States to consider issues of alternative market organization primarily in terms of a conflict between government intervention and private business choice. The true opposition is between the complex of forces favorable to initiative and progress, which may come from either government or private enterprise, and the obstacles to progress which may equally well come from either side. No nation is or ever will be free of the latter, because the impediments to economic progress are rooted in the search for reduction of uncertainty and in the impossibility of considering one's own and others' interests on perfectly equal terms.

The particular tensions at present turn on the conflicts between encouraging domestic competition as opposed to planning through producer groups, the possibility of moving toward methods of planning which would include power to block investment considered unnecessary by the group, the retention of external tariffs around the Common Market, and the extension of the Market itself to include new countries. On every one of these fronts, some well-intentioned government agencies are lined up with those business interests who would prefer orderly group coordination within well-defined boundaries. They are not against progress; they are simply in favor of the cooperative approach which would keep it tame. At the same time, newly vigorous firms aiming at independent growth of their own, and other government agencies favoring decentralized decisions channelled in the public interest by competition, are trying to break out of existing molds of behavior toward a more fluid world of less predictable change.

Neither of the two sides is completely right or wrong. Each represents a valid concern, one with preserving the economic structure from shocks beyond its capacity to absorb, and the other with fostering the forces of change necessary to keep the society from sliding back into a new set of rigidities. The weight of centuries of French economic policy, and the ease with which orderly coordination can drift into deadening stability, make the option in favor of continuing change most uncertain. There is enough poison in this system to bring it to an unpleasant end. There is enough vitality, and there are enough intelligent people pointing the economy toward the future, to encourage the belief that they will carry on the demonstration of the power of human choice to take an apparently deteriorating industrial structure and bring it back to vigorous life.

Bibliography

FRENCH GOVERNMENT PUBLICATIONS

1. Commissariat Général du Plan, *Rapport général sur le premier plan de modernisation et d'équipement*, Paris, November 1946—January 1947.
2. —— *Cinq ans d'exécution du plan de modernisation et d'équipement de l'Union française*, Paris, 1952.
3. —— *Rapport annuel*, vol. I, Paris, 1958.
4. —— *Rapport annuel*, vol. I, Paris, 1960.
5. —— Premier plan de modernisation et d'équipement, *Rapport Général de la Commission de Modernisation de la Sidérurgie*, Paris, May 1946—February 1947.
6. —— Deuxième plan de modernisation et d'équipement, *Rapport Général de la Commission de Modernisation de la Sidérurgie*, Paris, 1954.

7. Commissariat Général du Plan, Troisième plan de modernisation et d'équipement, *Rapport Général de la Commission de Modernisation de la Sidérurgie*, Paris, 1957.
8. —— Troisième plan de modernisation et d'équipement, *Rapport Général de la Commission des Industries de Transformation*, Paris, 1958.
9. —— Troisième plan de modernisation et d'équipement, Commission des Industries de Transformation, *Automobiles, Motocycles, Cycles et Equipements*, Paris, 1957.
10. Conseil Economique et Social, *Problèmes posés par la répartition de l'accroissement de la productivité, Rapport pour avis*, presenté par Bertrand de Jouvenel, Paris, March 17, 1960.
11. Institut National de la Statistique et des Etudes Economiques, *Annuaire Statistique de la France, 1952*, Paris, 1953.
12. —— *Annuaire Statistique de la France, Rétrospectif, Edition 1961*, Paris, 1961.
13. —— *Bulletin Mensuel de Statistique.*
14. —— *Les établissements industriels et commerciaux en France en 1954*, Paris, 1956.
15. —— *Les établissements industriels, artisanaux et commerciaux en France en 1958*, Paris, 1959.
16. —— *Etudes et Conjonctures.*
    a. L. Cahen, "La concentration des établissements en France de 1896 à 1936," September 1954, pp. 840–81.
    b. L. Cahen, "Un exemple de l'impossibilité de certaines comparaisons statistiques—la taille des établissements industriels dans les pays du Marché Commun," February 1959, pp. 197–208.
    c. A. Devaux, "Les coûts de main-d'œuvre dans l'industrie manufacturière des pays Européens et des Etats-Unis," March 1960, pp. 205–42.
    d. Jankeliowitch et Gervaiseau, "Situation et perspectives dans l'industrie et le commerce en novembre 1959 d'après les chefs d'entreprise," March 1960, pp. 179–98.
    e. J. Klatzmann, "L'évolution des revenues agricoles," December 1959, pp. 1067–76.
    f. J. Lemperière, "Structure et évolution des exportations des pays du Marché Commun et de La Grande-Bretagne depuis 1951," May 1960, pp. 420–54.
    g. A. Néel, "Effets de structure et de concurrence," May 1960, pp. 455–87.
17. —— *Etudes Statistiques.*
    a. P. de Castelnau, "Les salaires dans l'industrie, le commerce et les services en 1958," October–December 1960, pp. 325–33.

b. Liorzou, "L'industrie française de 1951 à 1956," January–March 1960, pp. 33–62.
c. R.-M. Monod-Broca, "La production industrielle en 1959," April–June 1960, pp. 89–104.
d. C. Piro, "La situation démographique en 1959," October–December 1960, pp. 245–78.
e. Sermage et Monod, "Les indices de la production industrielle sur la base 100 en 1952," July–September 1957, pp. 93–119.

18. —— *Mouvement économique en France de 1944 à 1957*, Paris, 1958.
19. *Journal Officiel: Conseil Economique*, "Le problème de la sidérurgie dans le cadre de la CECA," présenté par André Philip, April 2, 1954, pp. 359–69.
20. *Journal Officiel: Documents Administratifs*, Rapports de la Commission Technique des Ententes, January 14 and June 4, 1960; June 15, 1961.
21. Ministère des Finances et des Affaires Economiques, S.E.E.F., *Commission des Comptes et des Budgets Economiques de la Nation* (May 1954), Paris, 1956.
22. —— *Les Comptes de la nation*, vol. 1, Paris, 1960.
23. —— *Rapport sur les comptes de la nation de l'année 1960*, Paris, 1961.
24. —— *Statistiques et Etudes Financières*, October 1960.
25. —— "Les bénéfices industriels et commerciaux," March 1955 and May 1960.
26. —— *Tableau économique de l'année 1951*, Paris, 1956.
27. Ministère de l'Industrie, Direction des Industries Mécaniques et Electriques, "Principales Statistiques Annuelles, Année 1959," Paris, 1960 (mimeo).
28. *Rapport* présenté, Au nom du Groupe de Travail du Haut-Commissariat aux Affaires Economiques chargé de l'étude des économies d'importation et du développement des productions nationales, par M. A. Armengaud, Président, Sénateur, Paris, December 1958 (mimeo). "Note Complémentaire: Comment redresser la situation dans le domaine des biens d'équipement," Paris, February 1959 (mimeo).
29. République Française, *Plan Intérimaire*, 1960–61, Paris, 1960.

SOURCES OTHER THAN FRENCH GOVERNMENT PUBLICATIONS

A. General Studies of the French Economy

30. Warren C. Baum, *The French Economy and the State*, Princeton, 1958.
31. Jean Chardonnet, *L'Economie française*, vol. I, Paris, 1958.

32. S. B. Clough, *France, A History of National Economics, 1789–1939*, New York, 1939.
33. C. W. Cole, *French Mercantilism, 1683–1700*, New York, 1943.
34. Henry W. Ehrmann, *Organized Business in France*, Princeton, 1957.
35. François Hetman, "Croissance comparée des industries françaises," *Bulletin SEDEIS*, no. 786, supp., May 1, 1961.
36. Bert F. Hoselitz, "Entrepreneurship and Capital Formation in France and Britain Since 1700," in National Bureau of Economic Research, *Capital Formation and Economic Growth*, Princeton, 1955, pp. 291–337.
37. J. M. Jeanneney, *Forces et faiblesses de l'économie française*, Paris, 1956.
38. C. P. Kindleberger, *French and British Economic Growth and Slowdown*, forthcoming.
39. —— "The Postwar Resurgence of the French Economy," in *In Search of France*, Cambridge, Mass., 1963.
40. David S. Landes, "French Entrepreneurship and Industrial Growth in the Nineteenth Century," *Journal of Economic History*, 1949, pp. 45–61.
41. —— "Observations on France: Economy, Society and Polity," *World Politics*, April 1957, pp. 329–50.
42. Herbert Luethy, *France Against Herself*, New York, 1955.
43. Harold Lubell, "The Role of Investment in Two French Inflations," *Oxford Economic Papers, NS*, February 1955, pp. 47–56.
44. François Perroux, "Prise de Vue sur la Croissance de l'Economie Française, 1780–1959," *International Association for Research in Income and Wealth*, series V, London, 1955, pp. 41–78.
45. John E. Sawyer, "France's New Horizon," *Yale Review*, Winter 1959.
46. —— "Strains in the Social Structure of Modern France," E. M. Earle, ed., *Modern France*, Princeton, 1951, pp. 293–312.
47. John Sheahan, "Evolution de la productivité et des salaires en France et aux Etats-Unis depuis 1950," *Bulletin SEDEIS*, no. 759, supp., July 1, 1960.
48. Roland Tavitian, "Distorsions de structures en France depuis 1914," *Revue Economique*, September 1958, pp. 735–61.
49. United Nations, Economic Commission for Europe, *Economic Survey of Europe in 1954*, Geneva, 1955, ch. 7.
50. Gordon Wright, *France in Modern Times*, Chicago and London, 1960.

B. Competition and Concentration; Enterprise Size and Performance

51. M. A. Adelman, "The Measurement of Industrial Concentration," *Review of Economics and Statistics,* November 1951.
52. Joe Bain, *Industrial Organization,* New York, 1959.
53. Raymond Barre, "Quelques aspects de la régulation du pouvoir économique," *Revue Economique,* November 1958, pp. 912–24.
54. Robert Goertz-Girey, "Monopoly and Competition in France," E. H. Chamberlin, ed., *Monopoly and Competition and Their Regulation,* New York and London, 1954, pp. 21–42.
55. Daniel Hamberg, Statement in Hearings before the Joint Economic Committee, on *Employment, Growth and Price Levels,* 86th Congress, first session, September 1959, part 7, pp. 2337–78.
56. Fredrick Harbison, "Entrepreneurial Organization as a Factor in Economic Development," *Quarterly Journal of Economics,* August 1956, pp. 364–79.
57. —— and Eugene Burgess, "Modern Management in Western Europe," *American Journal of Sociology,* July 1954, pp. 15–23.
58. Jacques Houssiaux, *Concurrence et Marché Commun,* Paris, 1960.
59. —— *Le pouvoir de monopole,* Paris, 1958.
60. David S. Landes, "French Business and the Businessman: A Social and Cultural Analysis," in E. M. Earle, *Modern France,* Princeton, 1951, pp. 334–53.
61. W. R. Maclaurin, "The Process of Technological Innovation," *American Economic Review,* March 1950, pp. 90–112.
62. P. L. Mandy and G. de Ghellinck, "La structure de la dimension des entreprises dans les pays du Marché Commun," *Revue Economique,* May 1960, pp. 395–413.
63. Edward S. Mason, *Economic Concentration and the Monopoly Problem,* Cambridge, Mass., 1957.
64. Frederick Moore, "Economies of Scale: Some Statistical Evidence," *Quarterly Journal of Economics,* May 1959, pp. 232–45.
65. Paul Reuter, "A propos des ententes industrielles et commerciales," *Droit Social,* January 1953, pp. 1–12.
66. W. E. G. Salter, *Productivity and Technical Change,* Cambridge, England, 1960.
67. Charles L. Schultze and Joseph L. Tryon, "Prices and Costs in Manufacturing Industries," Study paper no. 17 prepared

for the Joint Economic Committee Study, *Employment, Growth and Price Levels*, January 1960.

68. Jacob Schmookler, "Technological Progress and the Modern American Corporation," E. S. Mason, ed. *The Corporation in Modern Society*, Cambridge, Mass., 1960, pp. 141–65.
69. Tibor de Scitovszky, "A Note on Profit Maximization and its Implications," *Review of Economic Studies*, Winter 1943, pp. 57–60.

C. International Trade and Economic Development

70. R. Bertrand, "Enquête sur les coefficients d'exportation de la production française," Institut de Science Economique Appliquée, August 1960 (mimeo).
71. C. P. Kindleberger, *Economic Development*, New York, 1958.
72. —— "International Trade and Investment and Resource Use in Economic Growth," with Comment by William N. Parker, in Social Science Research Council, *Natural Resources and Economic Growth*, New York, 1961, pp. 151–90.
73. —— *The Terms of Trade, A European Case Study*, New York, 1956.
74. Gerard Marcy, "Libération progressive des échanges et aide à l'exportation en France depuis 1949," *Cahiers de l'ISEA*, série P., no. 2, May 1959.
75. —— "La réglementation française du commerce extérieur depuis 1945," *Revue Economique*, May 1958, pp. 348–84.
76. Bertil Ohlin, *Interregional and International Trade*, Cambridge, Mass., 1933.
77. François Perroux, *L'économie du XXème siècle*, Paris, 1961.
78. —— "Les formes de la concurrence dans le Marché Commun," *Revue d'Economie Politique*, January–February 1958, pp. 340–78.
79. Romney Robinson, "Factor Proportions and Comparative Advantage: Part II," *Quarterly Journal of Economics*, August 1956, pp. 343–63.
80. Paul Samuelson, "International Trade and Factor Prices," *Economic Journal*, June 1948, pp. 163–84.
81. John Sheahan, "International Specialization and the Concept of Balanced Growth," *Quarterly Journal of Economics*, May 1958, pp. 183–97.
82. Jean Teissedre, "Le Commerce Extérieur," *Revue d'Economie Politique*, July–October 1961, pp. 630–49.
83. J. L. Vauzanges, "La Politique d'aide aux exportations," *Revue Economique*, May 1958, pp. 385–413.

D. Monetary and Fiscal; Business Finance

84. André Bisson, *Institutions financières et économiques en France*, Paris, 1960.
85. M. Lagache, *Les investissements privés et le concours financier de l'Etat*, Paris, 1959.
86. J. Meyer and E. Kuh, *The Investment Decision*, Cambridge, Mass., 1957.
87. Martin Norr, "Depreciation Reform in France," *Taxes*, May 1961, pp. 391–401.
88. Jacques Rueff, "The Rehabilitation of the Franc," *Lloyds Bank Review*, April 1959.
89. Delbert Snider, "French Monetary and Fiscal Policies Since the Liberation," *American Economic Review*, June 1948, pp. 309–27.

E. Nationalization and Government Enterprise

90. Bernard Chenot, *Les entreprises nationalisées*, Paris, 1956.
91. André G. Delion, *L'Etat et les entreprises publiques*, Paris, 1958.
92. Mario Einaudi, Maurice Byé, and Ernesto Rossi, *Nationalization in France and Italy*, Ithaca, 1955.
93. J. M. Jeanneney, "Nationalization in France," E. H. Chamberlin, ed., *Monopoly and Competition and Their Regulation*, New York and London, 1954, pp. 471–89.
94. John V. Krutilla and Otto Eckstein, *Multiple Purpose River Development*, Baltimore, 1958.
95. Georges Lescuyer, *Le contrôle de l'Etat sur les enterprises nationalisées*, Paris, 1959.
96. Monique Maillet-Chassagne, *Influence de la nationalisation sur la gestion des entreprises publiques*, Paris, 1956.
97. Thomas Marschak, "Capital Budgeting and Pricing in the French Nationalized Industries," *Journal of Business*, April 1960, pp. 133–56.
98. David H. Pinkney, "The French Experiment in Nationalization, 1944–50," E. M. Earle, *Modern France*, Princeton, 1951, pp. 354–67.
99. Université de Grenoble, *Le fonctionnement des entreprises nationalisées en France*, Paris, 1956.

F. Planning

100. Pierre Bauchet, *L'expérience française de planification*, Paris, 1958.
101. Jean Bénard and J. W. Hackett, "Planification indicative et

développement économique," *Cahiers de l'ISEA*, series D, no. 10, 1958, pp. 3–43.
102. A. Bienaymé, "La réorientation de la Croissance planifiée française et les risques de freinage par le commerce extérieur," *Cahiers de l'ISEA*, no. 104, supp., August 1960.
103. Bernard Cazes, "Capitalisme et planification, sont-ils compatibles?" *Cahiers de l'ISEA*, series M, no. 4, April 1959, pp. 113–59.
104. Harold Lubell, "The French Investment Program: A Defense of the Monnet Plan," Paris, 1951 (mimeo).
105. Pierre Massé, *Le choix des investissements*, Paris, 1959.
106. —— "French Planning," *French Affairs*, no. 127, December 1961.
107. P. Massé and R. Gibrat, "Applications of Linear Programming to Investment in the Electric Power Industry," *Management Science*, January 1957, pp. 149–66.
108. Wallace Peterson, "Planning and Economic Progress in France," *World Politics*, April 1957, pp. 351–82.
109. Political and Economic Planning, "Economic Planning in France," *Planning*, no. 454, August 14, 1961.
110. Stanislaw Wellisz, "Economic Planning in the Netherlands, France and Italy," *Journal of Political Economy*, June 1960, pp. 252–83.

G. Prices and Price Control

111. Louis Franck, *Les Prix*, Paris, 1958.
112. J. K. Galbraith, "The Disequilibrium System," *American Economic Review*, June 1947, pp. 287–302.
113. —— *A Theory of Price Control*, Cambridge, Mass., 1952.
114. Milton Gilbert and Irving Kravis, *An International Comparison of National Products and the Purchasing Power of Currencies*, Paris, OEEC, 1954.
115. Milton Gilbert and Associates, *Comparative National Products and Price Levels*, Paris, OEEC, 1959.
116. J. Laux, "M. Pinay and Inflation," *Political Science Quarterly*, March 1959, pp. 113–19.

H. Industry Studies:

1. *Aluminum*

117. Aluminum Association, "Increasing Free World Aluminum Consumption," New York, August 15, 1961.
118. G. A. Baudert, "L'industrie française de l'aluminium," *Revue de l'Aluminium*, November 1959, pp. 1179–85.
119. —— "1960, Année de développement majeur de la production

de l'aluminium en France," *Revue de l'Aluminium,* 1961, pp. 459–62.
120. —— "Le rôle du gaz de Lacq dans les récents développements de l'industrie de l'aluminium en France," *Revue de l'Aluminium,* 1961, pp. 55–60.
121. André Dumas, "L'aluminium et le progrès technique," *Revue de l'Aluminium,* no. 282, 1961.
122. —— "Aluminium et Marché Commun," conférence de la Chambre de Commerce Française de Bruxelles, April 19, 1961.
123. C. J. Gignoux, *Histoire d'une entreprise française,* Paris, 1955.
124. Merton J. Peck, *Competition in the Aluminum Industry, 1945–58,* Cambridge, Mass., 1961.
125. *Revue de l'Aluminium.*
126. Donald Wallace, *Market Control in the Aluminum Industry,* Cambridge, Mass., 1937.

2. *Steel*

127. M. A. Adelman, "Steel, Administered Prices and Inflation," *Quarterly Journal of Economics,* February 1961, pp. 16–40.
128. American Iron and Steel Institute, "The Competitive Challenge to Steel," New York, 1961.
129. Roger Biard, *La sidérurgie française,* Paris, 1958.
130. D. L. Burn, *The Economic History of Steelmaking, 1867–1939,* Cambridge, England, 1940.
131. —— *The Steel Industry, 1939–59,* Cambridge, England, 1961.
132. Chambre Syndicale de la Sidérurgie Française, *Bulletin,* série rose.
133. Jean Chardonnet, *La sidérurgie française,* Paris, 1954.
134. Otto Eckstein and Gary Fromm, "Steel and the Postwar Inflation," Study paper no. 2 prepared for the Joint Economic Committee Study, *Employment, Growth, and Price Levels,* November 1959.
135. H. E. English, "British Steel: A Unique Record of Public Regulation," *Canadian Journal of Economics and Political Science,* May 1960, pp. 241–64.
136. European Coal and Steel Community, High Authority, *Ninth General Report on the Activities of the Community,* Luxembourg, 1961.
137. —— Office Statistique, *Bulletin Statistique.*
138. Marc Gervais de Lafend, "Les investissements dans la sidérurgie française depuis la création de la Communauté Européenne du Charbon et de l'Acier," unpublished doctoral thesis, Université de Paris, 1959.
139. International Metal Workers' Federation, Iron and Steel De-

partment, "Survey of Wages and Conditions in the Iron and Steel Industry, 1955–57," March 1959.

140. —— "The Largest Steel Companies in the Free World," March 1959.

141. Louis Lister, *Europe's Coal and Steel Community*, New York, 1960.

142. OEEC, *The Iron and Steel Industry in Europe*, Second Half 1959, Paris, 1960.

143. N. J. G. Pounds and William Parker, *Coal and Steel in Western Europe*, London, 1957.

3. *Industrial Equipment*

144. M. E. Beesley and G. W. Troup, "The Machine Tool Industry," Duncan Burn, ed., *The Structure of British Industries*, I, Cambridge, England, 1958, pp. 359–92.

145. Bernard Cazes and Claude Vincent, "Deux perspectives pour la machine-outil française," and "Pour une politique de la machine-outil," *Cahiers de la République*, March–April 1960.

146. *Entreprise*, "L'industrie française de la machine-outil," May 9, 1959, pp. 13–35.

a. —— "Y-a-t-il place en Europe pour la machine-outil française?," August 20, 1960, pp. 12–15.

147. Eliane Mossé, "L'industrie française de la machine-outil, bilan et perspectives," *Bulletin SEDEIS*, May 15, 1958.

148. Organization for European Economic Cooperation, Trends in Economic Sectors, 5'th Year, *The Engineering Industries in Europe*, Paris, 1959.

149. Marcia Lee Stigum, "The Impact of the European Economic Community on the French Cotton and Electrical Engineering Industries," unpublished Ph.D. thesis, Massachusetts Institute of Technology, 1961.

4. *Automobiles*

150. Pierre Bauchet, "La structure d'une branche d'industrie française; l'automobile," *Economie Appliquée*, April–September 1952, pp. 359–99.

151. Maurice Bosquet, "Le marché automobile dans le cadre de la C.E.E.," *Revue du Marché Commun*, March 1960, pp. 100–07.

152. Hans Brems, "The Outlook for the Automobile Industry," *Current Economic Comment*, November 1958, pp. 25–38.

153. C.G.T. Force Ouvrière, "L'industrie automobile," *Bulletin d'Information du Bureau d'Etudes Economiques et Sociales*, May 15, 1960.

154. *Entreprise*, "Citroën," May 10, 1958.
a. —— "Peugeot, a-t-il eu raison?" January 5, 1957.
155. G. Maxcy and A. Silberston, *The Motor Industry*, London, 1959.
156. Janine Morice, *La demande d'automobiles en France*, Paris, 1957.
157. Eliane Mossé, "L'autonomie de la demande dans un mouvement de croissance industrielle," *Revue Economique*, July 1958, pp. 645–54.
158. —— "Dynamisme de la demande et croissance économique," Paris, 1957 (mimeo).
159. —— "Sur quelques aspects de la croissance de l'industrie automobile en France depuis la fin du XIXe siècle," *Bulletin SEDEIS*, February 1, 1958.
160. J. Pierjant, *L'industrie automobile*, Paris, 1956.
161. *Revue du Marché Commun*, February 1959.

5. *Cotton Textiles*

162. François Capronnier, *La crise de l'industrie cotonnière française*, Paris, 1958.
163. Penelope A. Mars, "An Economic Comparison of the Textile Industries in the U.S.A. and the U.K.," *Journal of Industrial Economics*, April 1961, p. 181–94.
164. Jacques Rabeil, *L'industrie cotonnière française*, Paris, 1955.
165. Syndicat Général de l'Industrie Cotonnière Française, Centre de Productivité, "Evolution de l'industrie cotonnière aux U.S.A. de 1950–51 à 1958," Paris, 1958.
166. Syndicat Général de l'Industrie Cotonnière Française, *Dossier de l'industrie cotonnière française*, Paris, June 1960.
167. —— *L'industrie cotonnière française, bilan du premier programme d'action*, 1953–58, Paris, June 1959.
168. —— *Industrie Cotonnière Française*, supplément "Statistiques 1959."
169. —— *Programme d'Ensemble de l'industrie cotonnière française*, Paris, 1953.

I. Statistical Sources; General Information

170. Board of Governors of the Federal Reserve System, *Industrial Production, 1959 Revision*, Washington, 1960.
171. Jacques Duhamel, "Le C.N.C.E. rénové au service des exportateurs," *La Vie Française*, May 6, 1960.
172. *L'Economie.*
173. Federal Reserve Bank of New York, "International Comparability of Unemployment Statistics," *Monthly Review*, March 1961, pp. 47–51.

174. Simon Kuznets, "Quantitative Aspects of the Economic Growth of Nations," *Economic Development and Cultural Change*, October 1956, pp. 5–94.
175. *Le Monde*.
176. Organization for European Economic Cooperation, *Demographic Trends in Western Europe and the United States, 1956–76*, Paris, 1961.
177. —— *Foreign Trade*, Series B.
178. —— *General Statistics*.
179. —— *Industrial Statistics, 1900–1959*, Paris, 1960.
180. Ingvar Svennilson, *Growth and Stagnation in the European Economy*, Geneva, 1954.
181. United Nations, *Yearbook of International Trade Statistics*.
182. United States, Department of Labor, Bureau of Labor Statistics, *Monthly Labor Review*.
183. —— *Wholesale Prices, 1954–56*.
184. United States Department of Commerce, *Business Statistics, 1961 Edition*, Washington, 1961.
185. *La Vie Française*.

Index